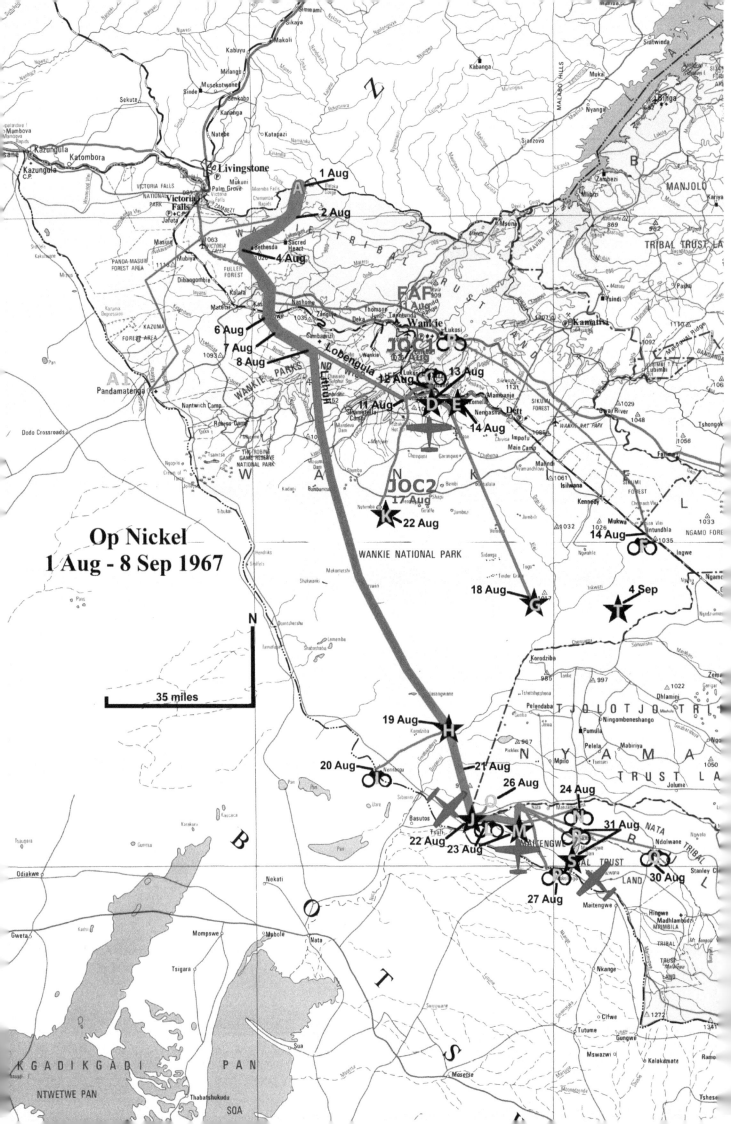

Op Nickel
1 Aug - 8 Sep 1967

Also from the RAR Regimental Association:

Masodja: Alexandre Binda
Chibaya Moyo: Andrew Telfer & Russell Fulton (Eds.)
Chibaya Moyo 2: Andrew Telfer & Russell Fulton (Eds.)

From Inyantue to Entumbane
The Rhodesian African Rifles
1965-1981

Colonel Michael P. Stewart, US Army

Published in 2021 by the RAR Regimental Association

ISBN 978-1-5272-8689-4

From Inyantue to Entumbane

The Rhodesian African Rifles
1965-1981

Colonel Michael P. Stewart, US Army

Why did they fight?
Why did they fight so well?
What became of this fine Regiment?

This study of the Rhodesian African Rifles, with its origins and history in WW1, WW2, the Malayan Emergency, and culminating in the 'Bush War', addresses these questions and others.

Stemming from a US Army Staff College project designed to examine the role of indigenous forces in modern wars, this book brings that study to life through enquiring into the culture and values of this once fine and loyal Regiment, at a time during which the trajectory of political and military forces in play were acting against it.

Front cover: two RAR soldiers in northern Matabeleland in 1967 during Op Nickel, the first contact of which was at Inyantue.

Back cover: two RAR MAG gunners in action at Entumbane in 1981.

CONTENTS

FOREWORDS

This is not the full history of the Rhodesian African Rifles, but Mike Stewart's Thesis at the US Staff College, which shows their worth during the Rhodesian Bush War from 1965 to 1980.

Mike Stewart's Thesis - The Rhodesian African Rifles: The Growth and Adaptation of a Multicultural Regiment Through the Rhodesian Bush War 1965-1980 - was presented to the Faculty of the US Army Command and General Staff College in partial fulfilment of the requirements for the Degree of Master of Military Art and Science: Military History.

He was awarded the Arter-Darby Award for Military History Writing, so, in addition to the next class at the Staff College being tortured by a picture of Mike Stewart on the wall for a few months, he received a $500 cash prize when he graduated. This he donated to the RAR Memorial Fund run by Mike Shute and Chris Vincent. In view of this he was made a Life Member of our Regimental Association.

Brigadier Pat Lawless, Chairman of our Regimental Association, who had previously been on the Directing Staff of the Staff College, Camberley, skimmed through the Thesis on its arrival and was amazed by the breadth and depth of Mike's work, and truly appreciated the volume of work that would have gone into its preparation, at a time when other aspects of his studies were competing for his attention.

The Thesis has been included word for word in this History and the only additions have been the operational maps and photographs which Mike had not been able to procure at the time. These have been included in the text by Alan Doyle, who was responsible for converting the Thesis into a historical book.

After more than sixty years' service in, and involvement with, the Rhodesian African Rifles, I can guarantee that this is an excellent history book, covering a wide range of knowledge.

Brigadier David Heppenstall, MLM
Lymington, Hampshire 2021

Colonel Michael Stewart's thesis gives an unprecedented insight into the mindset of the African soldier, or *masodja* as they called themselves in their vernacular. The publication has been further enhanced by the addition of numerous photographs, never previously published, of RAR soldiers of both races on operations.

From its early days in the Bush War, border patrols, follow-ups and the supreme skills of the trackers of the RAR were the norm. Well illustrated in this thesis are those hesitant days where the Regiment came to grips with a burgeoning counter-insurgency war, and developed the tricks of the trade while learning a new form of warfare in its own back yard.

Also well documented is the role of the RAR as it became embroiled in the Fireforce concept of aerial envelopment of the enemy, as devised by the Rhodesian Army. The RAR was to deploy companies on a continual rotational basis on Fireforce operations, both as helicopter-borne troops and as paratroopers. RAR paratroopers set records in military airborne operational history and to this day are ranked amongst the airborne units of Southern Africa.

It was such a pleasure to help in the compiling of this publication, drawing on my own experiences from the Entumbane operations, which were the swansong of the RAR. At Entumbane after Zimbabwean independence, the RAR performed as a fully-fledged combat group, which, although heavily outnumbered, carried out a multi-faceted operation with extreme professionalism and aplomb. This publication fully demonstrates the loyalty and professionalism of the RAR soldier, who fought a long protracted fight against sustained and increasing aggression.

John Hopkins
Llanelli, Carmarthenshire, 2021

EDITOR'S INTRODUCTION

Col Stewart's study is that most valuable of things: a lens that allows us to see how others see us. His thesis stands on its own and needs no embellishment. For the purposes of this book, however, accompanying material has been added to give some additional context to the themes investigated by Col Stewart

So, as Col Stewart's story of the RAR in the bush war begins with Op Nickel and ends with the Battle of Bulawayo, material has been included on both, from Brigadier David Heppenstall's papers, to which he gave unfettered access, and the resuscitated memories and personal collections of those who were there, in particular John Hopkins. Both David (a former CO of 1RAR) and John (who served at Entumbane) have been most generous with their time and patience as I raided their archives and their minds.

Those two operations, 13 years apart, are a useful comparison and contrast. Both battles were against the same enemy, ZIPRA, with SAANC men thrown into the mix in 1967, and with the addition of ZANLA ex-combatants in 1980-81. Some of what one RAR Major called "the country's collection of vintage aircraft" flew sorties in both. The BSAP (later ZRP) played a part in both. There the similarities end. Op Nickel, the first contact of which was at Inyantue, took place mostly in the uninhabited and parched expanses of Wankie National Park. The battles in and around Entumbane (named after King Mzilikazi's burial place) were fought in occasional guti in the densely populated western suburbs of Bulawayo. Op Nickel was a COIN operation: trackers, ambushes, and follow-ups. Entumbane was urban warfare in a highly charged political environment.

The cost of Op Nickel was high. Eight KIA on the part of the police and army (of which seven were RAR), and 15 wounded, of which 11 were RAR men. In 1980, three RAR men, off-duty in civilian clothes, were murdered at a ZIPRA roadblock, and two plainclothes ZRP CID men were murdered in 1981. Otherwise, Entumbane I and II involved no other deaths in action for the RAR, and only one seriously wounded. The escalating violence between the bands of ex-combatants in Entumbane I was successfully brought to an end without a shot being fired by the RAR.

Detailed maps of the operational areas have also been included, which I hope will spark memories for those who served, and enable readers to more easily find places referred to in the text. The final part of this book includes an RAR Regimental Roll of Honour for the bush war period, for all the various units of the RAR. My sincere thanks to Craig Fourie, Adrian Haggett and Dr Richard Wood for sharing their knowledge and expertise.

And finally, my gratitude to those who sent in photos from their private collections. As many as possible have been included. I hope they give a sense of what it was like to serve in the RAR, even if many of the images - inevitably - are of the laughter, the cigarettes and the beer rather than the blisters, the sweat, and the loss.

ACKNOWLEDGEMENTS

Heartfelt thanks to those who gave so much help in putting this book together:

Keith Adams; Roy Amm; Jo Amos; Rob Anderson; Andy Barrett; Alexandre Binda; Iain Bowen; Derek de Kock; Lionel Dyck SCZ; Andrew Field; Craig Fourie; John Garland; Peter Gill; Dave Grant; Piet Grobbelaar; Adrian Haggett; David Heppenstall MLM; John Hopkins; Mike Jones; Derek de Kock; Pat Lawless SCR; Ron Marillier BCR; 'Bugs' Moran; Richard Perry; Don Price BCR; John Ringshaw; Michael Shute OLM; Trevor Smith; Col Michael P. Stewart; Dr Richard Wood.

The standard responsibility-for-errors clause applies.

Alan Doyle
Sunbury-on-Thames, Middlesex, 2021

MAPS

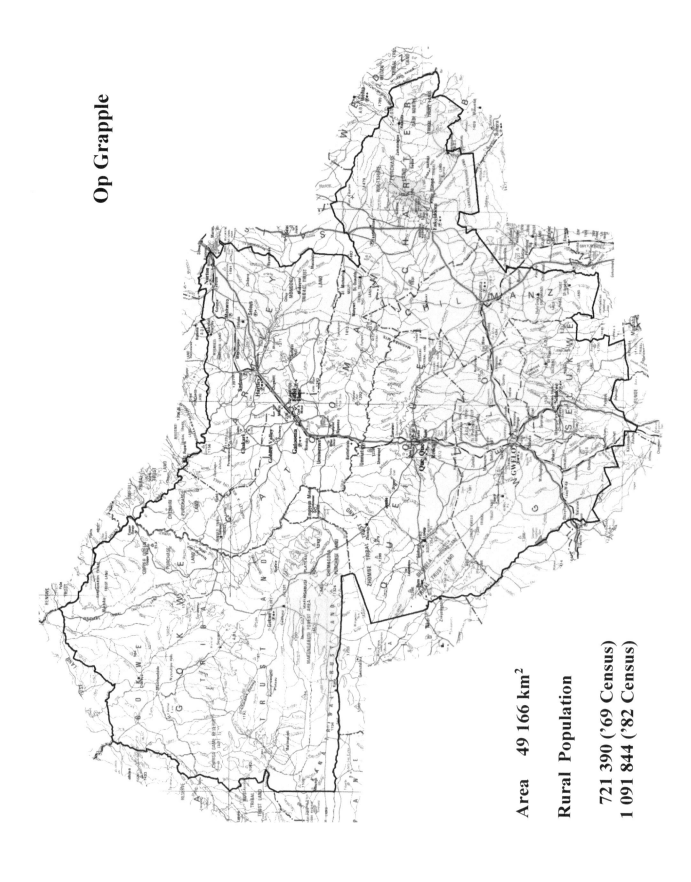

Op Grapple

Area   49 166 km²

Rural Population

721 390 ('69 Census)
1 091 844 ('82 Census)

Op Hurricane

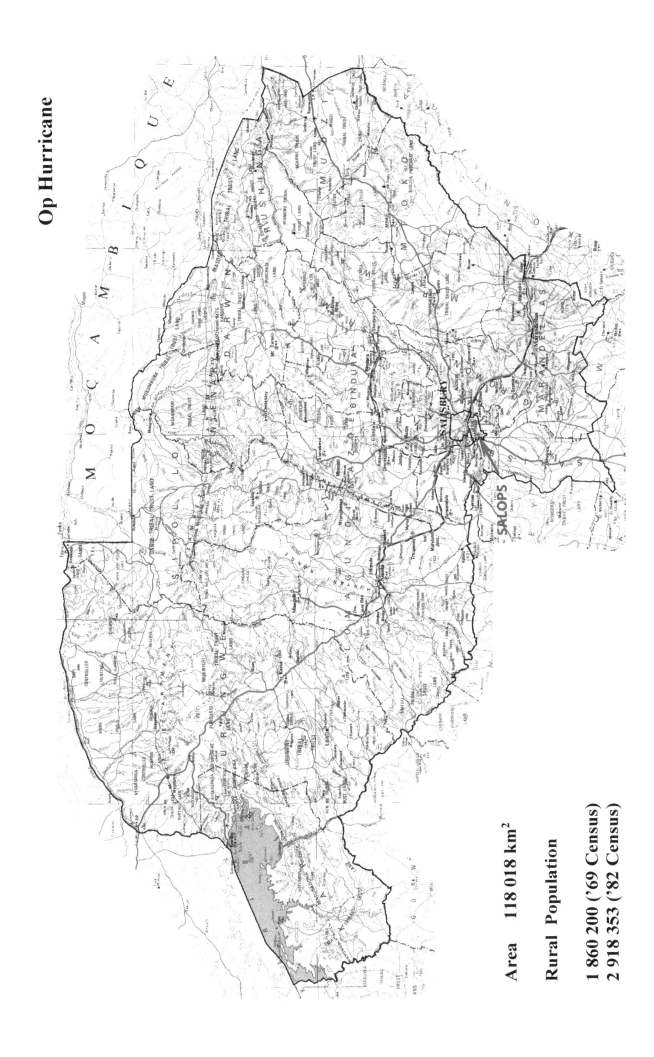

Area   118 018 km²

Rural Population

1 860 200 ('69 Census)
2 918 353 ('82 Census)

Op Repulse

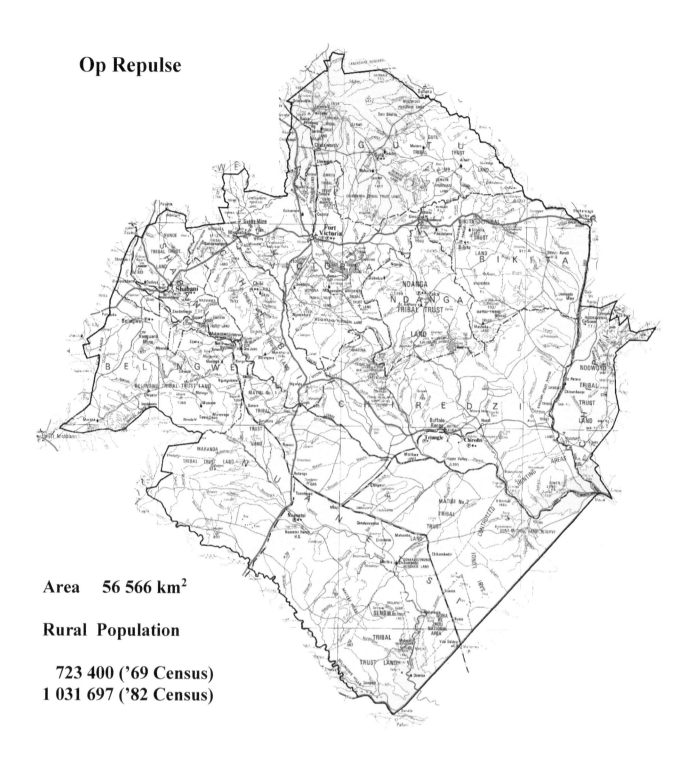

Area   56 566 km²

Rural Population

723 400 ('69 Census)
1 031 697 ('82 Census)

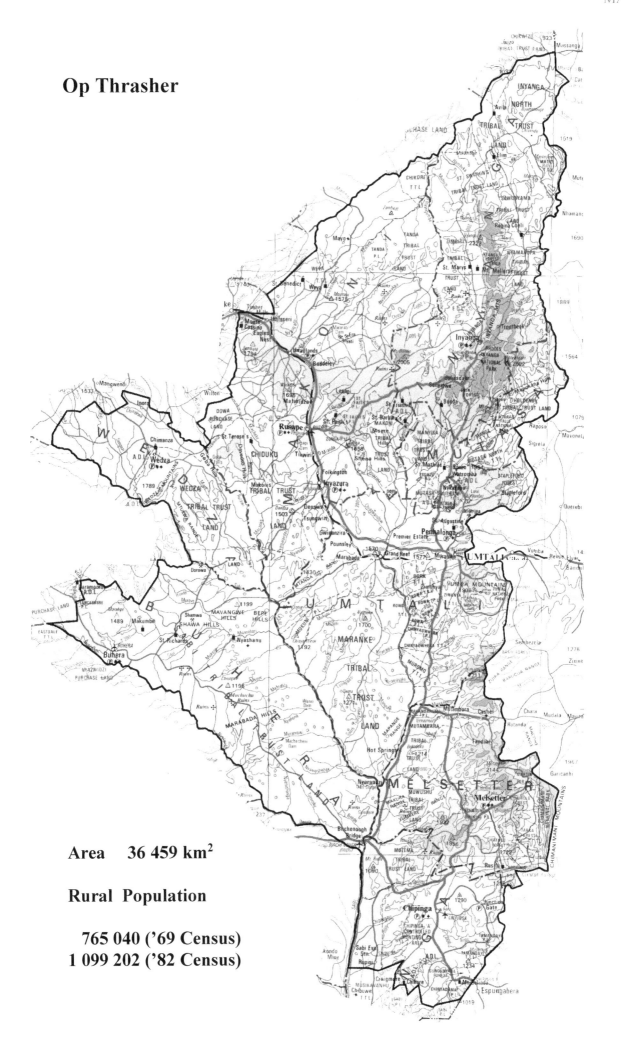

Op Thrasher

Area   36 459 km²

Rural Population

765 040 ('69 Census)
1 099 202 ('82 Census)

Op Tangent

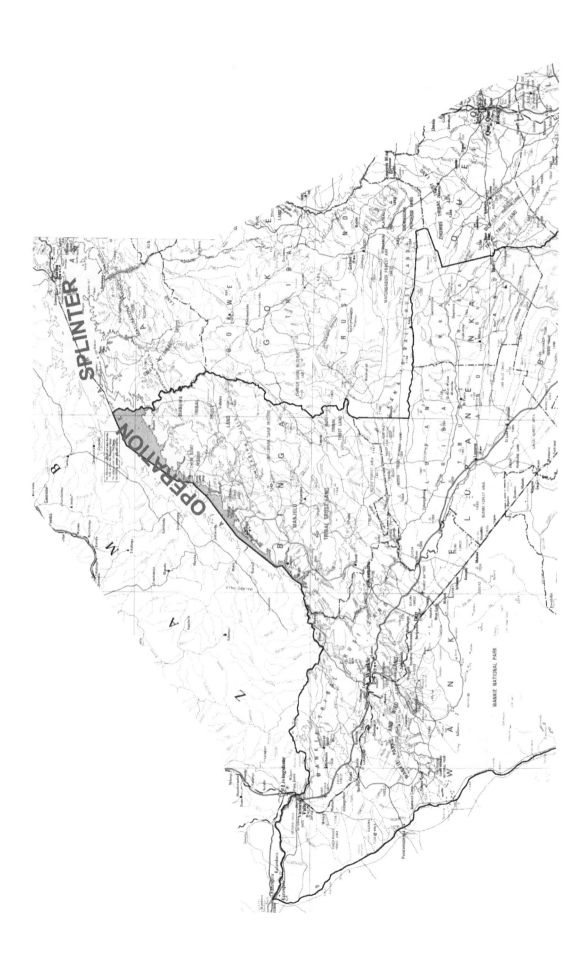

Area   129 197 km²

Rural Population

967 080 ('69 Census)
1 404 945 ('82 Census)

OP NICKEL TIMELINE
1 Aug 1967 to 8 Sep 1967

Please refer to the map on the front endpapers.

Note: The Army reports on Op Nickel state 79 men crossed the Zambezi on 1 Aug. Some are later named and some are not. The Special Branch report states list 81 men who crossed the river that day. Otherwise, the Army and SB reports are pretty much identical. This Timeline uses the SB list which enables most individuals in the two groups to be followed. Their names are largely noms de guerre.

1 Aug: Crossing of the Zambezi in the Batoka Gorge area by 81 CTs divided into three groups: the Lithuli Group of 13 ZAPU and 43 SAANC; the Lobengula Group of 14 ZAPU and 9 SAANC; plus two coloured SAANC men travelling separately – a total of 27 ZAPU and 54 SAANC. The Lobengula Group are headed east to the Nkai area, the Lithuli Group south east to Tjolotjo. The two coloured men are headed directly to Cape Town in South Africa. The overall commander is John DUBE aka Charles NGWEYA.

During the first two days, a total of eight CTs in two groups become detached from the main body. They eventually travel separately to Pandamatenga in Botswana, where one dies, seven are arrested, of which four escape. Three return to Rhodesia, and one makes his way from Botswana to Swaziland.

Dies: Don NCUBE
Arrested: Anderson DUMEZWENI; Rashid GAWAWO; Wilson MSWELI
Arrested and escapes to return to Rhodesia: Eric NDUNA; NGWANE; James NKONZO
Arrested and escapes to Swaziland: Jonathan MALAMA

5 Aug: The main body, now numbering 73, move south-west and south-east until they cross the Vic Falls-Wankie road and railway line on the evening of 5 August. That night, two more CTS become detached from the main body.

Detached: Peter TLADI; Alfred SCOTT

7 Aug: The main body of 71 are now camped due west of Wankie. That evening they move into the Wankie National Park and camp on the banks of the Deka River. During the day they move around freely and send out hunting parties for food.

9 Aug: Before dawn, the main body splits into two. The Lobengula Group of 22 (including Paul PETERSEN, one of the two SAANC men travelling separately) moves six or seven miles south-east, camps up for the day, and moves again on the night of 10 and 11 Aug. The Lithuli Group number 49.

10 Aug: 10 Pl, D Coy 1RAR under Lt NOBLE are returning to Bulawayo after a routine stint of Border Patrol. They are waved down by a BSAP Constable at Lukosi Mission, west of Wankie, who says a CT backpack has been found in the area. 10 Pl establish stop groups and a tracker team and Alfred SCOTT, one of the CTs who had become separated on 5/6 Aug, is captured and arrested.

1 Lobengula group captured: Alfred SCOTT

11 Aug: A JOC is established at Wankie. A platoon of 1 (Indep) Coy RR, and 10 Pl, D Coy 1RAR are deployed in the Wankie area. By dawn, the Lobengula Group are camped two miles south-west of Pongoro Siding. In the evening, two men accompany PETERSEN to Pongoro Siding. PETERSEN walks to Tshantanda Siding with the intention of boarding a train to Bulawayo the next morning.

12 Aug: Early in the morning PETERSEN is arrested by a railway security guard when he boards the train. He is taken to Dett Police station, where he draws a pistol and opens fire, injuring a BSAP Constable, and escapes. He steals a car and makes his way to Bulawayo.

1 SAANC arrested and escapes: Paul PETERSEN

By late afternoon, the Lobengula Group, numbering 21, are laid up close to Tshantanda Siding. A recce party is sent to the railway compound at Tshantanda to obtain food. The compound is deserted, but the party notices people at the siding, who are probably BSAP inquiring as to PETERSEN's movements.

Late that evening, A Coy 1RAR travels from Bulawayo to Pongoro Siding. At the same time, the Lobengula Group move south-east, reaching the Inyantue River, two miles south of Inyantue Siding early in the morning of 13 Aug 1967.

13 Aug: Capt HOSKING leads a patrol of seven from A Coy 1RAR plus three BSAP men and a civilian tracker to Inyantue Siding, and pick up tracks of five CTS. They are fired on, and a contact begins. Reinforcements are brought in by helicopter. The contact ends when the last SF casualties are evacuated at 22h00. Remaining Lobengula Group of 17 escape, including one with a serious arm wound.

2 RAR KIA: Pte Koroni KAMBANTE; Cpl Davison MUKOMBO
2 RAR wounded: Capt HOSKING, WO2 KEFASI
2 BSAP wounded: Insp PHILLIPS, SO TIFFIN
4 Lobengula Group KIA: James GOMAGOMA; Ben KOZA; Lameck MADUBA; Delmas SIBANYONI
17 Lobengula Group escape, including one with a serious arm wound: James MASIMINI

14 Aug: The wounded CT becomes separated from the main Lobengula body. Spotted at 14h00 to the east of the previous day's contact. Shot and killed by Lt NOBLE's patrol.

1 Lobengula Group KIA: James MASIMINI

14 Aug: Peter TLADI, who became detached from the main body on 5 August, is arrested at Intundhla Siding by a railway security inspector.

1 Lobengula Group arrested: Peter TLADI

17 Aug: PETERSEN leaves the stolen car in Bulawayo and travels to a farm near Figtree. He is shot and killed there by a BSAP SO.

1 SAANC KIA: Paul PETERSEN

17 Aug: JOC moved to Shapi Pan in Wankie National Park, FAF at Wankie. At 10h30 a pump attendant reports to the National Parks camp at Shapi Pan that two CTs (leader of the Lobengula Group, David MADZIBA, and Isaac LIZWE) had asked him for food the previous evening, which he refused. He had also spotted tracks at Gubolala Pan while travelling to Shapi. A platoon of A Coy 1RAR is sent to the attendant's hut and another - 3 Pl under Lt WARDLE - is sent to Gubolala Pan. Tracks are found and followed.

18 Aug: 10 Pl deployed as stops at Makona Pan at 11h00. At 12h30 Mortar Pl of Sp Coy 1RAR under Lt PIERS discover tracks near Makona Pan and follow them.

18 Aug: At 14h45, twelve miles north of Makona Pan, 3 Pl sees a CT lying under a fallen tree. He emerges when challenged. No reply is heard to further challenges, so 3 Pl opens fire, killing two CTs and capturing three others. Captured CTs are questioned and reveal there are more of their comrades hidden close by. Lt WARDLE challenges them, receives no reply, and fires towards the area, causing an explosion and a fire in the CT position. One CT is shot. Another escapes. When the fire dies down, more CT bodies are found. As helicopters arrive to remove the captured CTs, one is fired on by a CT in a slit trench. He is captured.

> **8 Lobengula Group KIA: Norman DHLAMINI; Tulani MADUNA; Charles MHAMBI; Daniel MHLEHLA; Jones MOKGOTSI; Andries MOTSEPE; Jack NDUNA; SHARP**
> **6 Lobengula Group captured: Peter BANDA; Lot CHIRUDZI; James HARMANS; Isaac LIZWE; Peter MOSES; Joseph ZAMI**
> **2 Lobengula Group escape: David MAZIBA; ?**

18 Aug: By this time the 47 men of the Lithuli Group have moved - undetected - a considerable distance south through the west side of the National Park. 45 of them set up camp near Leasha Pan. Two of their number - Ernest MUDULU and Christopher MOHALE - are sent to the Pan to shoot game.

At 16h00 the Mortar Pl, some distance north of Leasha Pan, find tracks heading south. They follow them and by 18h15 find a CT camp with equipment and fresh tracks. Mortar Pl base up for the night.

19 Aug: By 09h30 E Coy 1RAR are positioned as stop groups to the west of Leasha Pan along the game fence from Ngulube Pan to the border at Point 222, and south of Leasha Pan along the border from Point 222 to Point 290.

As the Mortar Pl approach Leasha Pan they are fired on. A follow-up finds one CT but he escapes. On its way back to its transport Mortar Pl shoot and kill Ernest MUDULU. The main body of the Lithuli Group move away two miles and lay low. Tracks leading west are lost.

> **1 Lithuli Group KIA: Ernest MUDULU**

20 Aug: Intensive patrolling by 1RAR reveals nothing. The Lithuli Group move further south and base up for the day on 21 Aug.

20 Aug: One of the two Lobengula Group escapees on 18 Aug is arrested by the Botswana Police at Point 308. This is the last of the Lobengula Group in Rhodesia to be accounted for.

> **1 Lobengula Group arrested: ?**

21 Aug: All available troops are brought to Leasha Pan, and patrolling begins eastwards towards Tjolotjo.

22 Aug: The Lithuli Group have now reached the western edge of Tjolotjo TTL near the Botswana border. At 10h45 1 Pl, A Coy 1RAR under Lt SMITH finds tracks at the game fence eight miles from the border. Tracks are followed to the south-east, and a sentry in the camp opens fire on 1Pl. Lt SMITH prepares to attack, unaware that he faces a 45-man Lithuli detachment which is dug-in in well-camouflaged slit trenches in an area 150 yards by 60 yards.

An overflying Provost aircraft is hit by ground fire. Lt SMITH and WO2 TIMITIYA are killed. Ammunition runs short. At around 15h45 1 Pl is charged by a group of CTs with bayonets fixed. Due to the shortage of ammunition, 1 Pl is forced to withdraw, leaving behind them two radios, some packs and several weapons. They reorganise about 100 yards away under L/Cpl MAVARADZE. Ammunition is redistributed, and three men are sent to get help. They withdraw to the National Park border road for the night.

> **2 RAR men KIA: Lt SMITH; WO2 TIMITIYA**
> **3 Lithuli Group KIA: Robert BALOI; Berry MASIPA; Charles SICHUBA**
> **3 Lithuli Group wounded: Peter MHLONGO; MBITSHANE; Sparks POOE**
> **2 Lithuli Group desert: Donald NKONKONI; George MLILO**

CTs remove the radios, packs, weapons, combat jackets, food and water. Peter MFENE uses a radio to contact a helicopter flying nearby and tries to persuade the pilot to land on the pretext of picking up casualties. The ruse fails.

The remaining Lithuli Group of 40 men move east that night with a stretcher party of five following behind the rest of the group in a skirmish line in front. One of the stretcher party deserts overnight, and one of the wounded dies. 38 remain. The group crosses the Nata River. Early on 23 Aug they are challenged by RAR men and a BSAP Constable guarding E Coy 1RAR's transport. They open fire. Pte MAHOHEMA is wounded in the head. Lt PEIRSON, in command of ambush positions nearby, goes to investigate the shots. He is accidentally killed by his own men on his return.

1 RAR KOAS: Lt PEIRSON
1 RAR wounded: Pte MAHOHEMA
1 Lithuli Group dies: Sparks POOE
1 Lithuli Group deserts: Matsobane RAMOSHABE

At 17h00 an African Game Ranger reports to the JOC at Shapi Pan that he has seen tracks near Nehimbe Springs. Lt WARDLE with a 3 Pl patrol moves to Nehimbe Springs and returns with one dead CT. This Lithuli Group man had escaped from the contact with Mortar Pl on 19 Aug near Leasha Pan at H, and had been killed by two National Park Wardens.

1 Lithuli Group KIA

23 Aug: At 09h10, Matsobane RAMOSHABE, the Lithuli stretcher bearer who had deserted the night before is captured by 13 PL, E Coy 1RAR under 2 Lt WINNALL. During questioning he reveals he is an SAANC member of a 30 strong group. Tracks are located and a follow-up by 13 Pl and 15 Pl, tracker dogs and two BSAP POs begins, and moves east. Mortar Pl is positioned in ambush on the Tegwani River.

1 Lithuli Group captured: Matsobane RAMOSHABE

An airstrike by two Hunters is called in at 16h44, ahead of 13Pl and 15 Pl. The RAR men are told to stay in an open vlei for identification purposes. While waiting for a Canberra strike at 18h00, Lt WINNALL decides to move the two platoons into thick bush to his front. This is observed by Lithuli Group men. Two of them, John DUBE and George DRIVER, wearing Army combat jackets removed from the 1Pl contact where Lt SMITH and WO2 TIMITIYA had been killed the day before, approach the two platoons posing as friendly forces. After exchanging a few words several other Lithuli Group men open fire. The Canberras arrive overhead at this point, but abort their attack due to the confusion on the ground and return to base.

After a short lull, the Lithuli Group launch an organised attack, followed by two more. Sporadic exchanges of fire continue until last light. The remaining 36 of the Lithuli Group remove more weapons, equipment, clothing and food and head north.

1 RAR KIA: L/Cpl MUSHURE
7 RAR wounded: Pte JONASI; PWO KISI; PWO OBERT; Pte SWONDO; L/Cpl TICHARGWA; Pte VANDIRAYI; 2 Lt WINNALL
1 BSAP KIA: PO THOMAS
1 BSAP wounded: PO HORN
2 Lithuli Group KIA: Jack SIBANDA; Nicholas DONDA

At 19h27 the JOC decides to move to Tjolotjo and 2 Cdo of 1RLI is sent from Salisbury to assist. D Coy 1RAR has moved from Methuen Barracks to the Nata River and is in position by 22h30.

24 Aug: The Lithuli Group continue their move to the junction of the Nata and Tegwani Rivers. A party of about eight of them leave the main group in search of food and water. The remaining 28 move to a better position beside the Tegwani River and wait until dusk on 24 Aug. The food-foraging group does not return so water is divided amongst the remaining members and the group moves off along the Tegwani River. Three men desert overnight. Thula SIZWE is later arrested near Chipinga on 23 Sep. The other two - KENI aka CAN CAN and Derek MKABELA - are thought to have been with him in that area. 25 remain.

3 Lithuli Group desert: KENI aka CAN CAN; Derek MKABELA; Thula SIZWE

A platoon from A Coy 1RAR under 2 Lt DUNCAN is sent to find the remaining members of 13 Pl and 15 Pl. They find them at 13h15.

At 18h05, BSAP PO Howse, 2 Lt SCHLACHTER and a patrol of D Coy 1RAR capture George MLILO and Donald NKONKONI, the two Lithuli men who deserted during the contact with Lt Smith and 1 Pl on 22 Aug.

2 Lithuli Group captured: George MLILO and Donald NKONKONI

25 Aug: Intensive patrolling around the Nata and Tegwani Rivers yields nothing.

26 Aug: A further body from the Lithuli Group is found near the contact with Lt Smith and 1 Pl.

1 Lithuli Group KIA: ?

27 Aug: The JOC decides to burn a large area by dropping frantan to facilitate patrolling the next day. Results are indifferent – the mopani scrub doesn't burn well.

27 Aug: Botswana Police arrest four of the Lithuli Group at Pt 171 on the border. The SAANC men with the main Lithuli Group leave for South Africa via Botswana. 17 are arrested by the Botswana Police on 3 and 4 Sep. The remaining eight of the Lithuli Group continue westward along the Tegwani River.

4 Lithuli Group arrested: George DRIVER; MASHIGA; NCAMBAZA; Perry NCUBE
17 Lithuli Group leave for Botswana: Victor DHLAMINI; Joseph HADEBE; Norman GUMBO; KENNETH; MANSHACK; Leslie MAREMA; Elliott MAROHA; MBITSHANE; Shooter MHAKAZI; Castro MCEBISI; Peter MFENE; Edwin NDHLOVU; NIKITA; Reuben NTHLABATHI; MJONO; Peter SITHOLE; Alfred WANA

28 Aug: The remnant of the Lithuli Group decide they can go no further without food and water. Two of the eight are sent to find food, but they desert.

2 Lithuli men desert: Dumisani DHLANGAMANDHLA; Stanley MEHLO

28 Aug: Four of the group of eight who left the Lithuli Group on 24 Aug are arrested by Botswana Police at Tutume.

4 Lithuli Group arrested: John DUBE; JAMBO; MLENZE; Christopher NKOSANA

29 Aug: Intensive patrolling continues around the Nata and Tegwani Rivers. Canberra strikes are put in over wide area, with no results. Tracks are followed to the Botswana border, made by the four who were arrested at Tutume the day before.

30 Aug: The two Lithuli deserters on 28 Aug are arrested by a BSAP patrol on a bus travelling towards Plumtree.

2 Lithuli men arrested: Dumisani DHLANGAMANDHLA; Stanley MEHLO

31 Aug: 7 Tp, 2 CDO 1RLI capture one Lithuli man who had gone to a kraal to obtain food, but whose presence was reported to the police. He led a joint force of 7 Tp under 2 Lt VILJOEN and 11 Pl under 2 Lt SCHLACHTER to the remainder of his comrades.

1 Lithuli man captured: Ambrose NCUBE

31 Aug: At 10h15 a short contact ensues. One RLI Trooper is wounded. Four of the Lithuli Group are killed.

1 RLI wounded: Tpr ENGELBRECHT
4 Lithuli Group KIA: Abraham MARIKITA; Peter MHLONGO; Donald NYATI; Goliat THEBE
1 Lithuli Group escapes: Haliman KOBOTSHWA

3 Sep: David MADZIBA, leader of the Lobengula Group, is arrested by the BSAP at St Paul's Mission in the Lupane District. He is the second of the Lobengula Group who escaped from the 3 Pl contact on 18 Aug.

1 Lobengula Group arrested: David MADZIBA

A dead rhino is found 20 miles SW of Intundhla Siding.

4 Sep: 10 Pl under Lt NOBLE follow tracks from the dead rhino. At 13h15 10 Pl come into contact with CTs. In the contact Pte PEDZISAYI is wounded and Pte Nyika MUCHAZOREGA is killed. Three CTS are killed.

1 RAR KIA: Pte MUCHAZOREGA
1 RAR wounded: Pte PEDZISAYI
3 Lobengula Group KIA: Eric NDUNA; NGWANE; James NKONZO

8 Sep: Op Nickel closed.

20 Dec 1967: KENI aka CAN CAN arrested by BSAP at Plumtree
12 May 1968: Derek MKABELA arrested by SAP in Durban
15 May 1968: Haliman KOBOTSHWA makes his way to Zambia

STATEMENT – JOHN DUBE AKA CHARLES NGWEYA

SECRET

MI/33/4

G (INT)

OP 'NICKEL' : REPORT BY TER COMMANDER

1.   On the 29th April, 1968 Tayson Makheto NDHLOVU was flown from BOTSWANA to ZAMBIA after being released from GABERONES jail. A search of NDHLOVU on his exit revealed a letter written to Lusaka by Charles NGWEYA, the overall Commander of the group which entered RHODESIA.

2.   A copy of the letter in the form of a report on events after the group entered RHODESIA is attached for your information.

3.   The above was received from a delicately placed source and it is requested that it be treated accordingly.

4.   The report is graded A.1.

13 May 1968.

(K.A. RADFORD)
Lt Col
DMI

VOC

Cy S

FJO 1

G (OPS)

G (INT)   13/5.

Please give me a lessons-to-be-learnt
extract from this report &
SECRET verify they appear in our
official lessons learnt
already published

13 May

<u>C O P Y</u>   SECRET

Dear Comrades,

Well I will say I am glad once knowing that I write
a report which will reach you. As you will realize this is not
the first one I have written and got no reply, so I agree. The
first day I crossed the river. I was on bank when it was day break
with whole detachment still coming behind. I placed the first
section of full defence of the way from river in order that the
whole detachment crossed whatever would happen. The detachment
kept coming up to 7 a.m. At 8 a.m. all commanders reported
the presence of all their detachments. Since it was day time
I order every detachment on position so that there is not too
much movement. I went around making sure of their position were
suitable. I was satisfied at 2 p.m. I ordered a detachment
of 6 people to recce. a distance of 4 to 5 miles from the river
and tell of the enemy front. They left well armed in case of
clash. I order them to report back before 5.15. I got two out
of this group reporting that the place had people upt to the
distance they returned. I had given them a man who knew the
local language in case they met civilians he should ask the place we
are. The two who returned said the other he said we shall get
them at a spot they turned. At 6 p.m. I ordered the march with
the two joining my recce. We marched 4 miles. The rec. said
they cannot get the other 4. I order a rest to the whole
detachment so that we should around for these 4 people. I
ordered the recomm. to look for they in the command of Isaac
<u>Lizivi</u> who had come the 4. It was very dark. When Isaac was
busy giving signal and calls another 4 from his group took
cover just near us. When Isaac came reported that he was
missing 4 people from the group. When I asked where he lost them
they had me. I heard them coming I asked where they were. They
said laying near by they did not hear the order well. So I gave
them a compass and told them to carry on the search. I had
wasted an hour and half. They broke the compass there. I
asked for another compass and gave them. I order the march and
we marched for an hour at a very slow pace. The rec. reported a
road. When they came to report somebody mistook them for an enemy.
The whole detachment began to cock their guns. Without an order
somebody shot by accident. I will say there was confusion in
the whole detachment. I had call all the commanders to put
the whole thing in hand. I crossed the road with all the
necessary precautions. I called for a rest and talked to the whole
detachment trying to give them moral - it worked. I never had such
a thing again. I marched on for three hours and ordered a days
rest thinking of all those behind. I thought I was going to be
followed. At 6 a.m. I took David and Mjolo for a round detachment
rec. I discovered I was amongst people. The terrain was
not very good. I went back to the camp. I tried utmost to ration
food. At 3 p.m. I sent another group back to try and find the
group of 6 of the past night and another group to contact the
civilians. All these groups were to fight if met by the enemy.
The group which went to the civilian came first for good news.
The man talked to us a friendly one and the group from river
arrived having no trace of the other 6. I decided to see the
civilian personally so I left orders that after food the detachment
should follow. I went with 4 people. I had put to guard the
village from a far in case there was anything the day. I went
and met this old man. He was very friendly. He gave us food and
water for everybody. He said he was determined to help in any way.
He gave me a road to follow and another friendly man I could buy
food. The detachment arrived. I started using the way given
by this old man. I arrived at the man described. I went personal
and bought food from him. He told me the way. These people
gave me the way passing 50 meters from one of the hospitals. I
passed well and marched on until day break. I ordered a

day/....

17

- 2 -

sleep. The detachment was in high morals and very attentive to any orders given. I expected the enemy, nothing happened again. At 6 I ordered another march. I moved the whole night up to 6 a.m. - had a day's rest. Moved off at 6. Crossed Railway and main road at about 3 a.m. Moved on up to 6 a.m. Had another day's rest. I thought they could trace our trail on the road but nothing before crossing the railway. These people when we had a ten minutes rest one of them his gun. I had to wait for him when he went looking for it. Before long they said he had come. I said we move on. When I made my day's rest I heard that this man had not returned. ✓ I asked, they said he had come. I could not get any answer. Davie reported one of his men missing. I ordered they to look for him. They looked but brought a negative answer. I could do nothing about all these people who were getting lost now and then. So I order all the commanders to report to me the presence of their men of every rest. This they did. I moved on, went all night. We were short of food. At 6 I ordered a days rest. I ordered some man to shoot some animals. They were many and the place had no people around. They shot one big animal. The detachment had a square meal. I started at 4 p.m. that day. We moved for some time, then Davie had to part with his detachment. I will say it was not easy for me to command such a big detachment for the first time. We parted with Davie. I moved on the whole night. Had a days rest, marched on for two nights still eating the animal that we shot before we parted. Water was short too. I was at a place where there was muddy water. I spent a day. I shot a zebra. In the evening we ate it and carried some meat for three days. The plane had no sign of man or animal. People were worn out. I had a day's rest and sent three men to recce. A sound which seemed sounding far away in the distance. They got lost. I had to remain in the same position for the night in case they came. I went out with another group in the morning but could not trace them. They turned up at about 2 p.m. I had seen a place in the morning which turned around us. They reported these three, a road which was very old. I decided to march on. I got the road and water in the morning. This road had not been used since it was made it seemed. I decided to follow it since it was going my direction. There was no food. I marched for 3 days without food. I ordered another rest. There was water at about a mile from where I was. I went to see the place and tried to see if I could get an animal. There was a lot of animal signs. ✓2 people I was going with volunteered to remain in case some animals could come and drink so I agreed. I went back. I hardly stayed on minute in Base. I heard the sound of a car. I was just about 20 metres away. A truck stopped. I ordered everybody to be ready. The enemy seemed not to see me. They went into the car. I passed on my nose. I think they found those 2 I left waiting for animals. I decided to change base at once. There was now two helicopters and a spotter plane overhead. In a very short time I moved the detachment for about a mile. The terrain was very bad. I lay low to wait for the 2 comrades. I heard shots. They shooting all over even towards us. We made no reply. At 6 I order a section to go where we were and see if the two had come and go and see if the enemy had caught them. They never came until next morning. The commander was not reliable so I prepared to move in the evening. The detachment was at its fourth day without food. Planes were more than 4 in the air. We remained under cover the whole day. At 6 p.m. we marched on for another 3 days without food. We could shoot a dive and share the soup to the whole detachment with the enemy behind. I came out of the Game Reserve at about 4 a.m. There were 3 roads both sides of the fence. I crossed. Cadri was completely finished. We had to carry him. When all of the detachment was only moving in separate I could not go far because of these difficulties. I made a base about 4 miles from the fence. There

SECRET
- 3 -

were cocks crowing at a distance. I sent two people to contact the people.
They met an old man who them some milk and information that we were
to be reported if seen. They got £50 per head of us. We had camped not
very far from their main base. The people were waiting for us. I
wanted to go and see this man so that I could orientate myself. When
I was preparing to go I was taken by heavy firing from my west flank.
Grenades were heavy on the detachment. I decided to go for them. So
I order most of detachment to turn to the enemy. We advanced in a
skirmish line. I caught them. When they saw me and heard my shouts
for orders to encircle them they run for their lives. We had to pick
them one by one by fire. When I came back I found I had three comrades
dead, 3 wounded, one was in a critical position. Before I started
the march he was dead too. I had nothing to use for burying these
fallen comrades. When I counted the enemy dead there were 8.? We
captured food. Almost all of their bags were there. 1 Bren, Gun, 2
F.N. rifles, 3 Sten guns, 2 radios, maps, grenades and ammunition.
I ordered our radio operator to remain by the radio since they had
no codes. They were scared to come for us so they lay an ambush for us
at the water. I was hearing all this in the radio so I marched and
avoided this place. When I was near their place of ambush 3 of their
men came running thinking we were their group. I opened fire on them.
2 were shot at the same time. The group which had run away went into their
own ambush. I heard heavy firing in their direction. I marched on
in the morning. They said they had killed 5 of their own people plus
the other 2. When I made a base I did not know the place, I was bucked
at a far distance. I sent 3 people to see and ask what place we were.
They went and reported no life nearby. At 2 p.m. somebody reported
people talking. I sent 2 people. They stayed too long. I decided
to follow them. I followed. It was not far. I saw a fire. I went
nearer. I could not make out whether these people were local or the enemy.
I decided to talk to them. I greeted them. They all lifted their heads.
They were scared. I could see in their faces. One just went for his Sten
gun and shot at me. Luckily the other 2 comrades I had sent saw me
and opened up from the other side of the enemy. They started jumping
over their commanders running. I could not fire. I went for reinforcements.
We had a long battle. They were coming. I grenaded them. Africans
were running away so we were engaged with their officers. They asked
for Helicopter reinforcement. They came too late. It was dark.
They asked them to fire even on themselves. The Helicopters refused and
left the at our mess. When the battle ended the enemy left everything behind. We captured 2 F.N. guns, 3 Sten guns, 3 radios, maps,
compasses, food and all their bags. I received 2 dead and one wounded.
Things were difficult to carry with all these wounded to be carried.
Water was the first thing we need. I decided to take the river direction.
I wanted to know the place I was very much. I got to a river
which seemed to have no water. The wounded were fainting in need
of water. I decided to take volunteers to go and get to Manzamnyama
of which I knew there was water. I got 8 people and started. Left
our bags. The place seemed near. I went about 6 miles. I got the
river and water and started back. When I counted 6 miles I found I
was not anywhere near the camp. I called the whole night, no
response, shot in the air, no response. I stopped at 4 a.m. I started
again at 6 a.m. I could not trace the place up to 4 p.m. We realised
we were not going these people. I decided to go where there were people.
When I asked how much rounds they carried they had very little to stand
any strong battle. I went on during the day and night thinking I was going
to pick where the group had walked by day. I failed to trace them. I
got people they were alright. I asked them to go with their cattle to

SECRET

see/..

SECRET

~ 4 ~

see if they can trace the main group. They reported a lot of the
enemy reinforcement. I remained at this point thinking I could get
an enemy. They enemy was too much for us. We were at this point
for 2 days and nights. The enemy was screaming, the civilians beating
them. Those who were going to the store were to say where they were
getting the money from. The boy we sent was caught and revealed us.
In the evening they came, so we had to jump this side. Most of the
things you will get from this man in a much detailed way.

SECRET

PREFACE

Occasionally in the study of military history, one finds a particularly exemplary organization whose story is not widely known but is worth retelling, and often. When I learned the history of the Rhodesian African Rifles, I saw precisely such a story and felt obliged to do the very best I could to capture that story, to describe the essence of the Regiment itself against the context of the broader wars in which it fought. I was honored and humbled to meet so many veterans of the RAR and the Rhodesian Army, and to hear their stories myself. Those stories - the research that led to this thesis - remain the greatest experience of my lifetime.

To the men of the Regiment, this story needs no description. But to those of us who did not live it, the history of the RAR is vitally important to understand. We see increasingly that the world divides us along every possible crack and fissure that defines groups of people living amongst one another. Like the men of the RAR, we must build and hone those forces that can bring us together to withstand the divisive forces around us. Their story was and remains an inspiration, and I hope readers and historians continue to find the very good example that the RAR set for us.

Col Michael Stewart
Seoul, Korea, 2021

Biography

Born in West Point, New York, Colonel Michael P. Stewart graduated and was commissioned from The Citadel in Charleston, South Carolina in 1998. His current assignment in the US Army is as the Chief of Fires for US Forces, Korea.

His previous assignments include command and developmental positions at all levels from Company and Battery through to Army Service Component Command. Before arriving at US Forces Korea, Col Stewart's most recent assignment was as a student at the US Army War College in Carlisle, Pennsylvania. Other previous assignments include: Company Fire Support Officer, Battery Executive Officer, and Infantry Battalion S-3 Air with the 173d Airborne Brigade in Vicenza, Italy; Battalion Fire Support Officer with 1st Battalion, 72nd Armor, 1st Brigade, 2nd Infantry Division in Camp Casey, Korea; Assistant Battalion S-3, Battery Commander, and Brigade Fire Support Officer with 4th Brigade, 101st Airborne Division in Fort Campbell, KY; Chief of Exercises at US Army Africa in Vicenza, Italy; Assistant Division Fire Support Coordinator, Battalion Executive Officer (3rd Battalion, 6th Field Artillery), and Brigade Executive Officer (1st Brigade Combat Team) at 10th Mountain Division in Fort Drum, NY; Chief of Fires, U.S. Army Cyber Command at Fort Belvoir, VA; Battalion Commander at 5th Battalion, 25th Field Artillery Regiment at Fort Polk, LA; and Chief of Doctrine for the Fires Center of Excellence at Fort Sill, Oklahoma. He has deployed numerous times, including three combat deployments to Iraq and Afghanistan as Battery Commander, Battalion/Brigade Executive Officer, and Battalion Commander.

Col Stewart is a graduate of the Field Artillery Officer Basic Course, the Field Artillery Captains Career Course, the Combined Arms Services Staff School, U.S. Army Command and General Staff College, US Army War College, Joint Firepower Control Course, Joint Targeting School, Airborne School, Ranger School, Jumpmaster School, Air Assault School, and Pathfinder School. He holds a Bachelor of Science degree in Civil Engineering from The Citadel; a Master of Military Art and Science degree in the Art of War from the US Army Command and General Staff College; and a Master of Strategic Studies degree from the US Army War College.

His awards and decorations include the Bronze Star Medal (third award), Meritorious Service Medal (sixth award), Army Commendation Medal (second award), Army Achievement Medal (fourth award), Meritorious Unit Citation (second award), National Defense Service Medal, Afghanistan Campaign Medal (with one service star), Iraq Campaign Medal (with two service stars), Inherent Resolve Campaign Medal, Global War on Terrorism Service Medal, Korean Defense Service Medal, NATO Medal, Combat Action Badge, Pathfinder Badge, Ranger Tab, and Senior Parachutist Badge.

Col Stewart is married to Jennifer, his bride of fifteen years. They have two children: Elizabeth, 12, and Patrick, 9.

ACKNOWLEDGMENTS

This work would not have been possible without the efforts of many others on my behalf. First and always, I must thank my wife, Jennifer, for her unwavering support and sacrifice during the many long hours of research and writing that kept me away from my family. Thanks also to Dr. Dan Marston, Dr. Nick Murray, and Dr. Scott Stephenson for your guidance and counsel, and to my colleagues at the Command and General Staff College Art of War Scholars Program - Eric, Darrell, Mike, Marcus, Art and Half-Pint. I also appreciate the gracious assistance of eminent Rhodesian historian, Dr. Richard Wood, who provided maps, insight, and continued correspondence throughout this project.

I am eternally grateful to the veterans of the Rhodesian Army and Rhodesian African Rifles, many of whom I had the privilege of meeting during the course of this study. These are remarkable men whose hospitality, openness and honesty were tremendous. I only hope this work is adequate representation of a worthy and noble regiment.

THE RHODESIAN AFRICAN RIFLES: THE GROWTH AND ADAPTATION OF A MULTICULTURAL REGIMENT THROUGH THE RHODESIAN BUSH WAR 1965-1980

A thesis presented to the Faculty of the U.S. Army
Command and General Staff College in partial fulfilment
of the requirements for the

Degree

MASTER OF MILITARY ART AND SCIENCE

Military History

by

MICHAEL P. STEWART, MAJOR, U.S. ARMY

Fort Leavenworth, Kansas 2011-02

ACRONYMS

2IC	Second in Command (Executive Officer)
ANC	African National Council
BSAP	British South Africa Police
CIO	Central Intelligence Organisation
CO	Commanding Officer
COIN	Counter-Insurgency
ComOps	Combined Operations
FRELIMO	(Frente de Libertaçao de Moçambique) Liberation Front of Mozambique
FROLIZI	Front for the Liberation of Zimbabwe
FPLM	(Forças Populares para o Libertaçåo de Moçambique) Popular Forces for the Liberation of Mozambique
GOC	General Officer Commanding
JMC	Joint Military Command
JOC	Joint Operations Command
KAR	King's African Rifles
NRR	Northern Rhodesia Regiment
OAU	Organisation of African Unity
OC	Officer Commanding
OCC	Operations Coordination Committee
OP	Observation Post
PATU	Police Anti-Terrorist Unit
PF	Patriotic Front
PRAW	Police Reserve Air Wing
PWO	Platoon Warrant Officer
PV	Protected Village
RAF	Rhodesian Airforce
RAR	Rhodesian African Rifles
RENAMO	(Resistência Nacional Moçambicana) Mozambican National Resistance
RhAF	Rhodesian Air Force (after 1970)
RLI	Rhodesian Light Infantry
RNR	Rhodesia Native Regiment
RSF	Rhodesian Security Forces
RSM	Regimental Sergeant Major
RR	Rhodesia Regiment (after 1970)
RRAF	Royal Rhodesian Airforce (pre-1970)
RRR	Royal Rhodesian Regiment (pre-1970)
SAANC	South African African National Congress
SADF	South African Defence Force
SAP	South African Police
SAS	Special Air Service
SB	Special Branch
TTL	Tribal Trust Land
UANC	United African National Council
UDI	Unilateral Declaration of Independence
WO	Warrant Officer
ZANLA	Zimbabwe African National Liberation Army
ZANU	Zimbabwe African National Union
ZAPU	Zimbabwe African People's Union
ZIPA	Zimbabwe People's Army
ZIPRA	Zimbabwe People's Revolutionary Army

CHAPTER 1 – INTRODUCTION

During 65 years of regimental history, men of different races with a common ideal had worked and fought together in a spirit of true comradeship and mutual esteem. In the process, a respect and understanding evolved between them which comes only to men who face conflict together and which cannot be described.

Without exception, all who served with the regiment were proud of it and would testify to the unique and profound effect it had on their lives.

Alexandre Binda, Masodja: the History of the Rhodesian African Rifles and its forerunner, the Rhodesia Native Regiment

The Rhodesian African Rifles (RAR) overcame profoundly divisive racial and tribal differences among its members because a transcendent "regimental culture" - described above as a "common ideal" - superseded the disparate cultures of its individual soldiers and officers. The RAR's culture grew around the traditions of the British regimental system, after which the RAR was patterned. The soldiers of the RAR, regardless of racial or tribal background, identified themselves first as soldiers and members of the regiment, before their individual race and tribe. Regimental history and traditions, as well as shared hardships on deployments and training were mechanisms that forced officers and soldiers to see past such differences. These factors enabled the RAR to withstand the racial and tribal tensions of the Rhodesian Bush War (1965-1980) and thrive as a combat effective and competent military force. The history of the RAR provides an example of how military culture, effectively developed, can prevail over cultural clashes among groups of mixed identity.

CULTURAL BACKDROP

The RAR principally recruited from three groups of people within Rhodesia: the officer corps primarily came from the white Rhodesian population, while the ordinary soldiers and most noncommissioned officers were from the Ndebele (Matabele) tribe of southwest Rhodesia and the Shona (Mashona) tribe of the north, east, and central portions of the country.

The ability of the RAR to bring together disparate racial groups is altogether more impressive when one remembers that the Ndebele and Shona tribes fought each other shortly before the arrival of whites in the country. The Ndebele were descendants of the Zulus, who lived further south, and they arrived in the southwestern portion of what would become Rhodesia around 1837. The warlike Ndebele immediately came to dominate the relatively disorganized Shona tribes of the area, raiding villages and generally treating Shona as inferior tribes within the Ndebele kingdom. Several decades of internecine rivalry ensued, until the arrival of white settlers in 1890[1].

The 1890 arrival of Cecil John Rhodes' pioneer column began to establish Southern Rhodesia - a British protectorate - based on mining rights dubiously granted to his British South Africa Company by King Lobengula of the Ndebele. Several years of sporadic fighting between the native tribes and Rhodes' pioneers ended in 1897 when the British South Africa Company defeated a tribal uprising. White settlers quickly established a government and economic system such that by 1931, most of the land and power belonged to the 50,000 whites, while the one million black Africans found themselves poor, uneducated and largely left out of the political process.[2]

The dynamics of racial and tribal differences in Rhodesia were rooted in this conflict, and were left simmering from the 19th century through to the 1961 nationalist movements. By 1961, the cause of black nationalism in Southern Rhodesia was led by the Zimbabwe African People's Union, a predominantly Ndebele but tribally mixed group. In 1963, a faction of ZAPU split off to form the Zimbabwe African

---

[1] Mark R. Lipschultz and R. Kent Rasmussen, Dictionary of African Historical Biography (Los Angeles, CA: University of California Press, 1989), 167-8.

[2] J.R.T. Wood, "Countering the CHIMURENGA: The Rhodesian Counterinsurgency Campaign," in Counterinsurgency in Modern Warfare, eds. Daniel Marston and Carter Malkasian (Oxford: Osprey Publishing, 2010), 192.

National Union (ZANU), which became a predominantly Shona group. These two movements derived from the same tribal populations as the RAR, yet they were never as successful at setting aside tribal conflicts and rivalries as the RAR was. Using only their own tribal culture to guide behavior, the soldiers of the RAR most likely could not have formed a cohesive unit - ZAPU and ZANU never did. It took a more powerful culture - a regimental one - to unite these disparate elements into one cohesive unit.

THE RHODESIAN AFRICAN RIFLES – A HISTORICAL OVERVIEW

The RAR was the oldest and largest regular regiment in the Rhodesian army. Its roots dated to the 1916 formation of the Rhodesia Native Regiment (RNR), which fought for the British in East Africa during World War I. When the regiment stood down in 1919, a cadre of the RNR formed the Askari platoon of the British South Africa Police (BSAP). When the Empire called again, in 1940, this cadre formed the nucleus around which Lieutenant Colonel Francis John Wane built the Rhodesian African Rifles. [3]

After training in Northern Rhodesia, Kenya and Tanganyika (Tanzania), the regiment deployed to Burma in 1944, where it distinguished itself in the fighting during the Arakan campaign, and again at Taungup and Tanlwe Chaung. [4]

After the Burma Campaign, Major Walter Walker (later General Sir Walter Walker KCB, CBE, DSO & Two Bars), said of the RAR:

> The conduct of the askari, most of whom had never experienced enemy fire before, deserves a lasting tribute. Their energy and endurance on the march and on patrol through some of the worst country in the Arakan, their constancy and discipline under the stress of persistent mortar and artillery fire, and their cheerfulness throughout the appalling weather conditions, which developed in the latter stages of the operation, were beyond praise. [5]

Further praise for the RAR came from a captured Japanese officer's diary, where he noted,

> "[t]he enemy soldiers are not from Britain, but are from Africa. Because of their beliefs they are not afraid to die, so, even if their comrades have fallen, they keep on advancing as if nothing had happened. They have excellent physique and are very brave, so fighting against these soldiers is somewhat troublesome." [6]

After World War II, the RAR remained active, guarding Royal Air Force training bases in Rhodesia, before briefly deploying to the Suez in 1952. After the regiment returned home from Egypt, Queen Elizabeth, The Queen Mother presented them with the Queen's and Regimental Colors on 12 July 1953[7]. The regiment deployed again, this time to Malaya from 1956-8, as part of the Federation of Rhodesia and Nyasaland fighting alongside the forces of other Commonwealth nations. While in Malaya, the RAR proved adept at jungle warfare, honing its skills hunting down communist terrorists in the southern Malayan province of Johore. [8]

After returning home again in 1958, the RAR was assigned to "duties in the aid of the civil power", and over the next several years was deployed into Northern Rhodesia and Nyasaland, where civil unrest was unraveling the Central African Federation - a British colonial administrative unit comprised of Southern Rhodesia, Northern Rhodesia and Nyasaland. With the breakup of the Federation in 1963, three

---

[3] Alexandre Binda, Masodja: the History of the Rhodesian African Rifles and its Forerunner, the Rhodesia Native Regiment (Durban, 30 Degrees South Publishers, 2007), 41; Christopher Owen, The Rhodesian African Rifles (London: Leo Cooper Ltd., 1970), 2.
[4] Binda, Masodja, 64-68.
[5] Owen, 63.
[6]Ibid.
[7] Binda, Masodja, 109; J.R.T. Wood, The War Diaries of Andre Dennison (Gibraltar: Ashanti, 1989), 372.
[8] Binda, Masodja, 115-133.

new states emerged - Zambia (formerly Northern Rhodesia), Malawi (formerly Nyasaland) and Rhodesia (formerly Southern Rhodesia).[9]

The RAR returned to the control of the Rhodesian Army in 1963, just as ZAPU and ZANU were beginning increasingly militant campaigns to overthrow the white Rhodesian government. ZAPU and ZANU each built military organizations, called the Zimbabwe People's Revolutionary Army (ZIPRA) and Zimbabwe African National Liberation Army (ZANLA), respectively. Rhodesia unilaterally declared independence from Britain on 11 November, 1965. From that date until 1980, the RAR served as a critical element of Rhodesian security forces, conducting hundreds of operations in the bush alongside other Rhodesian troops.

Of the RAR's performance during the Bush War, Army Commander Lieutenant General G. Peter Walls said:

> The men of this regiment are above faction or tribe or politics. They are an elite group of fighting men, both European and African, to whom the country owes an incalculable debt for their dedication and bravery. And their moral courage in the face of insidious assaults from those who would undermine their sense of purpose is nothing short of admirable …But not only are they brave and efficient soldiers. Their spirited approach to their task and their joie-de-vivre, their sheer love of serving are an example which many would do well to emulate. [10]

When the ZANU-Patriotic Front (ZANU-PF), led by Robert Mugabe, took control of the country following elections in 1980, the nation became Zimbabwe, and the RAR became the 1:1, 4:2, and 3:3 Infantry Battalions of the Zimbabwe Army.

The regiment continued to serve Zimbabwe as a multicultural organization, while nationalist ZIPRA and ZANLA factions fought one another based on tribal differences and feuds. In fact, the RAR intervened in clashes between elements of ZIPRA and ZANLA in holding camps after the elections.[11] Officers and soldiers of the RAR began to leave the regiment as the command of the Zimbabwe Army ordered the unit to sever its links to its traditions in order to incorporate the largely untrained and incompetent soldiers and leaders from ZIPRA and ZANLA into its ranks. The RAR officially disbanded in April 1981.[12]

Throughout its history the RAR served with distinction, first for the British Crown and the Commonwealth, then for its own country on its own soil, and ultimately - briefly - under the command of its former enemy, Robert Mugabe. Throughout all the changes and amidst all the competing cultural influences, the RAR remained a steadfast, professional military force. It was precisely this history and lineage that established the regimental culture of the RAR.

SYMBOLS, TRAINING AND SHARED HARDSHIPS

The symbols, training and shared hardships in the RAR enhanced values of loyalty, pride, and discipline, as well as the importance of regimental identity over that of the individual. Symbols, such as the regimental colors and badge, embodied the history and nature of the regiment. Training and deployment bonded the individual members of the regiment together through shared hardship and accomplishment.

For any regiment, the colors are the most visible symbol of the unit's history. The RAR was no exception. When the Queen presented colors to the RAR in 1953, she publicly and permanently

---

[9] Ibid. 169-173.
[10] Binda, Masodja, 268.
[11] Ibid. 380-389. At Entumbane, the RAR stood between ZIPRA and ZANLA elements of the newly created Zimbabwe Army and prevented escalation of the fighting into a full-scale civil war. This is covered in more detail in Chapter 7.
[12] Wood, War Diaries, 372; Binda, Masodja, 389.

acknowledged the regiment and major campaigns in which it earned honors.[13] The Queen Mother concluded her speech at the presentation of the RAR colors with the following words:

> In the short history of the Rhodesian African Rifles you have proved by your service in Burma that you can hold your own in battle. By your service since the war you have shown that you carry your duties towards the Queen, the Colony, and its people, with smartness and efficiency. I know how many of you volunteered to serve in the Middle East when help was needed. By this, you have shown that you are ready to take your share in the welfare of the Commonwealth, by all these things you have won the honour of carrying your Colours. I present them in recognition of your loyalty in the past, and in the faith that you and those that follow you in the Regiment will always guard its tradition and strive to bring new honour to its name.[14]

In addition to the battle honors, the Queen's colors represented the regiment's allegiance to the British sovereign, symbolized in the crown and the interposed crosses of St. Andrew and St. George on the Union Jack.[15] The single icon of the colors provided every member of the regiment, from the commanding officer to the newest private, a reminder of exactly what their predecessors had done. "The colours emblazoned with battle honours, commemorating some of the gallant deeds performed by members of the regiment, are a visible record. They keep a feeling of pride in past and present soldiers."[16] By learning the history behind the words and symbols on the colors, as instructed during their training, soldiers understood what was expected of them and they took pride in their regiment.

If the colors embodied the history, the RAR badge displayed the truly multi-cultural nature of the regiment. This badge, devised within months of the establishment of 1st Battalion in 1940,

> consisted of the Matabele shield (I-Hawu), in brown and white, upon which was vertically placed a knobkierie (nkudu) and crossed assegais. Across the bottom left to top right was the Shona digging spear (Museve) with the narrow sharp blade and an iron pick at the base of the shaft. Crossing from bottom right to top left of the badge was the broad-bladed fighting spear of the Zulu warrior (Umkonto). The badge was supported by a scroll bearing the inscription Rhodesian African Rifles, with black lettering on a red background.[17]

By capturing essential elements of the Ndebele and Shona cultures, the regimental badge symbolized the unity of these two historically hostile tribes within the RAR. The RAR created a new cultural symbol in which its soldiers, regardless of race or tribe, could take great pride. By breaking down the tribal barriers between individuals, this symbol allowed RAR soldiers to build loyalty, both to the regiment and between themselves.

The fighting spirit of the RAR evolved during its training and deployments. Training was tough, and shared by all members of the regiment - officers, soldiers and noncommissioned officers alike. Retired Australian Brigadier John Essex-Clark recalls his time as a lieutenant and platoon commander in the RAR, training his platoon to deploy to Malaya in 1956:

> We snap-shot at moving targets many times a week. The twenty-five metre ranges were less than a hundred metres away and were used day and night. I taught my askari to aim very low, at the crotch area, so they would hit the chest in the gloom of the jungle.

---

[13] Binda, Masodja, 225. The four battle honors earned by the RAR by 1953 were: East Africa 1916-18, Arakan Beaches, Taungup, and Burma 1944-45.

[14] Her Majesty Queen Elizabeth the Queen Mother (speech to the Rhodesian African Rifles, 12 July 1953).

[15] Unlike the RLI, the RAR never adopted the green and white Rhodesian President's Color to replace the Queen's color after UDI.

[16] Wood, War Diaries, 14.

[17] Ibid., 13.

Within a few months every askari in my platoon could, while blindfold, strip, clean, assemble, load and fire at level targets in front of them.

Their immediate action drills on automatic weapons were instantaneous and they could fix faults instinctively. They could pack up their gear and break camp at night within minutes. They could slip stealthily into ambush within seconds and most of them could hit with ease a moving 'figure' target at twenty-five metres.[18]

Training remained paramount through the bush war, particularly on marksmanship, as most African soldiers had little experience with firearms before joining the army. In conducting training, the RAR soldiers learned the capabilities of their officers, and learned to trust them.[19]

Loyalty to officers in the RAR was paramount. In 1977, when the regiment was designated for parachute training, many of the men had never even seen an aircraft before, let alone jumped from one. Their motivation to do such an unnatural task did not come from their faith in the aircraft, parachute or any training - in the end, as one RAR officer described, it was a matter of trust between the officer and his men. After explaining how everything functioned on the aircraft and the parachute, as well as detailing drop altitudes and possible malfunctions, one officer was reminded of the simplicity of the matter when a soldier said, "Ishe, if you go, I will follow".[20]

Ready for the Regiment. Intake of new soldiers at Depot RAR
Source: CE20110908G0001, former RAR officer (photo by Robal Studios).

The regiment deployed frequently throughout its history, particularly during the 1965-1980 Bush War while fighting ZIPRA and ZANLA. The rotation schedule during the Bush War was typically a six week deployment in the bush, followed by a ten day period to rest, recover and refit, then back out for six more weeks.[21] There simply was no time for racism in the RAR, nor was there room to accommodate tribal feuds. RAR soldiers and officers worried more about the level of training and competence of their men than tribal backgrounds. This cannot be said for ZIPRA and ZANLA. Tribal loyalties divided the two nationalist communist armies, and they proved unable to overcome their differences, even when mutual interest should have brought them together. In its heritage, symbols, training, and deployments, the RAR created an

---

[18] John Essex-Clark, Maverick Soldier: an Infantryman's Story (Burwood, Victoria: Melbourne University Press, 1991), 34.

[19] CE20110913M0001, former RAR officer, interview by author, Durban, Republic of South Africa, 13 September 2011.

[20] CE20110913M0001, former RAR officer, interview; CF20110920S0001, former RAR officer, interview by author, London, England, 20 September 2011; CE20110915B0001, Former RAR and SAS officer, interview by author, Cape Town, Republic of South Africa, 15 September 2011. Ishe meant "sir" or "chief" and was the term of respect from RAR soldiers to their officers.

[21] Ibid. This schedule was also reiterated in many other interviews with numerous former RAR officers.

overriding organizational culture that transcended tribal and racial differences by bringing diverse individual backgrounds into a common culture.[22]

The deep sense of loyalty between officers and soldiers remains immediately apparent among former members of the regiment today. An American Special Forces Vietnam veteran and former RAR company 2IC[23], commented that "[f]or those whites who served with African soldiers in the Rhodesian bush war there remains something that can best be called a 'Forever Sadness' caused by the separation after 'Independence' in the New Zimbabwe in March of 1980. I have a lump in my throat just thinking of the loss".[24]

PURPOSE AND CONDUCT OF THIS STUDY

The purpose of this study is to explore the regimental culture of the RAR, and to trace how that culture evolved throughout the Bush War, from 1965 to 1980. The aim is to answer the question: why would a black African fight to sustain a white-rule government in Africa? Logically, there should have been little willingness among the black population of Rhodesia to fight - often against family members - on behalf of a government that offered little social or political opportunity for blacks. The answer lies in the traditions, history, and culture of the regiment. Simply put, black soldiers in the RAR did not fight for the white government; they fought out of loyalty to their regiment and to each other. This is an attempt to explore and describe the depth of that loyalty.

The author, an active duty U.S. Army officer and combat veteran, has objectively researched the history and traditions of the RAR (particularly during the bush war of 1965-1980) to develop this study. The difficulties of developing and training multi-cultural military organizations present very real and current challenges to the U.S. military - in Iraq, Afghanistan, and increasingly in our expanding security cooperation role in Africa. This study offers insights into one successful historical example of a multi-cultural military unit, the RAR.

In conducting this study, the author interviewed over 30 Rhodesian Army veterans in South Africa, the United Kingdom, and the United States. Their memories and insights guide much of the discussion here. These veterans were mostly former officers in the RAR, although their ranks vary from warrant officer to major general and their regiments include the RAR, Rhodesian Light Infantry (RLI), Special Air Service (SAS), Rhodesia Regiment (RR), Rhodesian Army Education Corps, Grey's Scouts, and Selous Scouts. Many served in multiple regiments, some also served in other colonial regiments (such as the King's African Rifles and Northern Rhodesia Regiment), and most also served on the Rhodesian Army staff or the School of Infantry at least once in their careers. Several were company, battalion, and brigade commanders through key periods of the bush war. The critical missing piece of this research is the perspective of the black soldiers who served in the regiment. Time and circumstance did not allow interviews with these men during this study, but future studies in this field must capture their insights.

The insights gathered from interviews are injected into the context and events of the Bush War through the five phases of that war. These phases were first introduced by Dr. J.R.T. Wood (a former Rhodesia Regiment soldier and eminent historian on Rhodesia) in his book Counterstrike from the Sky. The events and details surrounding developments in each phase, as they affected the RAR, are described for the benefit of a reader who may have little prior knowledge of Rhodesia or the Rhodesian bush war. The aim is not to portray a complete picture of how Rhodesia lost the war. Other historical accounts have addressed such ideas[25], and many of these works may be found in the bibliography. The aim of this study

---

[22] CE20110909T0001, former RAR officer, interview by author, 9 September 2011; CF20110920S0001, former RAR officer, interview.

[23] 2IC is an abbreviation for "Second in Command". In the Rhodesian Army, as in the British Army, the 2IC for a company or battalion had essentially the same duties and responsibilities as an Executive Officer (XO) in the American military structure.

[24] CG20110927S0001, former RAR officer, interview by author, Portland, Oregon, 27 September 2011.

[25] Such broader analytical works include J. K. Cilliers' Counterinsurgency in Rhodesia; Paul Moorcraft and Peter McLaughlin's The Rhodesian War: A Military History; J.R.T. Wood's article in Counterinsurgency in Modern Warfare; and Greg Mills and Grahame Wilson's RUSI article, "Who Dares Loses? Assessing Rhodesia's Counterinsurgency Experience", to list a few.

is simply to follow how these events and details influenced (or did not influence) change in the culture of the RAR through the war.

Where referenced, the interviews are kept confidential: that is, the names of the interviewed officers are not disclosed here. This is not at the request of the men interviewed, but in adherence to the policies of the Art of War Scholars Program at the US Army Command and General Staff College.

CHAPTER 2 - WHY DID THEY FIGHT?

The white Rhodesians refused to accept an effective safeguard mechanism [of unimpeded movement toward majority rule] and instead, in a referendum on July 20, 1969, approved republic status which will end all ties with Great Britain as well as constitutional proposals which lay the groundwork for perpetuation of white control. The white minority - 4 percent of the population of Southern Rhodesia - made the decision; no more than a handful of the blacks voted. The minority of the 4.8 million blacks in Southern Rhodesia who are politically active have been expressing their opposition to the consolidation of white rule in two ways. A small segment have directly supported the liberation groups... Another small group has campaigned internally to get as many Africans as possible on the voter rolls.

U.S. National Security Council, Study in Response to National Security Study
Memorandum 39: Southern Africa, December 1969

When one studies the RAR's actions in the Rhodesian Bush War, one simple question surfaces along with a complicated answer: why would a black African soldier voluntarily fight to preserve a white-rule government in Africa? The above excerpt from a U.S. National Security Study in December 1969 highlights the essence of the Rhodesian struggle as it was perceived outside of Rhodesia. Notably, a third group of black Rhodesians - those who supported the government and joined the security forces to preserve it - is not considered. According to the U.S. National Security Council study, a "politically active" black Rhodesian had little cause to support the white Rhodesian government against the nationalist movements. Many did, however. By the end of the war, Rhodesian Security Forces boasted three battalions (nearly 80 percent of the regular army) of predominantly-black RAR, and many more RAR battalions could have been established. In addition, many of the BSAP policemen were black, and national service eventually placed black soldiers in the Rhodesia Regiment.[26]

To the RAR soldier, the regiment was a source of income, stability, and family pride - in many instances, he was doing the same job his father and grandfather had done before him. In the regiment, the RAR soldier was a respected member of a team rich in traditions and proud of its history. He was a part of a unique culture all its own. He was not a second-class citizen, nor was he viewed as inferior or incapable.[27] Leaders in the RAR - black and white - were tough, experienced, capable men who led by example and from the front, as do most good leaders in professional armies. While factors such as income, stability and

---

[26] CF20110920S0001, former RAR officer, interview; Nick Downie and Lord Richard Cecil, Frontline Rhodesia, DVD (Johannesburg: 30 Degrees South, 2007). In 1979, Prime Minister Muzorewa extended national service requirements to black Rhodesians. Prior to Muzorewa's governance, national service - that is, mandatory military service - only applied to whites. Throughout most of the bush war, black service was strictly voluntary.

[27] John Redfern, "Racial Discrimination in the Rhodesia and Nyasaland Army", Rhodesian Army memorandum, October 1962; John Redfern, "The Requirement for a Non-Racial Army in Southern Rhodesia", Rhodesian Army memorandum, October 1963. In 1962 and 1963, then-Captain (later Colonel) John Redfern at the Rhodesian Army School of Infantry wrote these two memoranda to the army commands of the Federal Army and Rhodesian Army respectively. In them, Redfern highlighted that racial practices of the Federal Army were unsuited for continued application, particularly in Southern Rhodesia. While his recommendations were not enacted at the time, it is noteworthy that the Rhodesian Army command concurred and forwarded them to the Rhodesian Air Force for action. The Air Force decided the status quo should remain, and the idea was not acted upon until 1977. The Rhodesian Army, and the RAR particularly, seemed far more open - much earlier - to racial integration than Rhodesian society as a whole (or American or British society at the time, for that matter). Additionally, during the course of researching this paper, the author personally interviewed over 30 Rhodesian Army veterans, from across the spectrum of service within the Rhodesian Security Forces (RSF). Without exception and in the most explicit terms, these men recounted their tremendous respect and admiration for the black soldiers with whom they had the privilege of serving. To say the African soldier was a respected member of a team is an understatement, as evident in how these men felt, and still feel, for their comrades.

family pride brought recruits to the RAR, they stayed and fought because of loyalty to the regiment and to their leaders.

Proud, professional RAR NCOs: Standing from left: Col C. B. McCullagh MBE, RSM
N. Tumbare MLM DMM, CSM Obert Veremu, CSM M. Pfupa, CSM Gobe, CSM Kisi,
CSM Kephasi. Source: Alexandre Binda, Masodja: The History of the Rhodesian
African Rifles and its forerunner, the Rhodesia Native Regiment (Johannesburg: 30
Degrees South, 2007), 257.

BLACK NATIONALISM VERSUS WHITE RULE

In exploring why black Africans fought for the Rhodesian government, one may ask its opposite question: why would they not? The seeds of black nationalism were well established by the 1960s. The white government offered little incentive, few opportunities for economic or political inclusion, and was viewed by many as a racist, colonial power. [28]

Black nationalist movements in Rhodesia dated back to the 1920s. Several incidents, including a 1948 general strike in Bulawayo, indicated a growing nationalist undercurrent within black Rhodesian society. The various movements for majority rule in Southern Rhodesia under the Central African Federation eventually became the Southern Rhodesian African National Congress (SRANC) in 1957 under the leadership of Joshua Nkomo. After it was banned in 1960, the SRANC reformed briefly as the National Democratic Party, then as ZAPU in 1961. ZAPU's agenda took a much more militant and hardline stance on immediate majority rule than its predecessors, conducting attacks on symbols of power structure and vulnerable white targets. This led to a ban on ZAPU in 1962, and the arrest of most of its leaders, including Nkomo.

In 1963, Ndabaningi Sithole and others disaffected with Nkomo's leadership of ZAPU (including Robert Mugabe, Herbert Chitepo and Rex Nhongo) split off and formed ZANU, which committed itself to

---

[28]Ronald Hyam, *Britain's Declining Empire: The Road to Decolonization 1918- 1968* (New York: Cambridge University Press, 2006), 365; Eliakim M. Sibanda, *The Zimbabwe African People's Union: 1961-87* (Trenton: Africa World Press, 2005), 78. Sibanda is a professor in the history department at the University of Winnipeg, and a former ZAPU member.

"a nonracial, democratic socialist, pan-Africanist state within the British Commonwealth"[29] , and pursued an even more hardline, militant movement for immediate majority rule. ZAPU and ZANU were Rhodesian manifestations of the larger black nationalist movements spreading across the African continent in the "post-colonial" period that began after World War II. By 1963, nationalist movements in Africa had swept from Algeria to Zambia, with varying degrees of successful transition.[30] As British Prime Minister Harold Macmillan famously stated in 1960, "The wind of change is blowing through this continent, and whether we like it or not, this growth of national consciousness is a political fact. We must all accept it as a fact, and our national policies must take account of it".[31]

On the surface, ZAPU and ZANU represented a revolutionary movement and were a part of the "wind of change". They promised a fundamental overhaul of the structure and governance of Rhodesia from minority (white) to majority (black) rule. They promised black Rhodesians their rightful share of the wealth and prosperity held by the tiny minority of whites under the Rhodesian system. Where that promise proved insufficient to secure support, they threatened and exacted horrific reprisals for any blacks who failed to support their struggle. Beneath the veil of good will, the true potential ugliness within the promise of ZANU and ZAPU was apparent to Rhodesia: to hand governance over to majority rule before that majority was ready to manage the country was inadvisable.[32] For Rhodesia, a quick glance north at the examples of the Congo, Zambia and Malawi provided ample evidence of the consequences of rushed majority rule. This coming wave of uncertainty and limited successful examples of transition to majority rule surely drove some politically aware black Rhodesians to defend the status quo of a stable (albeit exclusive) white government.[33]

The government of Rhodesia drew its heritage from precisely the imperial spirit of colonization and minority rule that was already obsolete. Cecil John Rhodes, the founder of Rhodesia, can quite objectively be described as the ultimate British imperialist[34]. White Rhodesia was founded upon commercial farming and mining. These industries relied on a steady supply of cheap, unskilled labor to support the endeavors of wealthy landowners and an efficient, business-friendly government to provide security as well as the economic mechanisms to maximize trade and profit. By 1961, this system had created a thriving economy that was unrivalled among African countries. It was truly the "jewel" of the continent. But a white

---

[29] Norma Kriger, Zimbabwe's Guerilla War: Peasant Voices (Cambridge: Cambridge University Press, 1993), 85. This quote is from ZANU's first policy statement under Ndabaningi Sithole.

[30] Kriger, 82-85; Paul Moorcraft and Peter McLaughlin, The Rhodesian War: A Military History (Johannesburg: Jonathan Ball, 2009), 24-27. From January 1960 to the end of 1961, the number of independent nations in Africa went from 8 to 26, including Congo, Nigeria, Tanzania, Malawi, and Zambia. Algeria became independent in July 1962, and Uganda by that October. The "wind of change" was blowing south; this fact was readily apparent to Rhodesians.

[31] Harold Macmillan (speech to South African Parliament, 3 February 1960).

[32] Ian Douglas Smith, The Great Betrayal: the Memoirs of Ian Douglas Smith (London: Blake, 1997), 149-50.

[33] CF20110920S0001, former RAR officer, interview.

[34] Cecil John Rhodes (1853-1902) was the founder of Rhodesia and a self-avowed advocate of the British Empire. Arriving in Natal, South Africa in 1870, Rhodes quickly began to speculate in diamond claims in Kimberley. These mining interests formed the De Beers Consolidated Mines and gained Rhodes a fortune and considerable political power in the Cape Colony, which he devoted to the furtherance of his own world views and the greater spread of British influence across southern Africa and the globe. Rhodes' second will, written in 1877, bequeathed his yet unrealized fortune to found a secret society that would extend British rule over the whole world and colonize most parts of it with British settlers, leading, among other things, to the "ultimate recovery of the United States of America" by the British Empire. In 1890 (the same year his British South African Company pioneer column moved across the Limpopo River into Mashonaland to found Fort Salisbury and Rhodesia) Rhodes became premier of the Cape Colony, where he began arranging his vision of a South African federation under the British flag. After sponsoring a failed raid into the Transvaal under Leander Jameson in 1895, however, Rhodes was forced to resign this position. After falling from power, he devoted himself to building a railroad from the Cape to Cairo to solidify British influence on the African continent and facilitate the spread of the British Empire. Ultimately unsuccessful in this endeavor, Rhodes died in Muizenburg, South Africa in 1902, leaving most of his £6 million inheritance to Oxford University in the form of scholarships for students from the United States, the British colonies, and Germany. For more on Cecil John Rhodes, read one of his several biographies, such as Cecil Rhodes: The Colossus of Southern Africa, by J. G. Lockhart and the Hon. C. M. Woodhouse (New York: The Macmillan Company, 1963).

government ruled it, and whites owned the key land. Black Rhodesians had little say in the governance of the country, they had no real vote, and they had very little share of the profitable farmland and mining properties. These issues were the fundamental reasons the militant black nationalist movement grew in Rhodesia, and they were the reasons the rest of the world refused to support the government of Ian Smith.[35]

These two sides - militant nationalism and incumbent white rule - grew increasingly polarized and vied for recruits among the black population. Military-aged black males in Rhodesia were often forced to choose their side.[36] Logically, there should have been little motivation for them to volunteer and fight to sustain the white-rule system. To many Rhodesian blacks, ZAPU and ZANU were not exactly the right answer. They represented hatred, communism and unbridled violence. For many more Rhodesian blacks, their lives in the rural tribal areas - politics aside - were increasingly interrupted by clashes and violence surrounding the issue of majority rule. To protest the atrocities of ZANU and ZAPU and protect their own livelihoods and tribal system, many black Africans voluntarily fought for white Rhodesia - in the RAR and in other elements of Rhodesian Security Forces.[37]

In fact, many more black recruits volunteered than could be accepted for service. One former RAR training officer stated that on recruiting days many more volunteers would stand outside the gates of the depot than required to fill 200 available training slots, from which about 130 trained soldiers would be selected and sent to the regiment after a six month training program.[38] This availability of volunteers did not substantially diminish throughout the bush war, even after fighting intensified through the late 1970s and the RAR was constantly deployed to fight increasing numbers of ZANLA and ZIPRA. In an interview with Illustrated Life Rhodesia in 1975, Lieutenant Colonel David Heppenstall, commander of 1RAR, stated that the regiment had no shortage of candidates, "often 100 per cent more than we require, and sometimes more than that percentage. I can recall one occasion when we required 100 recruits, and 500 applied".[39]

The RAR soldiers were never forced to fight against their fellow tribesmen in the nationalist organizations. However, they chose to do so in great numbers. The rest of this chapter will explore the reasons why many black soldiers made this choice.

INCOME

In 1963, the lowest entry-level African soldier in the RAR was paid about 10 percent of what his "European" or white, counterpart made in the RLI. This pay system was inherited from the Federal Army of Rhodesia and Nyasaland, and before that, from the British colonial army. The unequal pay scale improved only very slightly, until major reforms were made in 1977-8 to increase pay and opportunities among black and white soldiers in the Rhodesian army. Even so, the relatively modest pay for an African recruit in the RAR was on par or better than most of his other options and placed the RAR soldier in rather good financial standing among his counterparts in the villages and farms of Rhodesia.[40]

---

[35] Smith, The Great Betrayal, 149-50.

[36] CE20110909T0001, former RAR officer, interview. This former RAR officer recalled walking through a village near Fort Victoria late in the war to see nothing but old men, women and children. All of the military aged men were either in the RAR or in ZANLA. This effect on the population is often lost in military accounts of combat, but it had a tremendous effect on Rhodesian blacks. Neutrality was not an option.

[37] Only the RLI and Special Air Service (SAS) remained all-white through the end of the war. Black soldiers were recruited and served in the RAR, British South African Police (BSAP), Selous Scouts, Rhodesia Regiment, Guard Force, and eventually the more controversial Security Force Auxiliaries.

[38] CE20110908G0001, former RAR officer, interview by author, Johannesburg, Republic of South Africa, 8 September 2011. This officer recalled days when thousands of black Rhodesians stood outside the gates of Depot RAR to fill an advertised 200 open billets.

[39] Beverley Whyte, "An Elite Group of Fighting Men," A Pride of Men: The Story of Rhodesia's Army (supplement to Illustrated Life Rhodesia), August 7, 1975: 16-19, 18.

[40] Redfern, 1963, paragraph 6; James E. Dornan, ed., Rhodesia Alone (Washington, DC: Council on American Affairs, 1977), 36; The Internet Archive, "Employment and Climatological Data", http://www.archive.org/details/EmploymentAndClimatologicalData (accessed 21 November 2011); CE20110913M0001, former RAR officer, interview. The numbers to show salaries for military versus other occupations are difficult to find. However, interviews reveal that the RAR soldiers were generally better paid, with better opportunity for advancement, than their peers in other occupations. Redfern cites the African recruit's starting annual pay at £36.10.0 in 1963. According to 1973 data in Encyclopedia Rhodesia, 40 1/2 percent of black Rhodesians worked in agriculture and forestry (by

Most other black Rhodesians were unskilled laborers in the commercial farms or mines, or lived in the tribal areas as subsistence farmers. With little education and slim opportunity for advancement outside the army or police, there were few opportunities elsewhere. Within the regiment, however, an RAR soldier could expect a solid starting pay and excellent chance for advancement from private to senior NCO in a merit-based promotion system.[41]

STABILITY

The RAR provided family housing, meals, education and medical care to its African soldiers and their families. When the soldier was in the field, his family received free meals, and they drew from the support network of other families of soldiers and officers on the military barracks. Unlike their white counterparts, black soldiers did not pay into a pension program, nor were they charged for meals themselves.[42] African terms of enlistment were 7 years, compared to 3 years for white enlistments, which provided a stable employment environment and ample opportunity for the RAR soldier to learn his craft and become proficient. The Rhodesian Army Education Corps ran schools for children and wives, as well as for the soldiers themselves, so there was substantial incentive for an RAR soldier to stay with the regiment once he had a family. This system also allowed children of RAR soldiers to grow up with an appreciation of the familial atmosphere of the regiment, which encouraged them to follow in the footsteps of their fathers.[43]

FAMILY PRIDE

In selecting candidates for entry into the RAR, one of the easiest criteria to use was a family member's service and recommendation. The RAR recruited from all over Rhodesia, but most heavily from the Karanga, a tribe of the Shona people found predominantly in the Fort Victoria (now Masvingo) area in the central and southeastern part of the country. By recruiting heavily from one tribe, the regiment facilitated a family tradition among the Karanga, where grandfathers served in the Rhodesia Native Regiment during World War I, fathers served in the RAR in World War II, and sons counted the days until they too could stand the line as a masodja (soldier) like their forebears. By recruiting family members of RAR soldiers, the regiment gained known military skills from a ready pool of willing recruits.[44]

This is not to say the RAR was a Karanga tribal army. The demographics of the regiment were nearly identical to the black demographics of the nation. The RAR was about 85-90 percent Shona (not exclusively Karanga), 10-12 percent Ndebele, and a much smaller percentage of other tribes.[45] By comparison, the

---

far the leading occupation), which, according to a 1976 economic survey, paid Rh$125 per year, as of 1966. Converting between currencies, and accounting for inflation and the devaluation of the pound in 1972 precludes accurate analysis of these numbers. Interviews revealed, however, that African soldiers in the RAR had better opportunities in the regiment than in other occupations.

[41] CE20110913M0001, former RAR officer, interview; CF20110920V0001, former RAR officer, interview by author, London, England, 20 September 2011.

[42] Redfern, 1963, paragraph 11."European" soldiers were required to pay not less than 5 shillings per day for rations, and 7 ¼ percent of their income towards a pension plan. Africans did not pay for these benefits, although this accommodation by no means made up for the lack of pay and allowances for blacks.

[43] Redfern, 1963, paragraph 11; CE20110913M0001, former RAR officer, interview; CF20110919H0001, former Rhodesian Army Education Corps officer, interview by author, Aylesford, England, 19 September 2011.

[44] CE20110908M0001, former RAR officer, interview by author, Johannesburg, Republic of South Africa, 8 September 2011.

[45] Binda, Masodja, 12; CE20110909R0001, former RAR officer, interview by author, Johannesburg, Republic of South Africa, 9 September 2011. In addition, these percentages are consistent with the regimental demographics given by most Rhodesian veterans interviewed for this project. By comparison, ZANU recruited predominantly from the KoreKore Shona, in the northeastern portion of the country, and ZAPU was almost entirely Ndebele and Kalanga, both tribes from Matabeleland.

black Rhodesian population was approximately 19 percent Ndebele, 77 percent Shona, and 4 percent other tribes (Tonga, Venda, and Shangaan).[46]

REGIMENTAL TRADITIONS

The RAR was originally established as a colonial rifle regiment of the British Army. As such, its regimental culture was defined by the same basic traditions and heritage as other regiments of the British Army, particularly other British colonial regiments in Africa such as the King's African Rifles and the Northern Rhodesia Regiment. To define this tradition and heritage, one must first understand how the British regimental system was applied in Africa.

In establishing security for its colonies, the British Empire relied heavily on locally recruited security forces to maintain order, put down riots and assist the police. By statute, the employment of British regular forces was restricted "to the defence of maritime fortresses and coaling stations"[47]. The rest of the business of securing the empire was left to locally raised units under the control of civil authorities. This led to a dizzying array of colonial regiments loyal to the British Crown.

> From Wei-hai-Wei in North China to Port of Spain in Trinidad, and from Halifax in Nova Scotia to Hobart in Tasmania, there were soldiers organized, equipped and drilled in accordance with the manuals issued by the War Office in London. Some were called Scouts, others were named Levies, or Rifle Corps, or Guides, or Rangers, or Camel Corps, or Militias, or Military Police, or Defence or Frontier Forces. Seldom did their languages, organizations or roles exactly match and it was rare for the uniforms of any two to be precisely the same. But common to all, apart from the Drill Manual, was a dependence on the British Army to provide the officers and, in some cases, senior NCOs to command and train them in peace, and to lead them in war.[48]

The RAR was like any other colonial regiment, except in its lack of dependence on the British Army for its leadership. Because of its unique status as a self-governing colony after 1923, Southern Rhodesia recruited its own white officers into the RAR. Even the RAR's sister formations to the immediate north - the Northern Rhodesia Regiment and King's African Rifles - relied mainly on seconded officers and NCOs from the British Army, so the investment of RAR officers in fighting for their own regiment, for their own country, was quite a profound difference between the RAR and most other British colonial regiments.[49]

The colors and badge of the regiment, as mentioned in the previous chapter, represented the history and multicultural background of the regiment, respectively. The RAR took great pride in these symbols, as British military tradition demands. Each regiment of the British Army designs and produces its own badge, and the RAR badge was no different. The badge and colors were unique to each regiment - the RLI also had its own badge, as did the BSAP and Rhodesia Regiment - and these were proudly displayed by the soldiers of the regiment on their uniforms and on parade.[50]

---

[46] Peter Moorcraft and Peter McLaughlin, The Rhodesian War: A Military History (Johannesburg: Jonathan Ball, 2009), 18.

[47] James Lunt, Imperial Sunset: Frontier Soldiering in the 20th Century (London: Macdonald, 1981), 205.

[48] Lunt, xiii.

[49] CE20110908W0001, former RAR officer, interview by author, Johannesburg, Republic of South Africa. 8 September 2011; CE20110910H0001, former RAR officer, interview by author, Johannesburg, Republic of South Africa, 10 September 2011; CE20110908M0001, former RAR officer, interview. The British Army system of secondment allowed officers (and NCOs) to volunteer for service in colonial units, during which service they drew their regular pay plus pay from the colonial governments. In many British regiments, promotion or advancement often took a very long time, and service in regiments like the KAR or NRR frequently presented superb opportunities for better pay and more opportunity than continued service in regular British Army regiments. For more on how the secondment system worked in colonial regiments, read James Lunt's Imperial Sunset.

[50] CE20110915B0001, former RAR officer, interview. This officer also stressed that the badge and uniform of the RAR was earned, not given to, the soldiers, and these were a source of great pride and individual accomplishment.

Parades were extremely important events for the RAR. The regiment conducted parades for many occasions: trooping the color, the Queen's birthday, reviews for distinguished visitors, Regimental Week (called Tanlwe Chaung, after the RAR's famous fight in Burma), and countless other occasions. Pride in appearance and smart drill were distinct points of pride for the RAR, and the men took great satisfaction in displaying the highest military standards on parade. The RAR seemed to enjoy this formal military culture a bit more than its sister infantry regiment, the RLI[51] - not to say that they looked better or drilled better, but that parades had more value as manifestations of military precision to RAR soldiers than to their RLI comrades. This formal tradition was a tremendous source of self-esteem for black Rhodesians, who had few other opportunities to work as peers with their white counterparts.[52]

Uniforms were also a source of pride for the men of the RAR, very much in the British colonial mold. African soldiers had a reputation of paying particular attention to detail and proudly wore their uniforms. Early in the war, the RAR soldiers turned out in immaculately starched khakis complete with puttees around their ankles.[53]

The RAR bush hat was one item of uniform item that set the regiment apart. On the evolution of the distinctive RAR bush hat:

> In 1960, the commanding officer, Lieutenant-Colonel S. B. Comberbach, suggested that the RAR bush hat as worn by officers and warrant officers should be embellished in some way. The following year, a proposal was submitted to army HQ for the regiment to wear a three ostrich feather hackle in their bush hats. The commanding officer of 1KAR (Nyasaland) immediately objected, since his unit wore an ostrich feather hackle. The objection, of course, was upheld. One member of the Dress Committee then unkindly suggested that the RAR hackle should consist of Somabula bird feathers. The next sensible proposal, made by Major G. A. D. Rawlins, the battalion 2IC, was that the hackle should be made up of black ox-hair, the color worn by Lobengula's Mbizo Regiment whose former military *kraal* had been near the present-day Methuen Barracks. This Matabele impi, which had retained a strong Zulu strain, had worn black trimmings on their arms and legs.[54]

In the pattern of the British regimental system, once an officer was badged into the RAR as his parent regiment, he stayed on the regimental rolls, and continued wearing his RAR uniform (badge, hat and dress uniform) no matter where he was assigned. This created a sense of belonging and ownership between the individual and his regiment. Very rarely did an officer change his parent regiment, and only then with the expressed approval of the Colonel of the Regiment.[55]

AFRICAN TRADITIONS AND PRACTICES OF THE RAR

In addition to these British traditions, the RAR had a few traditions and practices of its own. Its mascot, songs, and habit of secretly "naming" officers were all generated by the men and added to the RAR's culture and esprit de corps. Additionally, Platoon Warrant Officers (PWOs) were a unique duty position within the RAR, created to provide black supernumeraries and role models for the soldiers within the platoons. For example, RAR soldiers killed in action usually had two funerals - one for the regiment and one for their family in the *kraal*. All of these traditions served to cement the bond of loyalty between the African soldier and his regiment, and these bonds proved strong throughout the war.[56]

The regimental mascot, a goat, came about after some selection. Originally, the regiment had chosen a zebra as its mascot, but in practice found both the zebra and its successor, a donkey, unfit for military life. Finally, in May 1965, "Chief Cronje of the Fingo Tribe (a people who had accompanied Rhodes' Pioneer Column) solved the problem by presenting the regiment with a three-month old goat, promptly named

[51] CE20110913M0001, former RAR officer, interview.

[52] CE20110913M0001, former RAR officer, interview; Alexandre Binda, The Saints: The Rhodesian Light Infantry (Durban, 30 Degrees South, 2007), 75.

[53] CE20110913M0001, former RAR officer, interview.

[54] Binda, Masodja, 170.

[55] CE20110913M0001, former RAR officer, interview.

[56] CE20110908M0001, former RAR officer, interview.

'Induna'.[57] " Induna rapidly became a favorite among the troops, and was trained to kneel on its forelegs and bow its head to "present arms". Induna lived to the age of eight, and on his death, was given a guard of honor, Last Post and Reveille, and was succeeded as the regimental mascot by another goat, Private Tendai.[58]

The soldiers had a habit of singing songs on route marches, details, at parties and anytime the opportunity presented itself. Accounts of the RAR songs marvel at the sound of the voice of the regiment, lifted in unison in "Sweet Banana", (the regimental song), or any other song relating to their experience in the war. It was quite common, particularly after some "lubrication of the throats" with a liberal dosage of chibuku (African home-brewed beer), for RAR soldiers to burst into boisterous song, mainly about their regiment and their history. These soldiers were extraordinarily happy, and justly proud of their achievements.[59]

African soldiers had a name for every officer in the regiment. It was a sign of acceptance for a white officer to be given a name by his soldiers, from Lt Col F.J. Wane (named Msoro-we-gomo, or "the top of the mountain"), who served with the Rhodesia Native Regiment in World War I and then rebuilt the RAR in 1940, to a young subaltern (named "Mr. Vice" after his father's position in the Rhodesian Air Force), or Captain (later Brigadier in the Australian Army) John Essex-Clark (named "Mopane", after the tall, slender hardwood found in the Rhodesian bush). The names were not always particularly flattering or exalting, but the existence of a nickname demonstrated acceptance of an officer among the ranks of his soldiers, and were shared with the officers only occasionally by the NCOs of his platoon.[60]

Platoon Warrant Officers (PWOs) were a highly effective group of senior leaders in the RAR. These leaders were absolutely essential to sustaining and perpetuating the regimental culture of the RAR. PWO was a rank between Colour Sergeant and Warrant Officer. The PWO was the primary noncommissioned officer in a platoon. Most PWOs had at least 12-14 years of service, and they were responsible for ensuring that the orders of the platoon commander were carried out, caring for the soldiers, and training the members of the platoon - including the young lieutenant in command. If the platoon ever lost its lieutenant, the PWO was there to lead them in combat. The PWO was the principal instrument of regimental culture in the RAR. He knew, taught, and exemplified the history and values of the regiment. Without exception, every former officer interviewed spoke with special respect and reverence for this class of leaders in the regiment. [61]

The RAR truly fostered a familial environment among its soldiers and officers. When the regiment lost a soldier, for example, "the war stopped" for his platoon. As previously mentioned, his fellow soldiers held a funeral service at the regiment's chapel before releasing his body to his family in the *kraal*, where his relatives would gather for a days-long remembrance, drinking chibuku and singing. On rare occasions, families invited white officers from the regiment to these events, and the officers were honored to attend. Those officers who did attend tribal funerals recalled the events with great reverence as a profound experience.[62]

LEADERSHIP

The RAR was blessed during the course of its history with some outstanding leaders. Like other British colonial units in Africa, the officers were all white (until 1977, when the first black officers were

---

[57] Binda, Masodja, 173. In Sindebele, the language of the Ndebele, "Induna means "great leader".

[58] Ibid. In chiShona, the language of the Shona, "Tendai is a female name meaning "thankful".

[59] CE20110908M0001, former RAR officer, interview; CE20110915B0001, former RAR officer, interview. Most officers interviewed recall the songs and voices of the African soldiers in the RAR as a great motivator for all ranks.

[60] Owen, 6; CE20110915B0001, former RAR officer, interview; Essex-Clark, 34. Owen describes Lt Col Wane's nickname; the young subaltern's came from an interview with the author, and Essex-Clark described his nickname.

[61] CE20110908M0001, former RAR officer, interview; CE20110913B0001, former RAR officer, interview by author, Durban, Republic of South Africa, 13 September 2011; CE20110913R0001, former RAR officer, interview by author, Cape Town, Republic of South Africa, 13 September 2011.

[62] CE20110908M0001, former RAR officer, interview; CE20110913M0001, former RAR officer, interview; CE20110915B0001, former RAR officer, interview.

commissioned), and most of the NCOs and all of the soldiers were black. By its nature, the RAR challenged a leader to adapt to cultural norms among his soldiers. Good officers in the RAR tended to be those who learned the languages and tribal customs of their soldiers, to understand what motivated them and what they feared.[63] Leading and training these soldiers took patience, as many of the problems presented by RAR soldiers - from multiple wives to witchcraft and spirit mediums - were completely foreign to white, "European" culture.[64]

Officers in the Rhodesian Army were very highly selected. In one typical officer intake in 1977, 650 candidates applied, 178 went to a selection board, and 45 were selected as officer cadets. Of these, 18 actually passed out of training as Second Lieutenants.[65] These 18 were then sent out to the Rhodesian Army based on where they were needed, and where their cadre saw that they fit best. According to a former officer cadet course instructor, "We paid great attention to the leaders we were going to use"[66]. Officers who were to serve in the RAR were selected after completing the 13 month officer cadet course at the School of Infantry in Gwelo, after which, "we knew those guys [officer cadets] as well as their dads did".[67] In selecting which newly commissioned officers were sent to the RAR, the selection committee looked for the more serious, more outgoing officers, who were able to interact with people, and who instinctively led by example.[68]

Leadership by example was among the most important traits of an RAR officer. "If clean boots were the order of the day, the officer had to have the cleanest boots."[69] This was what the soldiers expected of their officers. RAR soldiers did not respond well to being given an order and expected to operate with initiative, as could well be done within the commando structure of the RLI. To function best, the RAR officer had to lead from the front, and they were selected and trained to do just that.[70]

Equally important was the leadership of the black noncommissioned officers and warrant officers. The Regimental Sergeants Major (RSMs), Company Sergeants Major (CSMs), Warrant Officers (WOs) and Platoon Warrant Officers (PWOs) were the epitome of what a black soldier could strive to be, until the first black officers were commissioned in July 1977.[71] These men knew, lived, and taught the history and traditions of the regiment to soldiers and officers alike, and they were among the most capable soldiers in Rhodesia.[72]

---

[63] CE20110908M0001, former RAR officer, interview; CE20110913B0001, former RAR officer, interview; CE20110913R0001, former RAR officer, interview.

[64] Spirit mediums are a central piece of Shona culture. The Shona believe that all spirits are reincarnated after death, and that more powerful spirits continuously overlook the well-being of tribal areas and certain tribes. To the Shona, respect for the spirit medium is paramount. The 1897 Mashonaland uprising was led by two spirit mediums - Mbuya Nehanda and Kaguvi - both of whom were arrested and hung by the British South Africa Company. Before hanging, Nehanda promised that her bones would rise again to bring about a second uprising, or Chimurenga, which is what ZANU eventually claimed itself to be. Failure to understand the power of spirit mediums is a critical misstep for any foreign student of this culture. For more information on spirit mediums (which could easily fill a course of study on its own), see "The Social Organization of the Mashona, Part III", by C.J.K. Latham in the Rhodesia Native Affairs Annual 1979, http://www.archive.org/stream/TheRhodesiaNativeAffairsDept.AnnualFor1979/NADA2 #page/n3/mode/1uu.

[65] CF20110920V0001, former RAR officer, interview.

[66] CE20110913M0001, former RAR officer, interview.

[67] CE20110913M0001, former RAR officer, interview. Up to 1965, Rhodesian Army officer candidates went through the Royal Military Academy at Sandhurst. The cadet course at Gwelo stood up after UDI in 1965. It was modeled after Sandhurst, but tailored to Rhodesian Army requirements. One officer interviewed, a Sandhurst graduate, was charged specifically with establishing the cadet course at the Rhodesian Army School of Infantry after UDI.

[68] CE20110913M0001, former RAR officer, interview.

[69] CE20110913M0001, former RAR officer, interview.

[70] CE20110913M0001, former RAR officer, interview; CE20110915B0001, former RAR officer, interview.

[71] Binda, Masodja, 315. The first black officers were WO I Martin Nkatazo Tumbare and WO I Wurayayi Mutero, both former RSMs of 1RAR and 2RAR respectively. They were commissioned in June 1977.

[72] CE20110908M0001, former RAR officer, interview.

Leaders in the RAR understood the importance of morale. Napoleon's famous quote, "morale is to the physical as three is to one" was of utmost importance in training and leading African troops. "The aim was to create a unit with high morale; that is … the conquest of fear and the will to victory."[73]

To that end, officers of the RAR ensured the basic needs of their soldiers - pay, family, education, pride - were met, and that their soldiers were constantly involved, never bored. In preserving morale over time, RAR leaders ensured the lessons and values of the regiment endured across generations and through the challenging situations the regiment faced. [74]

CONCLUSION

The reasons black soldiers joined the RAR are best summed up by CSM Obert Veremu, who said in 1975:

> I joined the Army when I was 20 years old, in 1953. My uncle is a soldier, and I knew if I joined the Army, I would be all right. I enjoy the work very much, and also it is very good to have everything free - uniforms, rations (our wives, too, get free rations while we are away on active service); medical attention, and schooling for our children … These terrs are bad men. I have seen tribesmen who have been beaten to death by them. I also saw the woman whose lip they tore off with pliers. It is very bad what they are doing to their own people. [75]

In many respects, black Rhodesian soldiers enlisted for the same reasons most soldiers enlist in most armies - income, stability, pride, tradition, leadership. These pieces of regimental culture in the RAR are not virtues or characteristics that cannot be found anywhere else. The RAR is remarkable because these reasons and these bonds stayed true through the end of the war, through incredible pressure on black Rhodesians to succumb to the black nationalist groups and cast off a government that was portrayed to them as oppressive, racist and hateful.

The experience of the RAR in the bush war provides an excellent opportunity to examine why soldiers choose to fight. During the course of the war, the atmosphere in which these soldiers worked was constantly changing and fraught with racial, tribal, and international tension. The world in which the RAR soldier lived was turned upside-down, so that by 1980, his former enemy commander was his commander-in-chief. The enemy he had hunted down for 15 years, who had killed his friends, were integrated as peers into his formation. Militarily, the RAR was never defeated, but in the end, its war was lost. Loyalty for this soldier to anything but his regiment evaporated amidst the tremendous shifts resulting from the emergence of a majority-rule state of Zimbabwe.

Through to the end of the Bush War, and beyond, RAR soldiers remained loyal and steadfast to their regiment, and that must be their legacy. In the end, the values of the government - white-rule or otherwise - were irrelevant. It was the regiment that drew these men in, and their loyalty was more to their comrades and their heritage than to any particular government or cause.

---

[73] CE20110913M0001, former RAR officer, interview.
[74] CE20110913M0001, former RAR officer, interview; CE20110908M0001, former RAR officer, interview; CE20110913B001, former RAR officer, interview by author.
[75] Whyte, 18.

CHAPTER 3 - PHASE ONE: 1965-1972

The Rhodesian bush war, fought between the white-rule Rhodesian government and the black nationalist organizations ZAPU and ZANU, effectively began on 11 November 1965, when Rhodesia unilaterally declared its independence from British rule. Initial incursions of nationalist groups into Rhodesia prior to UDI were small, sporadic, and generally disorganized. By August 1964 both ZANU and ZAPU were banned from Rhodesia,[76] and operated exclusively from Zambia. Small strikes and raids were their *modus operandi*.[77] The first real contact, in April 1966, occurred during Operation Pagoda, when several groups of ZANU insurgents infiltrated from Zambia to attack various targets, including infrastructure, police stations and white farms.[78] Subsequent insurgent operations during this phase did not substantially change from a pattern of small elements (10-30 insurgents) crossing the Zambezi River, living in the bush and striking targets of opportunity. Their aim was not really to incite a popular uprising, but more to cause instability in Rhodesia and force British military intervention to keep the peace. Throughout Phase One, insurgent leaders genuinely believed the British would intervene if they could stir up enough trouble. This type of sporadic contact continued until December 1972 when insurgent operators, realizing the British would not intervene and under the increasing influence of Maoist philosophy (particularly in ZANU), executed a significant change in tactics which opened the second phase of the bush war.[79]

Rhodesian Army participation generally (and RAR participation specifically) in early contacts during Phase One was limited. Rhodesian police, principally the BSAP, saw terrorist incursions inside the borders of Rhodesia as criminal activities, falling exclusively under police purview. Once involved, the RAR found itself at the beginning of a learning curve in a new kind of conflict - unlike Burma, Malaya or Central African Federation deployments of recent memory. The regiment had much to learn as they faced their new enemies.

OPERATION PAGODA: THE "BATTLE OF SINOIA"

On the night of 1 April 1966, thirteen ZANU fighters crossed the Zambezi River from Zambia into Rhodesia. Seven additional fighters crossed the river the following night. These men were charged by ZANU leaders to begin the struggle to liberate Zimbabwe, in the hopes of securing funding from the Organisation of African Unity (OAU), rallying black Rhodesians to the ZANU cause while inspiring whites to leave the country, and generally causing enough unrest inside Rhodesia for the British to deploy troops.[80] These twenty fighters were organized into four groups. The first group of five men, code named the "Chimurenga" Group, were to go to the Umtali area in Eastern Rhodesia to attack the oil refinery and pipeline installations there. The second group, code named "Demolition" Group, consisted of two men and

---

[76] Originally banned in 1961, ZAPU continued to operate outside Rhodesia as "ZAPU" and inside Rhodesia as the People's Caretaker Council (PCC). In 1964, the PCC was also banned, along with ZANU.

[77] Kriger, 88.

[78] Moorcraft, 29; Binda, Masodja, 204-5.

[79] Wood, Counterstrike, 37. Historian Richard Wood's five phases of the Rhodesian bush war as outlined in Counterstrike will frame this paper's discussion of how the RAR adapted and changed through the war. Phase 2 began with the 1972 Altena Farm attack and ended with the 1974 Portuguese withdrawal from Mozambique, which opened the north eastern border area to ZANLA incursions, substantially increasing the number and frequency of contacts between RSF and CT forces that characterized Phase 3 (1974-1977). Phase 4 (1977-April 1979) saw massive concessions by the Rhodesian government towards majority rule, ending in the 1979 election of a black Prime Minister, Bishop Muzorewa. Phase 5 (April 1979-April 1980) was characterized by increasing international pressure, failure of outside states to recognize Muzorewa's government, and the election of Robert Mugabe as prime minister of Zimbabwe which ended the bush war.

[80] Wood, Counterstrike, 75; Binda, Masodja, 204-5; Moorcraft, 29-31. Moorcraft and McLaughlin's account of Sinoia varies slightly in accounting for the number and nature of the ZANU groups. They broke the Pagoda/Sinoia groups into 21 terrorists split into 3 groups. As Wood and Binda wrote much later after the war (The Rhodesian War was originally written in 1982), both had access to actual operational reports and other primary sources, so where numbers or dates disagree, Wood and Binda's data are used throughout this paper, as cited here.

was tasked to "blow up bridges and culverts along the road between Fort Victoria and Beitbridge".[81]. The third group, code named "*Gukula-Honde*", was made up of six men and was to "subvert locals in the Tribal Trust Lands south and west of Sinoia", then join the fourth group. This group, the "Armageddon" Group, was the seven-man element that crossed the night of 2 April. Their mission was to train the locals subverted by the *Gukula-Honde* group, then raid farms and attack police stations.[82]

On 12 April, three members of the Chimurenga group spent the night in the *kraal*[83] of one of the members about forty miles from Umtali, while the other two stayed with a sympathizer at Old Umtali Mission. Locals reported the pair at Old Umtali to police, who apprehended them the following morning. After interrogation, these two led police to the *kraal* where the remaining three members were also arrested. Once this group was more thoroughly questioned, police learned of the existence of the other three groups and began to search for them.[84]

Meanwhile, Special Branch (SB)[85] also learned the location of the Armageddon Group. During an Operations Coordinating Committee (OCC) meeting between the Rhodesian Army, Rhodesian Air Force (RhAF), BSAP and Central Intelligence Organisation (CIO) to decide whether to eliminate this group or follow them in hopes of uncovering their contacts, Police Commissioner Frank Barfoot insisted in the interest of public safety that they could no longer remain at large. The resulting massive police operation, involving 83 BSAP policemen supported by four RhAF helicopters, took place near Sinoia on 28 April. Armed with World War One vintage Lee-Enfield .303 rifles[86] and no radios capable of communicating with the helicopters, the largely reservist police force surrounded the rendezvous point between the terrorists and the SB informant, and a firefight ensued. Despite poor communication and several tactical blunders during the operation, police killed all seven members of the Armageddon Group, one from a helicopter-mounted MAG[87] after expending 147 rounds of ammunition.[88]

This operation was a major event for both sides. To ZANU, this was the start of the war in Rhodesia. In fact, 28 April - the day the Armageddon Group met their fate - is a public holiday in Zimbabwe marking this beginning of the "*Chimurenga*", or "War of Liberation". As ZANU spokesman Washington Malinga said on 30 April 1966, it was "only the beginning". For the Rhodesian forces, this began a contest for jurisdiction over counterinsurgency operations between the army and the police. The Army absolutely insisted on its inclusion in any future counterinsurgency operations - they were better trained, better equipped and more experienced in hunting and dealing with insurgents (in Malaya and Federal deployments) than the police. The police, on the other hand, had a much more sophisticated intelligence network inside Rhodesia, constant contact with the population, and no desire to cede control within its own borders to the army. For their part, the RhAF helicopter crews recognized the need to have effective radio

---

[81]Binda, Masodja, 204-5.

[82] 82. Ibid.

[83] *Kraal* is an Afrikaans corruption of the Portuguese *curral*, meaning cattle pen or enclosure. In Rhodesia, this word described an African village or dwelling.

[84] Binda, Masodja, 204-5.

[85]Special Branch of the BSAP provided much of the intelligence throughout the war. This organization had an extensive network of informers and operatives in the tribal areas and outside Rhodesia who reported to CIO and to the police. Integration of Special Branch intelligence with military operations was slow to evolve, and caused quite a bit of frustration within the army early in the war.

[86] Wood, Counterstrike, 77.The Armageddon group, like the other ZANU terrorists sent into Rhodesia, was armed with a mixture of semi-automatic "Soviet SKS 7.62mm rifles, French MAT-49 9mm submachine guns, German Luger 9mm pistols, Soviet F1 and RGD5 grenades", placing them at a distinct firepower advantage over the much older BSAP bolt-action Lee-Enfields.

[87]Mitrailleuse d'Appui Général, or General Purpose Machine Gun, designed by the Belgian company Fabrique Nationale (FN), was the standard issue machine gun used by the Rhodesian Army. It is an automatic, air-cooled, gas-operated machine gun firing belt-fed 7.62×51mm NATO ammunition from an open bolt. While it was experimentally mounted in helicopters, as noted here, it was far more prevalent among ground troops, issued at one per infantry rifle section (8-10 men), and later fireforce stick (4 man element), in the RAR and RLI. This machine gun was also adopted for use by the US Army and US Marine Corps in the mid-1980s as the M240. Rhodesian helicopters would later use twin Browning .303 machine guns and, eventually, 20mm cannons as armament.

[88] Wood, Counterstrike, 76-79; Binda, Masodja, 204-5; Moorcraft, 31; Ron Reid-Daly, "The War in Rhodesia" in Challenge: Southern Africa within the African Revolutionary Context, ed. A. J. Ventner (Gibraltar: Ashanti, 1989), 149

contact between the helicopters and ground units. Coming out of Sinoia, however, RhAF commanders began to resist future involvement of helicopters as gunships, seeing their role as exclusively support or troop transport.[89] All organizations recognized the need to train and prepare for future fights against ZAPU and ZANU in Rhodesia. While the RAR did not participate at Sinoia, the lessons learned there and passed across the Rhodesian Army directly contributed to future RAR experiences in the war.[90]

Operation Pagoda continued until 18 September 1966, resulting in the eventual death or capture of the remaining eight members of the Demolition and *Gukula-Honde* groups (as well as eleven ZAPU terrorists who infiltrated separately) by combined police and army operations involving small elements of both the RAR and RLI.[91]   Perhaps the most important result of the experiences during Pagoda was the formation and use of Joint Operations Centres (JOCs), consisting of army, air force, BSAP and SB officers, plus any other relevant agencies specific to an operation. The JOC structure was more focused than the OCC, as its members were oriented locally, rather than nationally. This "command by committee" would remain a part of Rhodesian operations throughout the war, resulting in a more streamlined coordination process, improved communication and sharing of intelligence at the local, tactical level.[92]

The RAR participated in a few other operations in 1966. During these operations, the regiment further familiarized itself with JOC procedures, operations with the police, and methods of tracking and apprehending terrorists. The RAR's mastery of these concepts would become critically important in the coming years of operations against insurgents, particularly in Operation Nickel in 1967[93].

OPERATION NICKEL

On 10 August 1967, a policeman stopped an RAR patrol along the Wankie-Victoria Falls road in the northwest corner of the country to tell them he had found a pack in the area and he believed there were terrorists nearby. The platoon set out stop groups and initiated a sweep operation[94], and quickly captured a terrorist. Interrogation would reveal this man to be a lost member of a 79-man combined ZAPU and South African African National Congress (SAANC) element that crossed the Zambezi and separated about four days previously. With one terrorist captured and a lead to many more, the RAR established a JOC at Wankie and brought in more police and soldiers. Operation Nickel was on, and it would prove one of the most formative experiences of the RAR in the Bush War.[95]

The ZAPU-SAANC group was divided into two subgroups. The first, code named Lithuli, was made up of 48 men (initially 54: 13 ZAPU and 41 SAANC),[96] and was to set up a base in the Tjolotjo area, near the Botswana border. The second group of 21 men (initially 23: 14 ZAPU and 9 SAANC) was code named

---

[89] Reid-Daly, Challenge, 156; Binda, Masodja, 224; Wood, Counterstrike, 61-63. Until 1973, RAF use of helicopters as gunships was largely experimental, and RhAF command continued insisted on using helicopters in a support, rather than combat role. This position would later be reversed at the army's insistence, RhAF Alouette helicopters equipped with MAGs, twin .303 Browning machine guns with reflexive sights, and by July 1974 with French Matra MG151 20mm cannons, were employed as "K-Cars" in fireforce operations with great effect.

[90] Moorcraft, 29; Wood, Counterstrike, 80; Reid-Daly, 149-50; Binda, Masodja, 205.

[91] Binda, Masodja, 206-10.

[92] Wood, Counterstrike, 80.

[93] Binda, Masodja, 206-7. Operations Grampus and Vermin are two such operations mentioned by name in the Regimental History. The JOC quickly became the central node of information, and its maturing process as a command element became evident as operations continued.

[94] Rhodesian Army, COIN Manual, Part II - ATOPS [Anti-Terrorist Operations] (Salisbury, 1975), 91-2. Rhodesian tactics frequently called for sweep operations using "stop groups" and "sweep groups". Typically, stop groups - the hunters - were placed in concealed positions along likely avenues of escape, crossing points or natural lines of drift. The sweep group - the hounds - then deliberately searched the entire area to flush the target out of hiding and into a waiting ambush at the stop group position. This tactic, refined and employed from helicopters, was the basis for fireforce and it was employed throughout the war.

[95] Binda, Masodja, 214.

[96] Binda, Masodja, 215. After crossing the Zambezi, 10 men were separated from the two groups, one of whom was captured by security forces. Two additional men of mixed race "were tasked with a separate mission in South Africa," bringing the initial total to 79, with 69 remaining when the RAR made contact.

Lobengula, and had Nkai as its objective, where it would receive assistance from members of the Zimbabwe Church of Orphans. From these two areas, each group was to establish recruiting and training bases to bring in local tribesmen, then attack European farms and police stations. After establishing these camps, the SAANC contingent would continue through Bechuanaland (Botswana) to the Sekhukuneland, Zululand and Transkei regions of South Africa.[97]

On 13 August, a BSAP patrol reported sighting insurgents near the Inyantue River area. Major Taffy Marchant, Officer Commanding (OC) A Company 1RAR, sent a seven-man section under the command of Captain Peter Hosking, his 2IC, along with two civilian trackers to follow up on this report. Marchant also sent a platoon led by Regimental Sergeant-Major (RSM) Aubrey Korb and Company Sergeant-Major (CSM) Timitiya shortly behind Hosking's detachment. Hosking made contact with what he believed to be a five-man terrorist element (it was actually the entire 21-man Lobengula Group) and called for reinforcements. More police and more soldiers arrived by helicopter, and in the ensuing firefight both Hosking and Platoon Warrant Officer (PWO) Kephasi were wounded, as well as police officers Tiffin and Phillips. Two RAR soldiers, Lance Corporal Davison and Private Koroni, were killed in action. The RAR soldiers pulled back into an all-round defense. The Lobengula Group lost three killed and one seriously wounded (he would later be killed) in the contact.[98]

Over the next few days, Rhodesian and Botswana police arrested three members of the Lobengula Group in separate incidents. The rest of the group was pursued by 3 Platoon, commanded by Lieutenant Ian Wardle, with 10 Platoon (under Lieutenant Graham Noble) and the Mortar Platoon (led by Lieutenant Piers) acting as stop groups. In another firefight, Wardle's platoon killed eight and captured six terrorists, completely accounting for the Lobengula Group.[99]

Meanwhile, the 47-man Lithuli Group, much more disciplined and better led (by a man named John Dube) than their counterparts, moved to the Leasha Pan, near the western section of the Tjolotjo Tribal Trust Land (TTL). On 19 August, the Mortar Platoon made contact with two members of this group, killing one of them. The platoon followed the tracks but lost contact. Dube assembled his men and quietly conducted two night movements into Tjolotjo TTL, while in the midst of security forces. By the morning of 22 August, the Lithuli Group had established a camp in the Tjolotjo TTL, complete with camouflaged positions in an all-round defense. Lt Nick Smith, commanding 1 Platoon, found tracks leading to this camp and followed them. At 1400, Smith's platoon made contact with the Lithuli Group. In the firefight that followed, both Smith and CSM Timitiya were killed. Lance Corporal Mavaradze recounted:

> We then carried on firing, knowing the enemy was still there. Firing stopped again because we had no more ammunition and the enemy formed up with bayonets fixed. We withdrew, leaving our packs, radios, some rifles, and two dead bodies. After we had withdrawn we took up an all-round defence and shared our remaining rounds. I then sent off three men to get help and later withdrew completely to the Wankie boundary road, and stayed there the night.[100]

The Lithuli Group had suffered three killed, three wounded, and two lost to desertion. They enthusiastically took the abandoned equipment, food, and water and continued to move east. While moving, the group opened fire on a group of RAR soldiers, wounding one. "Hearing this firing, Lieutenant Peirson, commanding several ambush positions not far away, unwisely left his ambush position to investigate; tragically, he was mistaken for the enemy and shot and killed"[101].

On 23 August one of the deserters from Lithuli Group was captured by 13 Platoon at Siwuwu Pools. Lieutenant Bill Winnall took 13 and 15 Platoons to pursue the lead resulting from his interrogation, and discovered tracks of approximately 30 men.

Estimating himself to be about 3 hours behind the enemy, Winnall continued pursuit while the Mortar Platoon deployed in an ambush position on the Tegwani River. While waiting for an airstrike against the

---

[97]Ibid.
[98] Binda, Masodja, 215-6.
[99]Ibid.
[100] Binda, Masodja, 218-9.
[101] Ibid. 219.

suspected enemy positions, Winnall decided to move his platoon into thick bush and establish a base for the night.

No sentries were posted and no clearance patrols were sent out, the soldiers being scattered about the area in groups of two or three, smoking and chatting.

Observing this carelessness, the enemy commander, Dube, seized the opportunity and, in company with one of his men, both wearing combat jackets (looted off 1Platoon's dead) casually sauntered over to the security force position. Exchanging greetings with the AS [African Soldiers], Dube rapidly assessed the troops' deployment and then called out the order to his men to open fire.[102]

In the ensuing engagement, Lance Corporal Cosmos and Patrol Officer Thomas were killed, eight men were wounded (including Lt. Winnall), and the patrol withdrew to form a defensive position and evacuate the casualties.

At this point, the JOC accepted an RLI Commando from Army Headquarters[103], in addition to 48 additional A Company soldiers and D Company 1RAR. These reinforcements arrived on 23 August, and immediately began patrolling in the vicinity of the Nata and Tegwani River junction, where Dube and his men were hiding. The JOC moved to Tjolotjo to better control security force actions.[104]

Dube then took seven men from the remnants of the Lithuli Group to find water and food. This small group got lost, and Dube was arrested in Botswana with three of his men on 28 August. When Dube failed to return to the main group, the remaining 31 men moved along the Tegwani on the night of 25 August. Without their leader, the group began to fall apart. Over the next two days, three more men deserted, the seventeen SAANC members split off to go to South Africa through Botswana, while the remaining eleven men, exhausted, stopped. On the morning of 28 August, two of these men deserted and were arrested. On 31 August, an insurgent named Ncube went to a *kraal* to get some food. While the old woman he had approached prepared his meal, she sent a girl to alert security forces, who promptly arrived and arrested Ncube. Ncube led 7 Troop, 1RLI with 11 Platoon, D Company 1RAR to the hide-out that he and five other insurgents occupied. In the ensuing firefight, four insurgents were killed and one fled.[105]

Through the next few days, security forces continued patrolling, looking for the rest of the Lithuli Group. While following up on tracks leading away from a dead rhino, on 4 September, Lt. Noble and 10 Platoon engaged three more insurgents. One of the insurgents threw a grenade, killing Private Nyika and wounding Private Pedzisayi. (at Inkundhla Siding.) This set off a fire, which cooked off the enemy ammo and grenades and kept the remaining RAR soldiers at bay. Once the fire died out, 10 platoon swept the area and recovered three dead insurgents. Patrolling continued until Operation Nickel concluded the morning of 8 September 1967. In December, one of the outstanding insurgents was arrested in Plumtree, and in May 1968, South African police in Durban arrested another.[106]

The results of Operation Nickel were immediate and far-reaching. On the enemy side, ZAPU did not consider the operation a failure. Not only was the war now underway, but they had killed security forces and they were able to capitalize on their own version of the truth back in Zambia, where ZAPU was working to establish themselves as the better Zimbabwean movement to the OAU and their Zambian hosts. For their part, ZANU praised the courage of the fighters involved but condemned as a "gross blunder" the alliance with SAANC, whose efforts ZANU believed should have been focused in their own country, not in Rhodesia.[107]

For the RAR, the results were somewhat humbling. At the outset of the war, the Rhodesian Army expected the RAR to have no problems defeating the incompetent insurgents, due to its previous experience in Malaya and Federal deployments. But the regiment committed a few tactical blunders that hurt its

---

[102] Ibid.

[103] Binda, Saints, 46. In 1965, the RLI restructured from a conventional infantry battalion into a "commando" battalion. While keeping its designation as a battalion, its subordinate units were called commandos rather than companies, and troops rather than platoons. The RLI had four commandos (numbered 1, 2, 3, and Support). Each commando was further subdivided into five troops of 25 men (as opposed to three platoons of 37 men), although they typically operated at strength of four troops due to manpower shortages and casualty rates. So, an RLI commando consisted of 100-125 men divided into 4-5 troops.

[104] Binda, Masodja, 219-20; Binda, Saints, 60.

[105] Ibid.

[106] Ibid.

[107] Binda, Saints, 64; Moorcraft, 32-3.

reputation. The lessons learned for the RAR were the value of confident and decisive junior leadership (as Lt. Wardle and Capt. Hosking displayed), and the disastrous results of tactical carelessness, as seen in Lt. Winnall's actions. Also, during Nickel, RAR troops only carried 50 rounds of ammunition to limit the amount of weight each soldier had to carry. This practice came from the regiment's experience in Malaya and recent experience against ZANU and ZAPU, where their enemy did not stand and fight, and soldiers rarely had the opportunity to fire. RAR soldiers were also firing their newly issued FN FAL rifles on automatic, wasting the little ammunition they had. These faults were immediately corrected.

Training subsequently focused on single, aimed shots, limiting the use of full automatic fire to lead scouts, and increasing the basic load for all RAR soldiers to 150 rounds.[108] Two ideas that were not immediately capitalized on, but would become crucial to success later in the war were the use of helicopters as fire support platforms (not just troop transport), and the importance of tracking - finding and following signs of enemy movement - to counterinsurgency operations.[109]

Perhaps of more strategic importance than these adjustments, however, was the subsequent offer of South African assistance to Rhodesia that came immediately after Nickel. The involvement of SAANC immediately brought the interest of the Pretoria government, eager to fight its own counterinsurgency away from home soil. Pretoria sent about 2,000 South African "police"[110] to assist Rhodesian Security Forces in COIN operations in the Zambezi valley. While Rhodesians considered their new South African allies to be clumsy, inefficient, and inexperienced - they were disparagingly called "ropes" (thick , hairy, and twisted) or "clumpies" (due to clumsy bushcraft) - for political reasons, they were welcome additions to the fight, and would eventually nearly equal the size of the Rhodesian regular army. South Africa would also add critical enablers such as helicopters and aircrews, along with tremendous economic assistance.[111] South African involvement in Rhodesia proved to be a "double-edged sword", however, as after the 1974 fall of Mozambique and Angola to communist guerrillas, South Africa became Rhodesia's only friend in the global community. South African Prime Minister John Vorster would use to his advantage later in the war.[112]

OPERATION CAULDRON

The RAR was deployed several more times through the first phase of the war, pursuing groups of terrorists across sparsely populated areas of the country, in constant cooperation with the police and with the willing assistance of the locals. In March 1968, a game ranger came across a wide track made by terrorists conveying supplies between several camps they had established near the Chewore River. He called in the police, and Operation Cauldron began, which was to be a "baptism of fire" for the RAR's sister regiment, the RLI. The RLI would emerge from Cauldron as a tested, proven and capable unit, earning the nickname, "The Incredibles", which would stick through the end of the war.[113]

The enemy in Operation Cauldron was once again a mixture of ZAPU and SAANC, a contingent of 100-125 men whose aim was to establish a number of base camps between the Zambezi River and Sipolilo in the north-central part of the country. From here, locals were to be trained and armed, and eventually unleashed on an unsuspecting Rhodesia at a later date. The RLI, with the SAS and limited participation from the RAR, put an end to those plans in the ensuing months, killing 58 terrorists and capturing a large number, while the rest limped back to Zambia.[114]

The RAR participation in Operation Cauldron consisted of 14 Platoon, E Company 1RAR, led by Lieutenant Ron Marillier. Although Marillier was awarded the Bronze Cross of Rhodesia for his actions during Cauldron, his platoon - and the RAR - drew heavy criticism from the RLI and Army command

---

[108] Binda, Masodja, 224; CE20110910H0001, former RAR officer, interview; CF20110920H0001, former RAR officer, interview by author, London, England, 20 September 2011.

[109] Reid-Daly, Challenge, 156.

[110] This number also included army and air force units, but the word "police" was used to obscure South African military involvement in what was internationally viewed as a British affair.

[111] Moorcraft, 32; Reid-Daly, Challenge, 158-9.

[112] Wood, Counterstrike, 53.

[113] Binda, Saints, 64.

[114] Binda, Masodja, 227.

(including Colonel Peter Walls, later the Rhodesian Army Commander) for multiple failures in the face of the enemy. Essentially, the RAR soldiers proved reluctant to move under fire and attack the enemy. Several attempts to rally these soldiers proved unsuccessful, and in their first contact, the RAR platoon and the RLI commando moving with them were forced to pull back and call in an airstrike against the enemy position. The RAR lost one soldier, Corporal Erisha, killed and two wounded, PWO Herod and Private Wilson.[115] Marillier had only taken command of his platoon the day before it was moved into Operation Cauldron, so he did not know the names of most of his men, nor did they know him. In contact, the men would not follow him, and control of the platoon broke down. These shortfalls can be attributed to the elevated sense of enemy capability amongst RAR soldiers coming out of Operation Nickel, and the fact that the RAR was still adjusting to its new war, discovering that their experience in Malaya and Nyasaland did not exactly apply against ZAPU and ZANU. Fortunately, both of these factors would evaporate rapidly in the coming operations, and the RAR was to become quite proficient at hunting and killing insurgents in the bush war.[116]

Operation Cauldron had a few significant outcomes. For its small part in the operation, the RAR learned more about how to fight its new enemy. Lessons from Cauldron, combined with Nickel, would be applied in future operations to bring the RAR back into the fold as a top-tier counterinsurgent force. Also, the RLI proved itself as an effective force, beginning its own sterling reputation. Unfortunately, a third outcome was that the Rhodesian Army - indeed the entire Rhodesian population - began to believe that the military situation was well in hand, and this war would not be a major problem. This was much to their detriment, as the years from 1968-72 are marked by an astonishing lack of pursuit, adjustment, and analysis by Rhodesian Security Forces against their enemy. The enemy, meanwhile, were adjusting their tactics.[117]

CONCLUSION

The RAR began the Rhodesian bush war as respected veterans of Burma, Malaya, and Central African Federation deployments - by far the senior regiment of the Rhodesian Army, expected to outperform its peers and emerge victorious from every fight. In its first two operations against ZAPU and SAANC, however, the regiment displayed some disturbing tactical blunders. The upstart RLI (only formed in 1961), however, came into its own during Operation Cauldron - in the face of a questionable RAR performance.

Between Nickel and Cauldron, the RAR proved that seniority did not instill competence, and that adjustments were required to succeed in this new war on Rhodesian soil. The Commanding Officer, Lieutenant Colonel Bill Godwin, recognized this need and immediately set out to make these corrections, and regain the vaunted reputation of the regiment. Valuable lessons learned by the regiment in these first operations - the value of tracking and moving small units around the battlefield, the price of overestimating the enemy (as Marillier's platoon did during Cauldron), and the necessity of competent, effective junior leaders - would lead to phenomenal success later in the war. Ironically, most of these shortcomings for the RAR were also lessons learned from Malaya, although some early accusations against the RAR concluded that its "Malayan Way" nearly caused failure in Operation Nickel.[118]

In 1972, several key events occurred which changed the face of the war. ZANU, under the influence and mentorship of Maoist Chinese advisors, realized that success in their protracted war depended on the support of the population, and their tactics shifted to coercion and collusion with rural villagers in Rhodesia. ZAPU followed suit, although much more slowly, and both groups increased their operational tempo. The regiment was about to get very busy.[119]

---

[115] Binda, Saints, 78. PWO Herod, while recovering from his wounds, was credited with saying famously to RLI Sgt Tim Baker, "We of the RAR used to laugh at your soldiers. To us they looked like boys. But they showed us how to fight. They have the faces of boys, but they fight like lions".

[116] CE20110910H0001, former RAR officer, interview; Reid-Daly, Challenge, 161-2; Binda, Masodja, 227.

[117] Moorcraft, 33; Binda, The Saints, 77-8; Binda, Masodja, 227.

[118] Reid-Daly, Challenge, 155; CE20110912G0001, former RAR officer, interview by author, Durban, Republic of South Africa, 12 September 2011.

[119] Wood, Counterstrike, 35-37.

CHAPTER 4 - PHASE TWO: 1972-1974

The problem of establishment of bases is of particular importance. This is so because this war is a cruel and protracted struggle . . . [S]ome part of our country - or, indeed, most of it – may...be captured by the enemy and become his rear area. It is our task to develop intensive guerrilla warfare over this vast area and convert the enemy's rear into an additional front. Thus the enemy will never be able to stop fighting. In order to subdue the occupied territory, the enemy will have to become increasingly severe and oppressive.
Mau Tse-Tung, On Guerrilla Warfare

From 1971 and leading to the December 1972 attack on Altena Farm in northeast Rhodesia, ZANU adopted a Maoist strategy to establish a base area in Rhodesia, spread security forces thin and collapse morale through consistent attacks on rural targets. In response, Rhodesian forces established a JOC at Centenary. This JOC became the headquarters for Operation Hurricane across the northeast portion of Rhodesia, and the first of six operational areas (Hurricane, Thrasher, Repulse, Tangent, Grapple, and Splinter) that would define the Rhodesian war effort.[120]

This period saw several security force developments, including the establishment of the first Operational Area (Hurricane); the start of the Protected Village (PV) program in contested areas of the country; the inception of the Selous Scouts; and the early development of a rapid airborne reaction force, called Fireforce, to quickly strike on actionable intelligence.[121]

Politically during this phase, the December 1971 rejection of the Home-Smith agreement for transition to majority rule stymied an early Rhodesian political solution to the growing insurgency and contributed to turmoil within and outside of Rhodesia. The Portuguese withdrawal from neighboring Mozambique in 1974, and subsequent handover of Mozambique governance to the Frente de Libertaçao de Moçambique (FRELIMO) guerrillas, effectively eliminated the Rhodesian government's crucial eastern ally. This left Rhodesia's sole remaining friendly ports and borders with South Africa. FRELIMO would also provide sanctuaries in Mozambique for ZANLA and open the north and east border regions to ZANLA infiltrations unencumbered by the more restrictive terrain of the Zambezi River along the Zambian border. Despite these developments, by 1974 security forces had reduced the number of insurgents in the country to 60 individuals, all contained in the northeast.[122]

THE HOME-SMITH AGREEMENT AND PEARCE COMMISSION

To understand the environment in which the RAR operated during this phase of the war, it is important to understand the significant political events that occurred. As the RAR began to consistently engage and pursue their enemy, much was in turmoil in Rhodesia.

In September 1965, the British Commonwealth Relations Office (CRO) established five principles for Rhodesian independence:

First, the principle and intention of unimpeded progress to majority rule, already enshrined in the 1961 constitution, would have to be maintained and guaranteed. There would also have to be guarantees against retrogressive amendment of the constitution. There would have to be immediate improvement in the political status of the African population. There would have to be progress towards the ending of racial discrimination. The British Government would need to be satisfied that any basis proposed for independence was acceptable to the people of Rhodesia as a whole. A sixth principle was

---

[120] These operational areas were permanent JOCs with attached subordinate units from RSF. The size of RSF forces in each operational area varied with the level of activity in them, but generally consisted of several infantry companies and sliced elements of BSAP, Special Branch, Selous Scouts, RhAF and any other security forces required for operations.
[121] Wood, Counterstrike, 37-39.
[122] Ibid., 39.

added in January 1966: no oppression of the majority by the minority, or of the minority by the majority.[123]

The first principle - unimpeded progress to majority rule - was the nominal reason Britain refused to grant independence to Rhodesia.[124] Under the 1961 constitution, which was referenced by the CRO above and annexed to the UDI seven weeks later, there were two voter rolls "A" roll and "B" roll. While these rolls were not explicitly racially divided, the A roll was restricted to higher thresholds of property, education and income - thus, higher contributions to income tax revenues - and was predominantly white. The B roll, with lower standards, was almost entirely black.[125]

The 65 seats of the Rhodesian Assembly were subdivided into 50 constituency and 15 district seats. Both rolls voted for constituency and district seats. However, the 1961 constitution had a "cross-voting" influence built in: that is, B roll votes were capped at 20 percent of the total vote for the 50 constituency seats, and A roll votes were likewise capped at 20 percent for the 15 district seats. The end result of this complicated voting system was that whites (A roll voters) had a controlling majority of 50 constituency assembly seats, while the black majority only effectively controlled 15 district seats. This breakdown was representative of contributions to "the fisc", or the income tax revenue of Rhodesia, but it was grossly out of step with the demographics of the country. In asking black leaders to accept this constitution, the Rhodesian government was effectively asking that they accept a long, slow road to majority rule: once enough blacks met the education, property and income requirements to qualify as A roll voters, they would gain parity in electing the constituency seats. Black nationalist leaders initially signed an agreement endorsing this constitution, but later reneged and urged the black population to reject the constitution during the 1962 referendum.[126]

In 1969, the Rhodesian Front proposed a new constitution, which declared Rhodesia to be a republic.[127] The UDI constitution still offered a viable path to majority rule, thus meeting the first principle laid out by the CRO,[128] but it was an even slower path than the 1961 constitution. Smith and the Rhodesian Front still believed they had made generous concessions toward majority rule, and had met the first four principles outlined in by the CRO.128 As a step backward on the path to majority rule, however, the UDI constitution alienated more of the moderate black population from the Rhodesian Front and provided a rich

---

[123] Colonial Relations Office to Prime Minister of Southern Rhodesia, 21 September 1965, as found in Hyam, 369-70.

[124] Smith,156. Smith (then Prime Minister of Rhodesia) suggests other reasons Britain did not grant Rhodesian independence. Chiefly, he states that the British government under Harold Wilson and the Labour Party was motivated to support black nationalists by its desire to "appease the OAU", while Ted Heath's Conservative Party, which won the 1970 British general election, was more interested in obtaining British entry into the European Economic Community than solving the Rhodesian problem. Whatever the reason, British attitudes regarding Rhodesian recognition certainly differed between Salisbury and London, and between the Colonial Office, Foreign Office and Prime Minister in both Labour and Conservative governments. The resulting duplicity of Her Majesty's Government confused both the Rhodesian government and black nationalist movements.

[125] Patrick O'Meara, Rhodesia: Racial Conflict or Coexistence (Ithaca: Cornell University Press, 1975), 15.

[126] O'Meara, 40-54; Smith, 151-2; Nyangoni, 57-8; Martin, 68-9.

[127] Smith, 151; O'Meara, 43. The 1969 "UDI" constitution also amended the Assembly seat allocation to 50 A roll, 8 B roll, and another 8 seats to be nominated by tribal chiefs. The cross-voting concept was removed, and the B roll was explicitly designated for "non-European" voters. For the first time, Rhodesian voter rolls were explicitly racially divided. The UDI constitution provided a means to increase the number of B roll seats in tandem with the increase in blacks meeting the standards for the higher roll (higher education, property and income tax contributions), up to parity at 50 B roll seats. Then, once blacks reached parity with whites, "a committee would be appointed to decide how to bring about an African majority government, and their suggestions would require approval by two-thirds of Parliament (essentially giving the white minority a veto power)". Ian Smith disagreed with the idea of racial division, believing that Rhodesia should "perpetuate the principle and continue our philosophy of trying to establish a genuine meritocracy in keeping with Rhodes's famous dictum: 'Equal rights for all civilised men.'" His efforts to exclude racial divisions were not accepted by the rest of the Rhodesian Front, and the racial language, which had not been in the Rhodesian constitution since the 1952 Federal constitution, remained in the 1969 document. In March 1970, a general election placed the UDI constitution into effect and formed the Rhodesian government into a republic, with the above division of voter rolls.

[128] Smith, 152.

opportunity for ZANU and ZAPU to capitalize on the Rhodesian Front's apparent unwillingness to share power.

In the April 1970 general election, the Rhodesian Front won all 50 A roll seats. In April 1971 the newly appointed Conservative British Foreign Secretary, Lord Alec Douglas-Home, flew to Salisbury to discuss the new Rhodesian constitution and assess the acceptability of this document as meeting the principles for British recognition of Rhodesia. From April to November 1971, Douglas-Home negotiated with Smith's representatives to create a compromise agreement. When Douglas-Home left for England in November, he assured Smith that London would be satisfied, pending a few formalities. The resulting agreement conceded additional B roll seats in the Rhodesian Assembly - giving black voters a total of 22 seats (still short, however, of a "blocking Third" to prevent additional amendments to the constitution). In the compromise Home- Smith Agreement,

> Rhodesia had to declare its intention to make progress toward ending racial discrimination; accept a new declaration guaranteeing individual rights and freedoms; include steps to enable more Africans to compete on equal terms with whites for civil-service jobs; review the cases of all detainees and restricted persons; and set up an independent committee to study racial discrimination and make recommendations to the Rhodesian government. Up to £50 million in British aid was to be given to Rhodesia over a ten-year period, and the Rhodesian government was to match this sum to promote educational and job opportunities for Africans.[129]

This agreement was accepted by both the Rhodesian Front and the British representatives as meeting the first four principles laid out by the CRO in 1965.[130]

To meet the fifth principle - satisfaction of the British Government that the proposal was acceptable to the people of Rhodesia as a whole - the British formed a twenty-one man commission, chaired by a British judge, Lord Edward Holroyd Pearce. Pearce's three deputy chairmen were Sir Maurice Dorman (former Governor-General of Sierra Leone and Malta), Sir Glyn Jones (former Governor of Nyasaland), and Lord Harlech (former British Ambassador to the United States). Neither Pearce nor Harlech had any experience in Africa, and while all of the other commissioners were former colonial officers in Africa, none of the commissioners were black, which instantly eroded any credibility of the commission amongst black nationalist leaders.[131]

The Pearce Commission arrived in Rhodesia in January of 1972 and began meeting with Rhodesians to determine their views on the Home-Smith Agreement (also called the Anglo-Rhodesian Agreement). From January to March, the commission met with about 6 percent of the black population amid violence between police and African National Council (ANC)[132] nationalists against accepting the agreement. In May, Pearce reported to Lord Douglas-Home and Parliament that black Rhodesians "roundly rejected" the Home-Smith Agreement and that British sanctions should continue.[133]

According to Ian Smith, the Pearce Commission's report was a fraud, because apart from the fact that "the vast majority of our black people were unable to comprehend what was taking place, the commission had seen less than 5 per cent of our black people - and yet they were prepared to submit a report purporting

---

[129] O'Meara, 42.

[130] Smith, 153.

[131] O'Meara, 46-7.

[132] J. K. Cilliers, Counter-Insurgency in Rhodesia (Dover: Croom Helm, 1985), 11. The ANC was formed by Bishop Abel Muzurewa (also spelled Muzorewa) in 1971 with the expressed purpose of actively encouraging black Rhodesians to reject the Home- Smith Agreement. In this endeavor, it was highly successful, as described here. The ANC, unlike ZAPU and ZANU never formed a military arm to take up arms against the Rhodesian government, and so was never banned from participating in Rhodesian politics. Muzorewa would come to be seen as a moderate nationalist leader, and would engage in talks over the next few years with the Smith government, ending in the Internal Settlement of March, 1978 and the establishment of majority rule in Zimbabwe-Rhodesia.

[133] Smith, 156; O'Meara, 54; Cilliers, 11; Kriger, 86; Wood, Counterstrike, 35; Lester A. Sobel, ed., Rhodesia/Zimbabwe 1971-77 (New York: Facts on File, 1978), 30- 1

to represent the views of 100 per cent!"[134] However, according to Dr. Wellington Nyangoni, a former ZANU member and African history professor at Brandeis University, "African opposition to the Anglo-Rhodesian Agreement was overwhelming, and their rejection of the Agreement rendered it unacceptable".[135] Whatever the cause for the Pearce Commission's findings, by 1971 it was clear that Rhodesia was beginning to fragment along racial lines, either at the urging of black nationalists of the ANC, ZAPU, and ZANU or because of an out-of-touch Rhodesian Front government.

Amidst all of this turmoil, the RAR continued to recruit, fight and thrive as a multicultural organization. None of the political or social dynamics in motion within the country were reflected within the regiment. The controversy surrounding the Home- Smith Agreement and the Pearce Commission did not affect the availability of black recruits for the RAR at all, nor did it seem to affect soldiers serving in the regiment.

Indeed, the regiment still had many more recruits than it could accept waiting outside its gates on recruiting days, and the soldiers serving in the regiment saw themselves as a staunchly apolitical force, undeterred by the political events surrounding them. Like most other RAR traditions, the absence of politics in the regiment was a British Army notion not copied in ZIPRA, ZANLA, or later in the Security Force Auxiliaries.[136]

OPERATION HURRICANE

In December 1973, ZANU insurgents attacked Altena Farm near Centenary "to study the reaction of the enemy and his tactics so we could decide upon our own tactics"[137], according to their commander, Rex Nhongo. ZANLA attacked from Chiweshe TTL, where they had established a base. The farm was randomly selected as a target, but the attack deliberately provoked a Rhodesian response, which ZANLA watched very carefully. ZANLA operators had been in the Chiweshe TTL for over a year, and had subverted the population in much of the northeast portion of the country. Their intent was not only to subvert the population but to force RSF to spread themselves out, resulting in constant attrition of troops and morale over time. ZANLA insurgents had given up on the idea that the British Army would intervene on their behalf if they could generate enough civil unrest. They were learning from their Chinese mentors, and their strategy and tactics shifted to a more popular struggle, focused on setting conditions for insurgency among the *kraal*s and tribal areas. Only once conditions were set among the population would ZANLA conduct any sort of military action, carefully avoiding costly direct confrontation with security forces, where ZANLA was at a disadvantage.[138]

The Rhodesian response to the attack on Altena Farm was to establish a JOC at Centenary and initiate Operation Hurricane to find and destroy the ZANLA forces in the area. To that end, a mixture of Rhodesian Security Forces (RSF), including elements of 1RAR, were deployed into the operational area as the first troops in what would be an eight-year operation. These troops immediately noticed that the locals were no longer as willing to cooperate with security forces - they were afraid of ZANLA reprisals, and their chief was a ZANLA supporter.[139]

Until Operation Hurricane, Rhodesian Security Forces believed they had the situation well in hand. They believed that black Rhodesians would fully support the white government's efforts against the insurgents, and that no major adjustments to their tactics were necessary, despite reports to the contrary

---

[134] Ibid. Smith's estimation of the percentage of Africans polled by the Pearce Commission (5 percent) differs from other accounts, which place the number at 6 percent. The discrepancy is noted here because Smith is quoted directly. Most other sources support the 6 percent number. Regardless, the Pearce Commission only met with a tiny sample of African population after much violence surrounding their arrival from both ANC activists and Rhodesian police. The Pearce Commission report acknowledged that fact but believed they had captured the predominant feeling of the black population, much to the consternation of Smith and the Rhodesian Front.

[135] Wellington W. Nyangoni. African Nationalism in Zimbabwe-(Rhodesia) (Washington, DC: University Press of America, 1977), 89.

[136] CE20110908G0001, former RAR officer, interview; CE20110908M0001, former RAR officer, interview.

[137] David Martin and Phyllis Johnson, The Struggle for Zimbabwe (London: Faber and Faber, 1981), 73.

[138] Binda, Masodja, 248; Wood, Counterstrike, 38; Martin, 73.

[139] Binda, Masodja, 262-3; Wood, Counterstrike, 38; Martin, 146.

(including documents captured during an SAS raid against a FRELIMO-ZANLA[140] base camp in Mozambique). It took the attack on Altena Farm to sound the alarm within the Rhodesian command. Once Rhodesian commanders realized that the paradigm of universal black support was an illusion, they made several adjustments in how they fought the war as well. The RAR would play a vital role in implementing these tactics.[141]

PROTECTED VILLAGES

One of the adjustments made by RSF was an effort to isolate the population from insurgent influence and create "no-go" areas[142] in sparsely populated regions by creating Protected Villages (PVs). The effectiveness of these villages was mixed - they did help create "no-go" areas for RSF pursuit of insurgents, but they failed to address the core issue of popular support for the insurgency.[143]

PVs were not new to the RAR soldiers, some of whom had experience in Malaya, as well as in Mozambique with Portuguese troops.[144] Malayan PVs - called "New Villages" - were highly effective at denying insurgent access to the population. The Portuguese versions of PVs, called *aldeamentos*, were not as effective because the Portuguese program in Mozambique was hastily executed and inadequately resourced.[145] The Rhodesian PVs were a blend of the Malayan and Portuguese concepts, and were a strategic failure of the Bush War.

According to counterinsurgency theorist Sir Robert Thompson, there are three main objectives of a PV strategy:

The first, a prerequisite for the other two, is the protection of the population...The most vital aspect of protection, however is the elimination within the hamlet of the insurgent underground organization. Until this is done, no hamlet will be secure against repenetration and treachery, nor can the people themselves be expected to take positive action on behalf of the government until insurgent agents and supporters within the hamlet have been removed. The second object ... is to unite the people and involve them in positive action on the side of the government. This can only be done by involving the people in a small way in national policies which both affect and benefit them, first in the defence of their community and secondly in its development. The third objective ... is this development in the social, economic, and political fields...The significant point here is that at the end of the [Malayan] Emergency very few families wished to leave their new homes and return to their old sites.[146]

---

[140]FRELIMO (Frente de Libertaçao de Moçambique), or Liberation Front of Mozambique, was the communist insurgent group in Mozambique fighting against the ruling Portuguese government. Because of their tribal similarities (the western portion of Mozambique was predominantly inhabited by Shona tribes) ZANU and ZANLA were able to make great allies of FRELIMO, using their bases for training, staging and operating extensively. ZAPU tended to operate out of Zambia throughout the war.

[141]Martin, 97.

[142]These were open areas for RSF to engage the insurgents without placing the population at risk by moving selected rural populations into consolidated compounds.

[143] Cilliers, 101.

[144] Binda, Masodja, 265; CE20110909R0001, former RAR officer, interview; CE20110913M0001, former RAR officer, interview. By this point, Rhodesian Army planners were working in Pretoria with both Portuguese and South African counterparts to drive policy decisions and compare experiences. Called Exercise Alcora, these planning sessions were largely influenced by the Portuguese contingent until their sudden withdrawal in 1974 (following the coup in Lisbon). Portugal was seen as the most experienced counterinsurgent force of the three parties involved. Once the Portuguese withdrew, the sessions became known as Exercise Oryx, and Rhodesian and South African military planners continued to meet in Pretoria.

[145] John P. Cann, Counterinsurgency in Africa: The Portuguese Way of War 1961- 1974 (Westport, CT: Greenwood Press, 1997), 159.

[146] Robert Thompson, Defeating Communist Insurgency (St. Petersburg, FL: Hailer, 2005), 124-5. Thompson refers to "strategic hamlets" to describe this concept. A veteran of Malaya himself, Thompson was also influential in adapting this theory for US commanders in Vietnam, where US and Vietnamese forces also attempted a strategic hamlet program, with minimal success. The concept is to create pockets of security and safety inside contested areas, allowing popular support to grow due to favorable security conditions, while denying resources and assistance to the insurgents. American counterinsurgency theorist John McCuen also describes this as the "oil spot strategy" in his book, The Art of Counter-Revolutionary War.

In practice, Rhodesian PVs did not separate the population from insurgent influence prior to moving them into the villages, nor was there ever enough investment in the infrastructure, social, economic or political fields to influence the population to support the government.[147]

In establishing the PV program, Rhodesian Deputy Minister of Law and Order Wickus de Kock emphasized that the purpose of the program was to create no-go areas, where access was restricted to "authorised members of the Security Forces".[148] This is a very different emphasis from the Malayan model, which focused on isolating the population from insurgents by first focusing on meeting security and infrastructure needs of the villagers themselves. In contrast to de Kock's policy, the Rhodesian Army stated that the intent of the operation that relocated people into PVs was "to deprive terrorists of their vital contact with the civilian population, particularly at night, when they force tribesmen to accommodate and feed them as they move through the area".[149] These two shades on the intent of the PV program reveal a rift between government policy and army practice, and neither of the stated intents addressed what was most successful in Malaya - safeguarding and improving conditions for the people.[150]

A third perspective on the intent of PVs came from an Internal Affairs planning document, which stated, "The short term objective is the removal of the African people from terrorist influence for the sake of national security, but the full attainment of this short term aim must surely result in our reaching the ultimate goal of more concentrated and more rapid development of the African people and the areas which they inhabit"[151]. The emphasis of the PV program never shifted to that second long term goal of development due to lack of resources, poor planning and misunderstanding amongst planners of the intent of the program.[152]

The result of this confused PV policy was the hasty establishment of poorly planned, insufficiently secured and under-resourced villages that inspired no confidence in the government and were still vulnerable to insurgent attacks. The civilians' situation had most certainly not improved, and in their view it had deteriorated. According to a black Member of Parliament, Aaron Mungate, the main objections to PVs among the black population were:

1. The only people who were protected were those within the keep itself (i.e. the guards).
2. In the majority of the Protected Villages no timely and adequate water supply had been installed.
3. People had been forced from their traditional, and in some instances, substantial homes with no compensation and no aid towards buying materials to erect new ones.
4. Because only the gates of the Protected Villages were guarded, the fences around the village did not prevent communication between the villagers and the insurgents.[153]

The Rhodesian PV program suffered from two main shortcomings in execution. First, there was "an over-emphasis on the short term goal of physically concentrating the local population and the freedom of action this would give the Security Forces". Second, the program never had the resources committed to it -

---

[147]Cilliers, 99.

[148] Ibid., 82. De Kock used the term "no-go areas" in his statement, which are defined in Rhodesian Army manual, Military Support to the Civil Power, as areas "from which all civilians are excluded by an order of the Protecting Authority, in terms of Section 4(1)(b) of the Emergency Powers (Maintenance of Law and Order) regulations … in order to ensure that they do not become involved in operations conducted by Security Forces against terrorists. Only authorised members of the Security Forces, on duty, will move in no-go areas and no action may be instituted against them for any death … or any act performed in good faith in the course of operations conducted during the time whilst the order is in force".

[149] Cilliers, 84.

[150] Ibid., 82-4.

[151] Ibid., 99.

[152] Ibid. Internal Affairs was the ministry of the Rhodesian government charged with administering the tribal areas. They were the lead agency for instituting the PV program, with the military in support.

[153] Cilliers, 85.

either financially or militarily - to succeed.[154] In the only truly successful example of population control the Rhodesians had (Malaya), the government committed adequate economic resources to the endeavor, resulting in New Villages truly becoming better places to live than their alternative. This was a lesson that the British had learned rather painfully by the time the RAR were deployed there in 1956. In Malaya, there were also more than enough security forces to isolate the villages from the insurgents - Rhodesia had neither the will nor the manpower to commit to PV security early enough to make a difference. Instead, PVs became unsanitary breeding grounds for contempt toward the government, and excellent targets for coercion and manipulation by the insurgents.[155]

The PV program is one area where the RAR could have played a tremendous role in turning popular support back to the government of Rhodesia. Had the Rhodesian government invested the time and effort into developing meaningful local protection of the PVs at their inception - possibly using RAR platoons as partners and trainers for village security forces, at least the security situation within PVs would have improved, and potential inclusion of the villagers in securing their own fate may have prevented their availability to the insurgents for psychological and physical attacks. Eventually, two security initiatives would attempt to redress the vulnerability of PVs and the surrounding tribal areas - Guard Force and Security Force Auxiliaries (*Pfumo re Vanhu*), mentioned earlier). Both initiatives were severely challenged in providing adequate training, equipment, and supervision. By the time these forces were stood up, they couldn't be trained fast enough to meet the threat.[156]

The RAR knew how to train African soldiers. They had established a rigorous selection and training program of their own, and understood quite well how to overcome the challenge of taking a raw recruit from a Rhodesian *kraal*, with very limited education, no experience with a rifle, and little cultural understanding of how the army was structured and turning him into a capable soldier - loyal and dedicated to his regiment. The development of such a force took time, as the RAR well knew.[157] In 1973, Rhodesia had time, but by 1977, when efforts to secure the PVs were stepped up and Guard Force was formed, time was up and the insurgents had the upper hand in the tribal areas.

SELOUS SCOUTS

By 1973, the Rhodesian Army realized that it had a real problem gathering actionable military intelligence on insurgent locations and activities. Until Operation Hurricane, counterinsurgency operations relied on intelligence primarily gathered by BSAP and Special Branch from willing locals. Due to the insurgents' shift to a Maoist strategy of coercion and intimidation of local populations, intelligence sources dried up almost completely in 1971, and something had to be done to get RSF back into action. The Rhodesians studied two very effective examples to accomplish this: the British experience against Mau-Mau guerrillas in Kenya, and the Portuguese example of the *fleches*,[158] a unit made up of local tribesmen

---

[154] Ibid., 99.

[155] Ibid., 88.

[156] CE20110912G0001, former RAR officer, interview; CG20110927S0001, former RAR officer, interview. In one interview, a former RAR officer said that he was placed in charge of *pfumo re vanhu* in 1979. On his assignment to work with *pfumo re vanhu*, this officer said that he had very little direction, and no understanding of what the intention was with the men he was to train. He - then a Lieutenant - and his CSM were given the task of developing a six-week program to conduct basic military training, then pushing the trainees out as quickly as possible.

[157] CE20110912G0001, former RAR officer, interview. See later discussion on SFAs. After initial training by Selous Scouts, the SFA program was run by officers of 1RAR. Guard Force was formed by Brigadier Bill Godwin, former CO 1RAR, brought out of retirement by Rhodesian Army HQ for the task.

[158] Former Selous Scouts officer, interview by author, 10 November 2011; Reid-Daly, Top Secret War, 109-11, 120. In standing up the Selous Scouts, Lt Col Reid-Daly admits openly to both the British and Portuguese influences. In fact, both British and Portuguese officers were directly involved with the development of Selous Scouts concept. Lieutenant Spike Powell, who worked in pseudo operations in Kenya (and was later killed in the second Air Rhodesia Viscount shot down by ZIPRA in 1979) collaborated in the early pseudo operations experiments in Rhodesia (as early as 1966), and Reid-Daly personally visited the *fleches* compound at Vila Pery (Chimoio), Mozambique to study their methods and tactics. Colonel Oscar Cordosa, commander of the *fleches*, would later lead several of his men into Rhodesia to join the Selous Scouts after FRELIMO took over Mozambique in 1974.

and turned insurgents used to great effect in Angola and Mozambique. Patterned after these examples, small groups of Rhodesian soldiers, with turned ZIPRA and ZANLA insurgents integrated into their organization, formed into gangs that imitated insurgent tactics to discover the support network and track movements of real insurgent groups. These experiments resulted in tremendous success, and the army formed a regiment to further develop and implement these "pseudo" operations in Rhodesian strategy. The regiment was called the Selous Scouts, named after the renowned Rhodesian hunter, Frederick Courtney Selous.[159]

The Selous Scouts' newly appointed CO, Lieutenant Colonel Ron Reid-Daly, was given top priority on selecting, equipping, and training personnel - black and white - from across the RSF. Recruitment for the Scouts was universal: anyone from any regiment could volunteer for selection, and no unit could refuse such a request. This resulted in some friction between the RAR and Selous Scouts, as Reid-Daly recruited heavily from the RAR to fill his ranks. For the RAR soldiers, selection to the Scouts meant more adventure in a special operations unit, more prestige as a highly trained special operator, and a significant increase in pay. The Selous Scouts offered equal pay for black and white members (unlike any other Rhodesian unit at the time), and they offered the additional incentive of a "special unit allowance" - an extra Rh$1.20 a day, which effectively made the average black Scout's pay the same as the RSM of an RAR rifle battalion. As a result, the Selous Scouts tended to draw out top-performing NCOs from the RAR, placing the regiment in competition with Reid-Daly's recruiters.[160]

The RAR was not the only source for black Selous Scouts, however. Many were also drawn from the BSAP, SB, and a great many were captured, "tame" insurgents whose experience in ZANLA and ZIPRA was critical to the Scouts' infiltration of the insurgents' networks. Many of the former RAR NCOs served with great distinction as Selous Scouts. While serving with the Scouts, former RAR soldiers earned seven Silver Crosses of Rhodesia, twenty-four Bronze Crosses of Rhodesia, one Member of the Legion of Merit, one Defence Forces Medal for Meritorious Service and thirteen Military Forces Commendations. Two of these men earned both the Silver and Bronze Crosses of Rhodesia, making them the most highly decorated NCOs in the Rhodesian Army.[161] As Reid-Daly stated in *The War Diaries of Andre Dennison*:

> Relations between the RAR and the Selous Scouts were not always cordial during the Rhodesian war. That is perfectly understandable from the RAR point of view, for they had to stand by and watch many of their best men poached for the Selous Scouts. But if one looks back dispassionately now, free from the stress and tensions brought about by the war, officers and soldiers of the RAR must only feel pride in the many deeds of valour performed by their men who served with great courage and distinction in the Selous Scouts.[162]

One Selous Scouts officer interviewed for this study recalled his selection course, which 175 candidates started, from whom only 12 were selected. At the tender age of 38, this officer struggled to finish the final forced march of the course, a tremendously long journey with full kit. He stopped to rest his aching feet, nearly at the end of his endurance, and a fellow candidate from the RAR stopped with him, picked up

---

[159] Reid-Daly, Top Secret War, 65-69. Selous, an Englishman, arrived in Africa in 1871 at the age of 19. He hunted elephants and other big game in what would later become Rhodesia, and was widely respected by the Ndebele and several notable characters, such as avid big game hunter and US President Theodore Roosevelt, Kaiser Wilhelm I and author Rider Haggard. Haggard later immortalized Selous as Alan Quartermain, the hero of King Solomon's Mines. At the outbreak of World War I in 1914, he attempted to join the army but was rejected because of his age (he was 62). However, he was later recruited by the War Office after it was determined that the Brits were losing too many men to the bush and diseases while chasing down German forces in East Africa. Finally brought into service and commissioned as a Lieutenant, Selous was a tremendous asset to the British army, but was killed by a stray bullet in a skirmish near the Rufiji River in Tanzania. Out of respect for his mastery and love of the African bush, he was buried where he fell and his grave stands today on a game reserve which bears his name.

[160] Ibid., 102-7. In his book, Reid-Daly describes an "insidious plot" within the RAR to undermine his recruiting efforts. After his initial recruiting drive, he received word that 90 percent of the candidates from the RAR had withdrawn their applications. At Reid-Daly's insistence, Army HQ subsequently ordered all who applied to go to selection, and Reid-Daly offered the candidates the opportunity to choose between the Selous Scouts and the RAR at the end of selection. Few chose to leave the Scouts.

[161] Reid-Daly, Challenge, 155.

[162] Wood, War Diaries, xii.

his rucksack and finished alongside the officer, carrying his own pack and the officer's the rest of the way. Such was the selflessness and spirit of these men. To be sure, the RAR was not the sole reason for the astounding success of the Selous Scouts, but "without the men of the RAR, the Scouts would not have been half as effective".[163]

FIREFORCE

> How do you force the guerrilla into confrontation situations (contacts) on your own terms, given the fact that the enemy's tactics and training make him adept at avoiding these situations?... Army actions alone (ambushes and fleeting contacts) seldom result in the guerrilla suffering significant casualties and follow-up operations on foot using trackers are also of dubious value. Air power used in isolation is similarly ineffective. In order to locate the guerrilla and force him to fight (or surrender), the peculiar attributes of ground and air forces acting in concert are required. Employed in the appropriate manner they provide the best possible chance of inflicting heavy casualties, and combined they provide a formidable fighting force.[164]

To act on the real-time intelligence gathered by the Selous Scouts and others, the Rhodesian Army needed a rapid reaction force on standby, with coordinated air support and ground troops ready to rapidly attack and destroy identified cells of terrorists before they could escape. To this end, the SAS began experimenting with dropping paratroops in Tête province of Mozambique to vertically envelop targeted insurgent groups. These experiments, combined with the refined insertion of heliborne troops from RhAF Alouette helicopters, led to the deployment of the first "fireforce" at Centenary in January 1974.[165]

Early fireforce deployments consisted of groups of four men, called sticks. In each stick was "a junior officer, NCO or senior trooper, armed with an FN rifle and equipped with a VHF A63/76 radio; two riflemen, one with first aid training; and a machine gunner carrying a MAG 7.62mm machine gun".[166] An Alouette helicopter could carry one stick of soldiers - the troop-carrying helicopters were called "G-Cars". The fireforce commander, usually the company or troop commander or 2IC, rode in a command helicopter, called a "K-Car". The fireforce commander was responsible for spotting terrorists on the ground, talking to the OP, coordinating all troop deployments, and integrating airstrikes from bombers and Lynx[167] aircraft with ground operations, while the K-Car pilot coordinated all helicopter movements and kept his aircraft in the fight. Within a few months of starting fireforce deployments (by June 1974) K-Cars were also equipped with 20mm Matra cannons, and were able to effectively engage ground targets while circling over the contact at 800 feet.[168]

Several sticks were deployed according to direction from the fireforce commander circling overhead in the K-Car. These sticks would serve as "stop groups" while another group (one or several sticks, depending on the situation) acted as a "sweep group", tasked to clear the open area to flush their quarry

---

[163] CB20111110S0001, former Selous Scouts' officer, interview by author, Fort Leavenworth, Kansas, 10 November 2011.

[164] Wing Commander Peter R. Briscoe, as quoted in Alexandre Binda's The Saints.

[165] Wood, Counterstrike, 90.

[166] Ibid. 102.

[167] A Lynx was a Cessna 337, armed with .30 caliber cannons and rockets. Lynxes were crucial enablers for Fireforce action, able to move in, stay low over a target area for a long period of time and provide immediate, accurate airstrikes when required, as well as guide in attacks from other strike aircraft.

[168] Wood, Counterstrike, 96-103.

into an ambush at the stop group locations. The circling K-Car provided fire support from its mounted gun, as well as coordinating strikes from Lynx and other aircraft.[169]

On 15 February 1974, the efforts of establishing fireforce were rewarded as 20 RLI soldiers were called in and arrived on five Alouette helicopters to assault an insurgent camp discovered by an Air Force pilot near Mount Darwin. Later that same month, one of the first Selous Scouts operations led by Lieutenant Dale Collett infiltrated a large group of ZANLA cadre operating in Rhodesia. By 18 April 1975, Lt. Collett's group had enough intelligence to call in a fireforce. Once again, the fireforce at Centenary - this time from B Company 1RAR - arrived and surrounded the insurgents.

The final result of this contact was 7 insurgents killed, 5 captured (one of whom died later), and 7 escaped (two of whom were believed wounded). Another body was found three weeks later. The results of these early fireforce operations were encouraging to the RAR and the RSF in general.[170]

There were lessons yet to be learned in employment of fireforce, and the weapons and tactics would continue to evolve for the rest of the war - notably the addition of 20mm Matra cannons to the Alouette gunships (called K-Cars) in June 1974, and the use of DC-3 Dakotas to drop paratroops in 1977 (until 1977 only the SAS were parachute qualified). The concept began with four or five sticks of troopers deploying by helicopter with additional sticks arriving via ground convoy (called the "land tail"), and would eventually evolve into large packages of hundreds of soldiers employed in "jumbo" fireforces conducting external raids into Zambia and Mozambique. The size of the fireforce was determined by the size of the enemy and the situation on the ground.[171]

The RLI and RAR were the principal units to execute fireforce operations. RLI commandos and RAR companies rotated through fireforce deployments at forward airfields scattered throughout the operational areas of the country. In later "jumbo" fireforce raids into Zambia and Mozambique the RLI and SAS operated almost exclusively, while the RAR tended to execute internal fireforce operations (that is, within the country of Rhodesia). This was because the RAR was generally better at pursuing insurgents through the tribal areas while operating amongst the population to gain intelligence and look for inconsistencies. The RLI's strengths - aggressive, fast-paced, initiative driven contact - were much better suited to external operations.[172]

Between Selous Scouts and fireforce, RSF made the innovations necessary to counter the Phase Two tactical shift to Maoist principles that ZANLA made in 1972. By the end of 1974, there were only 60-70 insurgents left operating in Rhodesia, all contained in the northeast part of the country and vastly outnumbered by the RSF. Militarily, Rhodesia had regained the military advantage and had the insurgents pressed nearly to the breaking point. The population had been moved into PVs in much of the area identified as insurgent stronghold, isolating (temporarily) them from insurgent influence.[173]

---

[169] The RhAF was able to employ an aging and tiny fleet of ground attack aircraft with tremendous effect on the battlefield. These included Hawker-Hunter FGA9 ground attack fighters, Vampire FB52 fighters, English Electric Canberra B2 light bombers, Provost trainers (adapted to carry .303 machine guns and napalm bombs). Sales of aircraft, engines and repair parts were the first round of sanctions imposed on Rhodesia by the United Nations after UDI, and so the fact that these aircraft continued flying throughout the war is a testament to the ingenuity and resourcefulness of the Rhodesian Air Force "blue jobs".

[170] Binda, Masodja, 265-6; Wood, Counterstrike, 91. Wood describes this action as a disappointment due to the RAR commander landing during the fight to direct action from the ground. Regardless, the results of this Fireforce, like the previous action of the RLI, resulted in higher insurgent kill rates than had been achieved prior to Fireforce. The RAR, like the rest of the Rhodesian Army, would continue to improve and adapt from this action.

[171] Wood, Counterstrike, 91-2. The DC-3 Dakota, called the "Paradak", could deliver up to 20 paratroops at a time. The Rhodesian use of paratroops in Fireforce was born of necessity, due to a shortage of helicopters: one Paradak delivered the same number of troops as five Alouette helicopters, and increasing numbers of Fireforce callouts against larger groups of insurgents called for airborne insertion in addition to heliborne insertion just to get enough forces on the ground to handle the situation.

[172] CE20110909T0001, former RAR officer, interview; Wood, Counterstrike, 96.

[173] Cilliers, 21-2; Wood, Counterstrike, 39; Trevor Desfountain, summary and background notes of a 1979 Rhodesian Strategy Revision Conference, compiled in 1984. Cilliers and Wood disagree on the number of insurgents operating in Rhodesia at the end of 1974. Wood cites that there were 60, Cilliers that there were 70. At any rate, the number was small, and the insurgents had lost the military edge they had started to gain with the attacks in Chiweshe in 1972.

LOSS OF AN ALLY: PORTUGAL WITHDRAWS FROM AFRICA

On 25 April 1974, the Portuguese Army in Lisbon staged a coup d'état (the Carnation Revolution) and took over the government. The new government in Lisbon, made up largely of disillusioned army officers tired of fighting costly colonial wars in Africa, promptly granted independence to all of its African colonies, and on 25 July 1974 Mozambique was turned over to FRELIMO as over 250,000 Portuguese inhabitants fled the country.[174]

The Portuguese withdrawal and the subsequent takeover of Mozambique by FRELIMO was a strategic disaster for Rhodesia. Portugal was a crucial ally to the Rhodesian government. They offered military cooperation, trade and access to ports on the Indian Ocean. Despite their tactical ineptitude and relatively poor military attributes,[175] the Portuguese had been fighting a counterinsurgency much longer than their Rhodesian counterparts, and the Rhodesians learned much about what to do (and what not to do) from their Portuguese allies and neighbors. In fact, the Portuguese contribution to joint military discussions were crucial in developing the early Rhodesian responses to nationalist insurgent operations. PVs and pseudo operations were both patterned after Portuguese examples (the former, unfortunately, was patterned more closely than it should have been). The formation of Grey's Scouts, a mounted infantry unit, as an effective counterinsurgency force was also a Rhodesian idea with Portuguese precedent.[176]

Without Portuguese Mozambique, Rhodesia only had South Africa to turn to for assistance, and that put the Rhodesian government at the mercy of its southern neighbor, under tremendous pressure of its own. As the new government of Mozambique, FRELIMO - already allied with ZANLA by tribal ties and as fellow nationalist groups - subsequently offered its direct assistance, bases and safe haven throughout Mozambique. FRELIMO ceased all assistance to the Rhodesian government, enforced the UN Embargo, and closed its ports to Rhodesian cargo. With FRELIMO assistance (and without Portuguese Army interference) ZANLA had unrestricted access to Mozambique and another 1,100 kilometers of border along which to stage incursions and strikes. The Rhodesian Army and the RAR would soon have an unsolvable problem on their eastern frontier - it would later prove no longer possible to militarily contain the growing insurgency.[177]

CONCLUSION

Those developments were yet to come, however. By the end of the second phase of the Bush War, RSF had overcome the insurgents' shift to a Maoist strategy by establishing the first permanent JOC in Operation Hurricane, and by adapting new tactics to isolate the population, increase intelligence and act decisively when that intelligence revealed a valid target. At the end of 1974, as at the end of 1971, Rhodesia had the war very much in hand militarily. This would not continue. The loss of the friendly Portuguese government in Mozambique increased regional pressure on Rhodesia, and left the Rhodesian Front government with very few options. From this point forward, factors beyond Rhodesian control would drive the pace of the war.

For its part, the RAR remained steadily and increasingly employed throughout this period. The advent of fireforce increased demands on the regiment. The RAR had learned valuable lessons since Operation

---

[174] Binda, Masodja, 266.

[175] Al J. Venter, "Why Portugal Lost Its African Wars", in Challenge: Southern Africa within the African Revolutionary context (Gibraltar: Ashanti, 1989). Rhodesians who worked with their Portuguese counterparts in Mozambique saw little military competence or bushcraft in the largely metropolitan Portuguese Army. With notable exceptions, such as the *fleches*, most Portuguese soldiers had little knowledge and less interest in African affairs, and their attitude was manifest in their lack of military intensity. Nonetheless, Portuguese withdrawal from Mozambique, and the subsequent turnover of governance to FRELIMO, was a tremendous loss for Rhodesia.

[176] CE20110909R0001, former RAR officer, interview; CE20110913M0001, former Grey's Scouts officer, interview; Cann, 139. Exercise Alcora was a crucial joint collaborative effort between Rhodesian, South African, and Portuguese military planners, in which the Portuguese had the leading role. Portuguese dragoons, or *dragões*, began operating in Silva Porto, Angola in 1966 and by 1971 were also in Mozambique. This idea predated Grey's Scouts, a Rhodesian mounted infantry unit formed in 1976. The use of horse-mounted troops in the southern African bush was highly effective.

[177] Cilliers, 19-20; Binda, Masodja, 266.

Nickel, and proved its effectiveness in conducting fireforce operations, patrols, and observation post missions against an increasingly familiar ZANLA opponent.

The political uncertainties of the Pearce Commission and increased insurgent intimidation in the tribal areas and *kraals* had surprisingly little effect on the availability of black volunteers for service in the regiment. While never explicitly employed in protecting Protected Villages, the RAR could have provided a valuable service by committing to the development of PV security forces during this critical period. Later attempts to secure PVs (discussed in subsequent chapters) would be hastily conceived and poorly executed.

With the formation of the Selous Scouts, many of the best NCOs left the RAR for better pay and more adventure as trackers and pseudo operators under Lt. Col Reid-Daly. While the loss of these NCOs did degrade 1RAR slightly, the regiment still retained its reputation as a superb counterinsurgency force and did not suffer tremendously.

The loss of Portuguese influence in Mozambique would have profound effects on the RAR, as the increased tempo of the war stretched its companies more thinly across a wider area of the country. The numbers of insurgents encountered by fireforce operations would quickly increase from dozens to hundreds, while the RLI and SAS strikes targeted thousands of insurgents in external raids.

CHAPTER 5 - PHASE THREE: 1974-1977

Phase three of the war, from 1974-77, initially saw a negotiated détente and a ceasefire brokered by South African Prime Minister John Vorster during a December 1974 conference with the "frontline" states of Zambia, Tanzania, Botswana, Angola and Mozambique. This ceasefire was quickly broken by ZANU and ZAPU, and the war intensified again through 1976. ZANLA and ZIPRA continued to build strength and recruit from among the black rural population, as large numbers of whites, mostly from the urban centers, began to leave the country. Rhodesian forces responded to the insurgent violation of the ceasefire agreements by attacking into Zambia and Mozambique, targeting ZIPRA and ZANLA base camps. To control a growing military operation within and outside of Rhodesian borders, Ian Smith established a Combined Operations (ComOps) organization, deploying increasing numbers of security forces and striving to "contain the war". [178]

The increased demands on security forces caused the Rhodesian government to create a second battalion of RAR, among other changes to National Service and Territorial Force structures. This period also saw the commissioning of the first black officers in June 1977, followed by parachute training for both RAR and RLI soldiers later that same year. Political activity was marked by increased outside political pressure from South Africa, Britain and the United States to force Ian Smith towards majority rule. [179]

DÉTENTE

In late 1974 South African Prime Minister John Vorster agreed to enter into a détente with the frontline states to resolve the situation in Rhodesia. The aim was to unite ZANU, ZAPU and ANC under the leadership of Bishop Abel Muzorewa, and then to negotiate a settlement between the united nationalist movements and Smith's government. If this scheme worked, the front-line states promised to recognize white-rule South Africa, buying the apartheid government time and influence among its neighbors, albeit at the Rhodesia's expense. The terms of the ceasefire - as dictated by the leaders of Zambia, Mozambique and Tanzania - were an immediate end to hostilities, withdrawal of South African forces from Rhodesia, the lifting of bans on ZANU and ZAPU, and release of political detainees. The released nationalist leaders and Smith's government would attend a constitutional conference in Lusaka to negotiate the transfer of power in Rhodesia to majority rule. In exchange for these terms, the frontline states would use their influence to discourage ZANLA and ZIPRA military actions in Rhodesia; prevent incursions from frontline states into South Africa; bring Nkomo, Sithole and Mugabe to the negotiating table; and host the Lusaka conference. [180]

Ian Smith's Rhodesian Front government, still attempting to cope with the loss of its eastern trading partner and ally, and facing a five-fold increase in its front line (which now included the entire Mozambique border, as well as the Zambian and uncontrolled Botswana borders), had little choice but to accept the terms of détente. Refusal of these terms would have cut crucial ties with South Africa and completely isolated Rhodesia. So, on 11 December 1974, Smith agreed to the ceasefire and released all detainees, among whom were Joshua Nkomo (ZAPU), Ndabaningi Sithole (ZANU), and Robert Mugabe (ZANU). RSF pulled back and stopped pursuing insurgents in Rhodesia. The consequences of this would prove disastrous. In discussing détente, Smith said:

> We were on the brink of dealing them a knock-out blow - we had them on the run - of this we had no doubt. In our minds, the détente exercise undoubtedly saved those terrorists remaining in Rhodesia because our security forces abided by the terms of the ceasefire. We pulled back in order to give the terrorists time to comply with their part of the bargain. However, before long it became clear the enemy had no intention of keeping its promise. This not only affected us militarily, but, more importantly, psychologically. The terrorists cashed in on our withdrawal by telling the locals that they had won the war and that we

---

[178] Cilliers, 67-8, 197; Wood, Counterstrike, 43-4.
[179] Binda, Masodja, 267-8; Wood, Counterstrike, 40-44.
[180] Martin, 145.

were retreating. Our actions (and those of the departing South African police units) substantiated their claims. This was probably the most important aspect of all.[181]

Smith was right - ZANLA was nearly militarily defeated before détente. Fighting in the northeast during Operation Hurricane had taken its toll on trained insurgent fighters and leaders, and the nationalist movement was starting to melt down - not without some assistance from Rhodesian Central Intelligence Organisation (CIO). In November 1974, a rebellion broke out within the ranks of ZANLA over the detached lifestyle of the ZANU and ZANLA leadership in Lusaka, lack of supplies and poor administration of the war. While newly recruited ZANLA soldiers fought and died in Rhodesia, some of the ground commanders for ZANLA saw their leaders' opulent lifestyles outside the country as hypocrisy. Called the Nhari Rebellion, this revolt was ultimately put down by the ZANU Chief of Defense, Josiah Tongogara.[182] The two leaders of the Nhari Rebellion were executed, along with others. A few months later, in March 1975, ZANU Chairman Herbert Chitepo was also assassinated in Lusaka.[183]

Between the Nhari Rebellion, Chitepo's assassination, and subsequent rivalry amongst ZANU members, the Zambian government soon tired of ZANU. By 28 March, Zambia arrested most of ZANU's members in the country and closed their offices, saying ZANU were "prejudicial to the maintenance of peace, order and good government".[184]

After this humiliation of ZANU's leadership and Zambia's refusal to continue to support their movement, the remaining ZANU members in Zambia fled to Mozambique. This left the Rhodesian nationalist movement in Zambia exclusively to ZAPU and ZIPRA. Additionally, the OAU now insisted on funneling its funding through Muzorewa's ANC, so resources, logistics, and leadership for ZANLA were all getting even more scarce in 1975. The new chairman for ZANU, Robert Mugabe, began to establish himself and his organization in Mozambique. This move temporarily shut down ZANU operations in Rhodesia for much of the year. By Rhodesian intelligence estimates, in December 1975 there were only three groups of 10 ZANLA insurgents each operating in Rhodesia.[185]

Then an idea surfaced among the nationalists to form a "third force", to unite ZIPRA and ZANLA into one organization committed to the armed struggle for the liberation of blacks in Rhodesia. Led by Rex Nhongo (ZANLA) and Alfred "Nikita" Mangena (ZIPRA), this organization called itself the Zimbabwe People's Army (ZIPA). While the union lasted quite briefly, ZIPA did carry out attacks along the new open border between Manicaland (in eastern Rhodesia) and Mozambique. In response to these attacks, Rhodesia established Operation Thrasher in February 1976, based out of Umtali, and increased call-ups among Rhodesian army reserves. This increased activity also led to the creation of a second RAR battalion. 2RAR, like 1RAR, was completely filled by black volunteers. Many more potential recruits were still turning out to enlist in the RAR than could be accepted.[186]

2RAR

At the breakup of the Central African Federation in 1963, the Rhodesian Army recommended to the government that the RAR be comprised of two battalions with three line companies each. The idea was that it would be much easier to grow each battalion to accommodate four or five rifle companies and a support company, should the need arise, than to build a new battalion on short notice - potentially in the middle of

---

[181] Pat Scully, Exit Rhodesia (Ladysmith: Cotswold Press, 1984), 52.

[182] Cilliers, 34; CE20110909R0001, former RAR officer, interview. Of note, many of the "Nhari rebels", including Thomas Nhari, were relatively new commanders recruited from the area of Operation Hurricane, in the northeastern part of Rhodesia. They were Shona, from the KoreKore and Zezuru tribes. Joseph Tongogara and the ZANU high command were all Shona Karanga tribesmen who joined ZAPU much earlier in the war, before splitting to form ZANU. The KoreKore and Zezuru resented what they saw as Karanga tribal monopoly of ZANLA's key leadership.

[183] Smith, 174-5. Years later, the Rhodesian CIO chief, Ken Flower, would reveal that Chitepo's assassination was a CIO operation, which happened to be timed perfectly to coincide with existing ZANU discord. Everyone in Zambia, including the Zambian government, believed Tongogara assassinated Chitepo. Chitepo's death would lead to more infighting in ZANU.

[184] Martin, 159-167, 179.

[185] Moorcraft, 41.

[186] Ibid., 41-2.

a war. The Rhodesian government refused this request, and decided instead to keep the RAR strength at one battalion, adding a fifth company, "E" Company, in 1964. "Regrettably, the Rhodesian Front did not trust the African soldier".[187]

Distrust of black soldiers had two principal sources: past experience during the establishment of Rhodesia, and the Congo Crisis of 1961. After the tribal uprisings of the 1890s, Rhodesia was wary of creating a black regiment (the RNR), for fear that a trained, armed force of blacks could easily overthrow the relatively small white security forces - many of whom had personally experienced the events of the 1890s. The RNR exhibited no such tendencies however; nor did the RAR during any part of its existence. Suspicions of black troops rose again in June 1960 with news of the Congo Crisis. In the southern Congo region of Katanga, black soldiers of the Force Publique mutinied against their white officers and "attacked local white civilians, looting, raping, and inciting a mass exodus of Belgian officers, administrators and settlers during the summer of 1960". The fear of a black mutiny on the heels of the Congo Crisis led to the creation of all-white regular army units in the Central African Federation - the RLI, SAS, and Armored Car Regiment - to balance the four "African" battalions in the Federal Army (the NRR, two battalions of KAR, and the RAR). This move was to mitigate a perceived vulnerability of the white population against a similar mutiny in the Central African Federation amidst "subversive activities of nationalists in Nyasaland and Northern Rhodesia". This fear was not founded in any evidence of such activity in the RAR, but seemed to be the source of hesitation in the Rhodesian government to follow the army's recommendation and create additional RAR battalions early on.[188]

Once the bush war began, in the late 1960s, the Rhodesian government also failed to:

> heed warnings from the army that, despite the presence of two 100-man companies of South African police, its regular component was overstretched when merely assisting the BSAP with border control. The retired former Federal Prime Minister, Sir Roy Welensky, suggested raising 10 RAR battalions, but, because the immediate threat seemed so minor, and funds were short, the Treasury and the Department of Defense were fatally deaf to all pleas.[189]

It took the government over a decade to realize that more black troops were absolutely necessary to keep up with the demands of the war. By 1975, Rhodesia could no longer sustain the notion that black troops were an unnecessary risk.

In the early part of 1975, accurately predicting imminent increasing demands for troops after FRELIMO took power in Mozambique, the RAR began to form the nucleus of a new battalion by increasing the number of trainees at their training wing. These 230 recruits passed out in July and formed "A" Company, 2nd Battalion RAR (2RAR), under the command of Major André Dennison.[190]

The battalion, commanded by Lieutenant Colonel Peter Hosking, adopted the motto "Tinowira Kukunda", which meant "We fight to win". 2RAR was tasked to rapidly form and immediately commence

---

[187] CF20110920H001, former RAR officer, interview by author; Wood, War Diaries, 12. As the officer interviewed indicated, the Rhodesian army's response to the government's lack of trust of black soldiers was "absolute rubbish."

[188] Owen, 2-3; Banda, Saints, 20; James Dobbins et al., The UN's Role in Nation-Building: From the Congo to Iraq (Santa Monica, CA: RAND, 2005), 5.

[189] Wood, "Chimurenga", 199.

[190] Major Dennison rose to be a legend within the Rhodesian Army. Born in Bradford, England, he served in the British Army in several regiments, including 22 SAS in Borneo. He was seconded to the Malaysian Rangers from 1965-68, to the Malawi Rifles from 1969-71 and retired from the British Army in 1975 to accept a three year commission with the Rhodesian Army. Enroute to Rhodesia, Dennison stumbled across a mercenary ring forming up to attack Rhodesia from Zambia. When he notified the Director of Military Intelligence, Lt. Col. Peter Hosking (later the CO, 2RAR), Hosking agreed he should join the group and act as an informant. During a party for the mercenary group on the eve of their departure for Lusaka, the group drew too much attention to itself and lost its sponsor. The group dispersed, and on 1 October 1975, Dennison joined 2RAR to command A Company. He was a no-nonsense leader and an outstanding fireforce commander, "who inspired his men by example, professionalism and dedication to defending the hard-pressed people of all race groups in Rhodesia". Andre Dennison was killed on 3 June 1979 by friendly fire. Wood, War Diaries, viii, 5.

operations, based out of Fort Victoria in the central-eastern part of the country. E Company 1RAR was entirely transferred over to form C Company 2RAR, and B Company 2RAR formed shortly after with recruits passing out of the newly established Depot RAR. By November 1975, A Company 2RAR was deployed around Chipinga, in the Manicaland province along the southeastern border of Rhodesia. These were the initial stages of what would become Operation Thrasher. The formation of 2RAR was a tremendous undertaking, as 1RAR provided most of the NCO leadership for the new battalion. That this endeavor was completed with minimal impact on continuing operations, and that 2RAR was immediately available for combat is a testament to the professionalism, training, and leadership of the RAR. It also proves that there was still an ample recruiting base for RAR soldiers in 1975, as the additional strength requirements were adequately met with volunteers.[191]

RAR machine gunner, ready for action
Source: Alexandre Binda, Masodja: The History of the Rhodesian African Rifles and its forerunner, the Rhodesia Native Regiment (Johannesburg: 30 Degrees South, 2007), 363.

With the shared heritage and leadership between 1RAR and 2RAR, the two battalions naturally had much in common. One key difference between the two battalions of RAR, however, as noted by a former 2RAR subaltern, was 2RAR's lack of emphasis on many of the older, more formal colonial British traditions practiced in years past. According to this officer, "we [2RAR] were less regimental" than 1RAR. In 18 months of service with the battalion, for example, this officer only wore his "Number one" dress uniform once, to a funeral for another officer. By this point in the war, 1RAR was not practicing much formality either - both battalions were busy enough fighting the war. But from its inception, 2RAR never had the opportunity to practice many of the formal traditions of its predecessors. Importantly, the business of fighting the war - and the carried-over knowledge of imported NCOs from 1RAR - served as ample replacement for British regimental traditions, and 2RAR never had any problems among race or tribe within its ranks, either. By this point, the soldiers were more concerned with whether or not the man next to them could shoot and perform his duties than whether he was Shona or Ndebele - or whether his boots were properly shined, for that matter.[192]

INCREASED INSURGENT ACTIVITY AND RHODESIAN RESPONSE

As a result of the increased activity along the Mozambique border, Rhodesian forces established two new Operational Areas in 1976: Thrasher in February, and Repulse in May. In addition to the newly formed 2RAR, additional national service call-ups increased overall troop strength by about 20,000, but the pressure from insurgent activities continued to build through 1976.[193]

---

[191] CE20110910H0001, former RAR officer, interview.
[192] CE20110909T0001, former RAR officer, interview.
[193] Moorcraft, 42; Wood, War Diaries, 51. In May 1976, national service was extended from 12 to 18 months, and national servicemen in the field due to stand down were retained on active service. Territorial forces (comprised of national servicemen) were kept in the field. This trend would continue as the tempo of the war continued to increase and whites began to leave the country in larger numbers.

With ZIPA attacking further south along the Mozambique border and ZANLA rebuilding itself in border camps in Mozambique, the eyes of the OAU now turned to ZAPU to carry on the nationalist movement. ZAPU had been focused on equipping and training its Soviet-trained ZIPRA forces in Zambia, sending leaders to Soviet Eastern Europe and Cuba for indoctrination and training. They had not conducted any major operations in Rhodesia for quite some time.

By mid-1976, the OAU told ZIPRA to start fighting or lose their funding. ZIPRA duly began infiltrating across the Zambezi River in northwest Rhodesia and northeast Botswana. In August 1976, Rhodesian forces established Operation Tangent to counter the increased ZIPRA activity. Thus, in less than one year, RSF operations went from one operational area to four, as insurgents took advantage of the détente and changing circumstances to increase their activity.[194]

Increased operations brought more need for a unified command to manage what was now a nationwide military operation. Rhodesians knew the Malayan example of a "Director of Operations" quite well, and in March 1977, Ian Smith formed the Ministry of Combined Operations somewhat after the Malayan model, appointing Lieutenant General Peter Walls as the Commander of Combined Operations (ComOps). While this resulted in increased coordination, Lt. Gen. Walls was never afforded the same supreme authority over all efforts and agencies as the Director of Operations was in Malaya - he was even outranked within his own organization by the Chief of the Army, Lieutenant General John Hickman. Quite often the ComOps organization bogged down in bureaucratic inertia, as other agencies sent deputies and generally were not bound to obey the directives coming from Lt. Gen. Walls. However, the organization of ComOps, while far from perfect, was a positive step towards unifying the war effort across government agencies at the strategic level.[195]

One of the tendencies of ComOps and the JOC system used by the Rhodesian Army was that battalions seldom operated as entities of their own. Each JOC commanded elements of several different regiments (RAR, RLI, RR, BSAP, Selous Scouts, etc.) attached on rotational duty. In fact, within weeks of assuming command of 2RAR, one former commander was placed in command of the JOC in Chiredzi, where none of his companies were assigned. He didn't see his own troops for several months, during which time they were farmed out to other operational areas. [196]

During one deployment in 1975, D Company 1RAR deployed to an operational area and integrated with a company of national servicemen of the Rhodesia Regiment (RR). For the entire six-week rotation, the two units broke down into integrated teams, and one RR NCO recalled that two of his soldiers, both of Afrikaans descent, drew an assignment to work in a four-man stick under a black RAR corporal with black RAR lance corporal as a MAG gunner. These two white soldiers each owned farms which employed hundreds of blacks. They were not accustomed at all to taking orders from black men, and expressed their hesitation to spending time in the bush under the command of a black NCO. But at the insistence of their NCO they duly set off for a six week duty with their RAR colleagues.[197]

At the end of six weeks, the RR NCO anxiously waited at the rendezvous for his soldiers to return from their patrol. His curiosity peaked when he saw the RAR corporal walk in from the bush with an extra ruck sack on his back and an extra pair of boots slung over his neck. The RAR lance corporal walked in behind him, also with extra boots and an extra ruck sack in addition to his machine gun. When the RR NCO asked the RAR corporal if he had any problems with the two men, the corporal said, "No, absolutely not". Then, the two white soldiers came staggering in, obviously exhausted, with a new-found respect for their black counterparts. They had learned the ability of the RAR soldiers to conduct extended patrols over long distances in the Rhodesian bush, and had trouble keeping up. They came away with an intimate knowledge of this and learned to respect their black colleagues' capabilities.[198]

---

[194] Binda, Masodja, 284-94; Moorcraft, 41-3; Binda, Saints, 185.

[195] Wood, Counterstrike, 43-4; Desfountain, paragraph 7.

[196] CE20110910H0001, former RAR officer, interview.

[197] CE20110910W0001, former RR NCO, interview by author, Durban, Republic of South Africa, 10 September 2011.

[198] Ibid.

EXTERNAL OPERATIONS

With ZANLA and ZIPRA establishing camps and assembly areas just across the borders in Zambia and Mozambique, Rhodesia was faced with a military problem common to many counterinsurgency operations. In order to effectively attack the insurgents before they came into the country and dispersed into smaller groups, Rhodesian forces needed to conduct offensive operations within other sovereign nations, namely Zambia and Mozambique. Given the extreme political pressure on the Rhodesian Front government, this was a tough problem to solve. As they had done in the past, the neighboring governments would condemn any such attacks on "refugee camps", and demand further international retribution, which Rhodesia could ill afford (particularly from its only remaining friendly neighbor, South Africa).[199]

In the face of evidence, however, Rhodesia could hardly sit and wait for large groups of insurgents gathering across the borders to enter the country and overwhelm security forces there. In one case, Selous Scouts conducted a reconnaissance between 27 May and 4 June 1976, identifying a large ZANLA-FPLM camp on the Mudzi River, about 30 kilometers inside Mozambique. True to Mao's teaching that "you cannot win at the conference table what you have not won on the battlefield", Mugabe was preparing a massive attack by ZANLA into Rhodesia to coincide with the Geneva Conference, planned for October 1976. According to reports, approximately 2,000 insurgents were operating inside Rhodesia by the end of October, with another 8,000 ready to enter from Mozambique. As one officer described the situation, if Rhodesia allowed the buildup to continue unabated in Mozambique, they would find their current problems to be "the thin end of a very thick and ugly wedge to come".[200]

In response to the intelligence gathered, and to weaken Mugabe's position going into the Geneva Conference, RSF planned Operation Mardon, a set of preemptive attacks to destroy the Mudzi Camp and others, disrupting the logistical support and infiltration routes in to northeastern Rhodesia. Shutting down these bases and routes would also force ZANLA to infiltrate further south along the Mozambique border, where terrain favored Rhodesian detection and fireforce operations. In August 1976, the Selous Scouts had conducted a major attack near this area, killing over 1,000 insurgents in a major ZANLA base at Nyadzonya.[201]

Operation Mardon called for SAS, RLI, Grey's Scouts (horse-mounted infantry) and two companies of RAR (D Coy 1RAR and A Coy 2RAR) to simultaneously attack targeted camps on 31 October to maximize surprise and prevent the insurgents' escape. Of all forces involved, D Coy 1RAR had the most success against its target, the Mudzi Camp. After conducting a night march in through extremely difficult terrain under heavy combat loads, D Company arrived at their target, which they believed to be a few dozen ZANLA fighters transiting between other camps. What they found was actually training camp teeming with over 800 ZANLA recruits under the protection of FRELIMO and Tanzanian troops. Unexpected delays in the approach march caused the attack to shift a day later than planned. Without air support (the limited sorties available were supporting strikes on other targets), Lieutenant David Padbury and the 2IC, Captain Glenn Reed (an ex-American Special Forces soldier) planned a hasty attack on the 800 insurgents inside the camp, setting stop groups in ambush on the backside (east side) and a sweep group assaulting across the camp from west to east.

With D Company moving into stop positions on the eastern side of the camp, Padbury set up a command post on the high ground to the west. Capt. Reed began moving the sweep group and mortars into position along a ridge south of Padbury's position, but before the sweep group was in place, a group of

---

[199] Cilliers, 172-5.

[200] Reid-Daly, Top Secret War, 338; J. R. T. Wood, "Counter-punching on the Mudzi: D Company, 1st Rhodesian African Rifles, on operation 'Mardon', 1 November 1976", Small Wars and Insurgencies 9, no. 2 (Autumn 1998): 64.

[201] Reid-Daly, Top Secret War, 321-406. In August 1976, Operation Eland, a flying column of Selous Scouts, with 14 vehicles and 84 troops, armed with vehicle mounted 20mm cannons (taken from scrapped Vampire fighters), twin MAG machine guns, 12.7mm anti-aircraft guns, twin .30 caliber Browning machine guns, and 81mm mortars drove 30 km into Mozambique to a ZANLA training base on the Nyadzonya River known to contain over 5,000 insurgents. The Scouts arrived on the camp wearing FRELIMO uniforms just after ZANLA's morning parade - as planned - and opened fire, killing between 1,000 and 1,300 insurgents before driving back across the border to Rhodesia. Captured documents and insurgents from the raid clearly indicated the purpose and intent of this camp as a training facility for ZANLA, but ZANU and FRELIMO, as was to be the standard, insisted that Rhodesians were murdering civilians in refugee camps.

Tanzanian soldiers walked into Padbury's position, triggering a premature firefight. The sweep group and mortars quickly moved into position and began to assault across the camp, under effective mortar fire. The stop groups, nearly in their ambush positions, opened fire on the fleeing insurgents. In the ensuing battle, one RAR soldier was burned by a phosphorus grenade and Capt. Reed called for a casevac using fireforce helicopters stationed nearby. The helicopters also provided additional fire support from their guns, as well as observation platforms to spot hidden insurgents. In the end, over 30 insurgents were killed at Mudzi camp, smaller numbers were killed elsewhere during the operation, and Rhodesian forces withdrew, having effectively disrupted the logistical base and infiltration routes in the area.

The RAR only participated in few external operations - notably, Op Mardon and Op Murex later in the war. The great strength of black soldiers in the RAR was in their superior bushcraft and ability to observe and interact with the local population. ComOps tended to employ the RAR inside Rhodesia rather than on larger raids into Zambia and Mozambique that became defining roles of the RLI and SAS. RAR soldiers, while quite capable of these types of strikes, tended to be less aggressive and more thorough in executing their missions. Their abilities to observe and communicate with the population inside Rhodesia was crucial to internal operations.

PARACHUTE TRAINING

By late 1976, increased fireforce actions were starting to reveal the limitations of the small fleet of Rhodesian helicopters. Army Headquarters decided that the only other way to rapidly get troops into a fireforce action was by airborne insertion, and so in late 1977 the RLI and RAR began parachute training. The addition of paratroops to fireforce allowed commanders to get many more troops on the ground in the first wave, resulting in more successful fireforce contacts. The first unit of the RAR to become airborne qualified was B Company 1RAR in October 1977, with the rest of the regiment following closely behind. Initially, there were concerns that black Rhodesian soldiers would not jump out of airplanes, or that their superstitious nature would cause them to panic on the aircraft, but the RAR proved all critics wrong, and were enthusiastic about being airborne. "A" Company 2RAR, under Maj. Dennison's leadership, was one of the most capable and respected fireforce elements in the Rhodesian Army.[202]

RAR soldiers proved themselves capable of every task they were ever asked to do. They participated in fireforce, limited external operations, extended patrols in the bush, and airborne operations. They earned respect for their loyalty, spirit and discipline. But they truly found their strength patrolling the bush, working with the local population, and manning Observation Posts (OPs) for extended periods. They were much more patient and attuned to local customs than their RLI counterparts. In one example, an RAR soldier on an OP with an officer observed three women walking down a path towards a village, one of whom was carrying a suitcase. The white officer thought nothing of it, but the black soldier said, "Ishe, the one with the suitcase is a terrorist". "How could you possibly know?" asked the officer. "She is carrying the suitcase in her hand. Our women carry things on their heads". A patrol caught up to the "women", who were in fact insurgents dressed as women walking into a village. This was the strength of the RAR as a counterinsurgent force. They knew the tribes and customs, and could instantly spot what was out of place.[203] On another occasion:

> A group of male civilians, walking along, was spotted from a distance. The [RAR] OP pointed out one of them as an insurgent, even though at first glance nothing distinguished him from the rest of the men. He was picked up, however, and found to be carrying an AK concealed beneath his coat. When quizzed, the RAR soldiers said that they knew he was an insurgent as he swung only one arm when walking (the other held the weapon against his body).[204]

---

[202] CE20110910H0001, former RAR officer, interview; Peter J. Hosking, foreword to The War Diaries of André Dennison, by J. R. T. Wood (Gibraltar: Ashanti, 1989), viii- ix.
[203] CE20110913M0001, former RAR officer, interview. The RAR soldiers' strengths on OP missions are also documented in Binda, Masodja, 310-11.
[204] Binda, Masodja, 311.

RAR paras waiting for a fireforce call-up
Source: CE20110908G0001, former RAR officer (photo provided by RAR officer).

The ability of RAR soldiers to notice and blend into the culture around them, obviously, came from the fact that they grew up in the same culture they were observing. This fact, however, was not always to their advantage, especially when their identity as RAR soldiers was revealed to insurgents operating near their family homes.

WAR ON THE HOME FRONT

One of the unfortunate circumstances RAR soldiers (and black soldiers in other units of the Rhodesian army) faced was that their extended families were in the same *kraals*, indeed were the same families, from which the insurgents recruited and relied for support. It was not uncommon, therefore, for an RAR soldier to return to his *kraal* on leave to find insurgents infiltrating his village and intimidating his family. A few soldiers were killed when their identity was known to insurgents. In at least one such incident, however, an RAR private home on leave was able to coordinate, and then participate in, a fireforce on a group of ten insurgents who had arrived in his *kraal* requesting food.

Private Wilfred, of A Company 1RAR, reported the "terrs" to a local farmer, providing descriptions of the men in his village that assisted the K-Car in identifying them. Then, he "was given a rifle, webbing and combat jacket and became a member of Stop 1." The subsequent contact killed nine of the ten, and a follow up ambush was set for the tenth insurgent but he was not seen again.[205]

POLITICAL PRESSURE

As the pace of the insurgency increased during 1976, so too did the political pressure on both the Rhodesian government and nationalist sides to compromise and end the conflict. The frontline states were economically affected by the ongoing war, and the OAU was increasingly frustrated by the inconclusive efforts of the nationalist organizations. For their part, Britain wanted to end to an embarrassing problem while maintaining the relevance of the British Commonwealth in Africa. South Africa was looking for a

---

[205] Ibid. 295.

way to gain more time and recognition for their own international pariah of apartheid government. At this point, US Secretary of State Henry Kissinger, the master of "shuttle diplomacy", stepped in to attempt to mediate and bring both sides to an agreement.[206]

Entering Africa on the heels of two embarrassing recent US failures in Vietnam and Angola,[207] Kissinger was eager to:

> co-opt the program of moderate evolutionary reform, that is to say majority rule, and minority rights. At the same time we sought to create a kind of firebreak between those whose radicalism was ideological and those whose radicalism was geared to specific issues. We could meet the demands for majority rule; we never thought we could co-opt the ideological radicals; our goal was to isolate them.[208]

Kissinger had a deadline of his own - by September 1976, it was becoming increasingly apparent that Jimmy Carter would win the upcoming U.S. presidential elections. This would hurt the process, as any deal brokered by a "lame duck" American administration would expire under the new administration. This allowed the PF to bide their time and see if a better result would come of waiting for the new U.S. president.[209]

In September 1976, Kissinger and Vorster invited Ian Smith to Pretoria. In a frank discussion, the two impressed upon Smith that his efforts were doomed to failure if he stayed his course and continued to fight a transition to majority rule. They presented a plan, drafted by the British and agreed upon by the frontline states and black Rhodesian nationalists. This plan proposed an interim government, half-white and half-black, to preside over a two year transition to majority rule. Smith's options, as presented by Kissinger and Vorster, were to accept these terms and attend a conference with the nationalist leaders to decide how to implement the plan, or reject the offer and immediately lose all financial and military support from South Africa. Faced with such options, Smith returned to Salisbury and conferred with his cabinet and the caucus, and the Rhodesian government ultimately accepted the terms proposed by Vorster and Kissinger. A conference was set for October 1976 in Geneva to settle the details and set a course for transition to majority rule. Joshua Nkomo, Robert Mugabe and Ndabaningi Sithole all attended the conference. After two months of abortive attempts to reach an agreement, the conference ended with no results. The fighting continued.[210]

Perhaps the greater impact of the Kissinger talks and the Geneva Conference was the revelation of a rift between the South African and Rhodesian governments. This was a new development, and its impact on white Rhodesia, when combined with the prospects of more war, increased national service, and tougher economic times ahead, was devastating. At the end of 1976, the numbers of whites leaving Rhodesia was

---

[206] Smith, 198-9. Shuttle diplomacy is the use of a third party to resolve a diplomatic crisis, in this case the introduction of the United States as an intermediary between Britain and Rhodesia. Kissinger used this technique most famously in the 1973 negotiation of the cessation of hostilities after the Yom Kippur War between Israel and the Arab states led by Egypt and Syria. Kissinger's technique was to isolate each party, extract demands and possible concessions, and shuttle between the two until a compromise was accepted by both parties. The Rhodesian situation was complicated by the fact that although Britain was not a belligerent party, they were legally required to endorse any compromise government in order for Rhodesia to gain international recognition and for sanctions to be lifted. As such, Kissinger treated the black nationalist groups (ZANU, ZAPU and ANC), and the leaders of the frontline states, as a third leg of the agreement.

[207] In April 1975, the People's Army of Vietnam forces entered Saigon, destroying the US backed government of the Republic of Vietnam and creating a unified communist state. This came after the US withdrew all troops and support for Vietnam, and was widely viewed as a strategic failure of the United States in stopping the spread of communism. Also in 1975, the US was further embarrassed by its involvement in backing the FPLA in Angola against Cuban and Russian communist-backed MPLA. The MPLA soundly defeated the FPLA, and the US was smeared with a second consecutive foreign policy debacle. For more on the US in Vietnam, see John Nagl, Dale Andrade, or Richard Hunt's works. For more on Angola, see Fred Bridgland or John Cann's works.

[208] Stephen S. Rosenfeld, "Henry Kissinger on the U. S. and Rhodesia", Washington Post, 3 July 1979.

[209] Smith, 189.

[210] Ibid., 202-222.

greater the number of whites entering the country.[211] The "white flight" had begun, due in large part to the perception that Rhodesia was friendless and hopeless. This dramatic change in attitude among white Rhodesians would also affect the war in the coming years. Ian Smith observed that the doubts among the white Rhodesian community "were not about the British, Americans, Europeans or the communist-inspired Commonwealth, whom we had known all along we could not trust. Instead, they were about the South Africans, whom we had believed would stand together with us".[212]

CONCLUSION

This period of the war saw tremendous changes in the Rhodesian Army and the RAR. From its relatively confident position in 1974, the Rhodesian Army was stressed to its limit when the pace of the war increased through 1976. The 1975 détente was a complete failure, which ultimately ceded momentum and the initiative over to the insurgents, severely damaging morale across the Rhodesian Army.

Faced with larger groups of insurgents training in safe havens in Zambia and Mozambique, Rhodesia chose a strategy of external strikes against large targets, integrating parachute training across its principal infantry units: the RAR and RLI. Intent on limiting insurgent capacity to infiltrate Rhodesian tribal areas, these external raids increasingly committed a large percentage of the army away from the country, leaving the population even more vulnerable in the tribal areas.

Despite the creation of 2RAR and increased national service commitments, RSF did not have nearly enough troops to secure the population where it was most vulnerable, in the *kraals* and tribal areas and along the borders with Zambia and Mozambique.

---

[211] Wood, War Diaries, 60. "[D]uring the first half of 1976 Rhodesia had endured a net loss of 2,271 whites, compared with a net gain of 1,590 whites in the first half of 1975".
[212] Smith, 223.

CHAPTER 6 - PHASE FOUR: 1977-1979

During phase four, from 1977-79, the Rhodesian government began to genuinely move towards majority rule, with negotiations beginning in late 1977 and ending with the March 1978 Internal Settlement. Bishop Abel Muzorewa, Ian Smith, Ndabaningi Sithole and Chief Jeremiah Chirau formed an interim government with an eye toward a popular election and a path to increased black participation in the political process. ZANU and ZAPU formed the Patriotic Front coalition and refused to participate in this process, but remained aligned against each other and in separate camps in Mozambique and Zambia as they stepped up attacks in Rhodesia. Rhodesian military actions focused on external strikes at the core of ZANLA's and ZIPRA's support structures in Mozambique and Zambia, while political militias and "turned insurgents" formed into Security Force Auxiliaries to provide security in tribal areas.[213]

There were also some significant changes to the RAR during this period. The first black officers were commissioned in June 1977, and with the advent of majority rule following the Internal Settlement, national service was extended to the blacks, bringing in the first black conscripts into the Rhodesia Regiment and the RAR.

INTERNAL SETTLEMENT

After the failed conference in Geneva, Ian Smith believed that continued reliance on Great Britain, South Africa and the United States to solve the Rhodesian problem was futile. The disparate and constantly fluctuating agenda of outside influences were not constructive in finding any meaningful solution, nor was it truly in their interests to do so.

> "We all came to the conclusion that our salvation lay in working together with our internal black leaders - in spite of their shortcomings they seemed more reliable than our so-called 'friends' of the free world."[214]

So in late 1977, Smith met with moderate black leaders to work on a settlement. Smith's objective was to determine and agree upon a way to implement the Anglo-American Agreement presented by Kissinger in 1976. Participating black leaders were "Muzorewa, Gabellah (from Matabeleland), Chikerema, Ndabaningi Sithole, and the two chiefs, Chirau and Kayisa Ndiweni".[215]

As Ian Smith explained in his New Year's Message to Rhodesia on 31 December 1977:

> The British have been trying to settle the Rhodesian problem in a manner which would best settle their own interests, rather than the interests of Rhodesia.
> Rhodesians have thus come to the conclusion that their best bet is to bring Rhodesians together around the settlement table, to the exclusion of outside interference. The talks are proceeding well and I believe all delegations will agree that we have made significant progress. The basic position remains the same. In exchange for acceptance of the principle of majority rule, we are negotiating the inclusion in the constitution of those safeguards necessary to retain the confidence of our white people, so that they will be encouraged to go on living and working in Rhodesia and thus continue to make their contribution to the economic progress of the country.[216]

The settlement discussions continued from January through March, making slow progress towards a final agreement. Both Joshua Nkomo and Robert Mugabe were absent from these discussions, having

---

[213] Wood, Counterstrike, 44-6.
[214] Smith, 237-8.
[215] Ibid., 242
[216] Ibid. 241-2.

elected instead to meet as the newly formed "Patriotic Front" (PF) [217] with the new British Foreign Secretary (David Owen) and the new American Ambassador to the UN (Andrew Young) in Malta.

The Malta Conference resulted in the Patriotic Front accepting a UN role in supervising elections, and called for a ten man Governing Council made up of two representatives from each of the delegations in Geneva (Mugabe, Sithole, Nkomo, Muzorewa, and Smith) and a Resident Commissioner, presumably British. Additionally, and particularly objectionable to Smith, was a requirement that the Chief Justice, Police Commissioner and Secretary to the Cabinet vacate their posts, presumably the first of many required to do so. Not only did Smith reject the outcomes of Malta and a follow up conference (called "Malta Two") held in Dar es Salaam, but David Owen and US Secretary of State Cyrus Vance - the hosts of Malta Two - agreed that the PF's insistence on dominating any settlement was "unacceptable".[218]

The results of the Rhodesian government's meetings from January to March 1978, however, ended in a signed agreement among all participants (Smith, Muzorewa, Sithole, and Chirau) on 4 March 1978. The resulting interim government, run by an Executive Council of the four signatories, was tasked to "organize a cease-fire, to remove racial discrimination, to draft a new constitution and to hold elections later in the year before a handover to 'black' government at the end of December".[219] Smith negotiated an assurance that the white minority retained a voice by securing 28 seats of 100 in parliament and requiring a three-quarters majority to enact any constitutional change.

Nkomo and Mugabe completely rejected the Internal Settlement because the military and police remained under white control, and they objected to whites retaining a blocking minority in the parliament.[220]

The interim government, as designed in the Internal Settlement, went into effect and proceeded to undertake the immense tasks before it. The most immediate - and perhaps most difficult - challenge facing the interim government under Muzorewa's government was the actual achievement of a cease fire. The Patriotic Front, staunchly opposed to any progress that did not grant its ringleaders immediate and uncompromised personal power, set out to prevent any semblance of progress by Muzorewa and Smith's government. The three black signatories to the Internal Settlement were dubbed the "blacksmiths", and ZANLA declared 1978 "the Year of the People", to be filled with preparations for Gore re Gukurahundi, or the "Year of the People's Storm", in 1979. By mid-1978, ZANLA had infiltrated 13,000 guerrillas into Rhodesia, spread across the country and training local forces to support the insurgency.[221]

For its part, ZIPRA also escalated the war, attempting to discredit the Interim Transitional Government. On 3 September 1978, ZIPRA insurgents shot down an Air Rhodesia civilian aircraft with a SAM-7 missile as it was taking off from Lake Kariba with 52 passengers aboard. Horrific stories later emerged of ZIPRA guerrillas murdering the survivors of this attack, and public revulsion of Nkomo and ZIPRA was palpable. A second attack on another Air Rhodesia aircraft in February 1979, killing 59 civilians, further cemented hatred for ZIPRA among Rhodesians whites and the RAR.[222]

---

[217] Formed in October 1976, the Patriotic Front (PF) was the latest attempt by the two nationalist parties – ZANU and ZAPU - to work together. The formation of the PF was a direct response to Nhongo and Mangena's formation of the ZIPA in January 1976, as well as an attempt to negotiate with the newly elected Democratic administration of the United States, and Labour Party government of Great Britain. Previous attempts at unifying ZANU and ZAPU, some mentioned in earlier chapters, were the Joint Military Command (JMC) formed in February 1972, the Front for the Liberation of Zimbabwe (FROLIZI), formed in October 1974, the unification of ZANU, ZAPU and FROLIZI under Muzorewa's ANC in December 1974, and finally the uniting of elements of ZANLA and ZIPRA to form ZIPA in January 1976. Every attempt was brought about due to outside pressure, and each ended in failure. In fact, by the end of the war, ZIPRA and ZANLA were fighting each other in Rhodesia when they weren't fighting the RSF. For an excellent discussion on Zimbabwean attempts at unity, see Daniel R. Kempton, Soviet Strategy Toward Southern Africa (New York: Praeger, 1989), 118-125.

[218] Smith, 252.

[219] Martin, 293.

[220] Ibid.

[221] Ibid. 292.

[222] Binda, Masodja, 327, 364; CE20110913M0001, former RAR officer, interview.

"THE SPEAR OF THE PEOPLE": SECURITY FORCE AUXILIARIES

In bringing about a ceasefire between the government and the vast network of insurgents in the country, the Executive Council believed that Muzorewa's ANC (now called United African National Council, or UANC) and Sithole's faction of ZANU[223] could bring their followers over to the government side. With majority rule achieved, the government assumed that the insurgents would have no more reason to fight. Both Muzorewa and Sithole claimed to be in control of the majority of ZANLA forces, and each duly called for their "armies" to switch sides and become auxiliaries to RSF. Called the "Spear of the People" - *Pfumo re Vanhu* in Chishona, or *Umkonto wa Bantu* in Sindebele - the Security Force Auxiliaries (SFAs) were hastily established to feed, clothe, train, and pay turned insurgents who accepted the offer to fight for the Interim Transitional Government.[224]

The real problem was the loyalty of the SFAs to their respective political factions rather than to Rhodesia itself. Whereas the RAR - indeed, all of the RSF - were staunchly apolitical[225], the SFAs were defined as political forces. In this respect, they were similar to ZANU and ZAPU. Training these men was a difficult process, as they did not believe they had anything to learn from the RSF. Once employed, they worked in tribal areas, and Security Forces were not allowed into those areas. In effect, the SFAs were allowed to operate like ZANLA or ZIPRA and feed off the population (most of them, as mentioned, were new to this idea), as long as they did so in the name of the Interim Transitional Government, rather than ZANU or ZAPU.[226]

In practice, the SFA program was a failure. Neither Muzorewa nor Sithole had a solid connection to the actual ZANLA forces in Rhodesia. The vast majority of Muzorewa's and Sithole's followers who turned out for SFA training had never been insurgents - most were rounded up by UANC and ZANU(Sithole) from the villages in order to add to the numbers of each faction's "army". Training for the SFAs was initially the job of the Selous Scouts. As Reid-Daly notes, "[n]either my officers nor I viewed the new order of things with any marked enthusiasm, because none of us could see it working, but orders were orders, so the Selous Scouts swung into disciplined action". The selection of Selous Scouts to train former insurgents to fight for the interim government was an interesting choice. If any actual ZANLA insurgents ever discovered their trainers were the hated *sku'zapo*[227], this would surely introduce unnecessary tension into the situation. But, as most of the new trainees had never actually been insurgents, and the Scouts were very careful not to reveal their identity, it never became a problem.[228]

Needless to say, the real ZANLA took some exception to the SFAs. In at least one instance, a recently trained group of Muzorewa's SFAs were moving into the Wedza TTL to establish themselves, only to be captured by a ZANLA group operating there. The ZANLA group stumbled upon a few newly trained SFA soldiers who had separated from the group, and quickly ordered two of them to return to the main SFA group and arrange a meeting. The inexperienced auxiliaries agreed, and were promptly taken prisoner by ZANLA. Most of these auxiliaries were summarily executed. Forty-one corpses were discovered by a

---

[223] Sithole never really relinquished leadership of ZANU after he was deposed by Robert Mugabe. The resulting split in ZANU meant that a small faction remained loyal to Sithole and operated inside Rhodesia while the vast majority of the movement was controlled by Mugabe from Mozambique. The smaller group is commonly referred to as ZANU (Sithole). Reid-Daly, Top Secret War, 564.

[224] Reid-Daly, Top Secret War, 563-5.

[225] CE20110913M0001, former RAR officer, interview.

[226] Reid-Daly, Top Secret War, 567.

[227] Reid-Daly, Top Secret War, 146. *Sku'zapo* was the nickname used by the insurgents to describe the Selous Scouts. According to Reid-Daly, "'*Skuz*,' is a corruption of the English, excuse me, while *apo* is the Shona word for here in the immediate sense. Thus, in direct translation *Skuz'apo* might mean: Excuse me here . . . or: excuse me for what I have just done". In context, it refers to the way two pickpockets approach their victim, one bumping the target and muttering "*skuz'apo*" while the other takes advantage of the distraction to lift his wallet. The Selous Scouts took great pride in their nickname, and their distinct unpopularity among the enemy.

[228] Ibid. 565-6; CB20111110S0001, former Selous Scout officer, interview. No clear reason is evident for the selection of the Selous Scouts as the training force for the SFAs. Reid-Daly suggests that by this point his force had become a "go-to" force for nearly any unsolvable problem - indeed, that may be true. Or perhaps, as one former Scout officer proposed, their status as former insurgents may have helped in understanding the minds of their new trainees. And as hated as the Scouts were, they certainly commanded the respect of the insurgents. The SFA training mission would pass to the RAR in 1979.

Police Reserve Air Wing pilot overflying the area. The few who escaped reported back to police what had happened. The Scouts quickly made contact with the ZANLA group and within a week killed 29 of them, either directly or by calling in fireforce.[229]

The RAR took over training the SFAs in August 1979. As with the Scouts, the RAR were not enthusiastic about the mission, but they carried out their orders. In recalling the SFA training program, one former RAR officer stated that he (a Lieutenant at the time) and his CSM were called aside, given a task to develop and execute a six- week training program for the *pfumo re vanhu*. Unsure exactly what the program was or why they were involved, the Lieutenant and NCO duly executed a very basic training program, consisting of marksmanship and fundamental military skills before passing out their trainees less than two months later.[230]

RAR ACTIONS

Much of the RAR's activity during this phase was fireforce action and night patrols. A typical fireforce call-up, involving A Company 2RAR, occurred on 9 October 1978, when a Selous Scouts OP in Operation Area Repulse reported 50 insurgents between the Lundi River and a smaller tributary.[231]

A Lynx aircraft initiated contact, marking the target for a strike by Hunter fighter- bombers of the RhAF. Following this bomb run, the K-Car carrying the company commander, Maj André Dennison, arrived overhead. Two "stop groups" were inserted by helicopter (G-Cars) along likely avenues of escape, while four sticks of paratroopers jumped in to form a sweep line and flush out the insurgents. In the ensuing firefight, the troops on the ground, guided by Dennison and the K-Car pilot, conducted multiple sweeps, displaying aggressive and thorough pursuit of the enemy. In the end, up to 38 insurgents and trainees were killed, one insurgent was captured, and six escaped. Because only 16 weapons were found, however, SB only credited the fireforce with 16 kills.

Dennison disputed this claim - according to him, the target was a training camp, so not all the trainees were armed but most had webbing and several had hand grenades. While directing the action from the K-Car, Maj Dennison was shot through his knee but remained overhead for another hour and fifteen minutes until the K-Car had to refuel. Dennison and the sweep group commander, WO2 Dick Mandava, were later recommended for the Bronze Cross of Rhodesia for their actions that day.[232]

At dusk on 11 August 1978, an eight-man patrol from Support Company 1RAR, led by Lieutenant Pat Lawless, were operating in the Devil's Gorge area of Zambia[233] in conjunction with a simultaneous SAS operation. Lawless' patrol made contact with three insurgents, killing two and fatally wounding the other. As the wounded man was dying, Lawless interrogated him and learned of a nearby insurgent company of about 100 men.

Lawless laid an ambush for the night - he had two MAGs. He also set up a claymore mine along the track but nothing happened. However, at first light, as they began to dismantle the claymore, preparatory to moving on, they saw some 70 insurgents approaching along the track. Every soldier immediately squirmed back into his position and waited for Lawless to spring the ambush. As soon as the enemy was in the killing ground, the order was given. Eight insurgents were killed and 15 wounded in this initial attack.

A further 20 men, initially unseen, tried to outflank the patrol by sneaking down the hillock behind their position. However, Corporal Ernest Rashamira noted the move and, leaping up, charged them, firing bursts from his MAG, killing three.[234] After continuing the attack for several hours against such

---

[229] Reid-Daly, Top Secret War, 570-1.

[230] CG20110927S0001, former RAR officer, interview.

[231] Binda, Masodja, 344-5; Wood, War Diaries, 273-5.

[232] Binda, Masodja, 344-5; Wood, War Diaries, 273-5.

[233] The RAR did conduct external operations, like the one described here, into Zambia and Mozambique. These patrols routinely submitted false Location Station (LOCSTAT) reports to prevent enemy knowledge of their operations.

[234] Binda, Masodja, 349.

overwhelming odds, the small patrol, low on ammunition, withdrew. Lawless was later awarded the Silver Cross of Rhodesia for this and other actions.[235]

In many instances similar to the two described above, the RAR continued to demonstrate their ability to engage and destroy their enemy. The lessons learned from early operations like Nickel and Cauldron were well-learned and the regiment was emerging as a superb counterinsurgent force. Recruiting continued, and young black Rhodesians volunteered in droves to join the RAR as operations continued across the country (and beyond).

CHANGES TO THE RAR

As early as the breakup of the federation, the Rhodesian Army had begun to consider commissioning black officers for service in the regiment. In the early 1970s, one former RAR officer recalls evaluating a number of black candidates for selection to the Cadet Course at the School of Infantry in Gwelo. The Officer Selection Board was sufficiently impressed with the black candidate's attributes - after a five day selection course he was among the top five of twenty candidates. In the end, however, the Brigadier in charge of the board decided it was still too early to send one black cadet through the course by himself. As the RAR officer recalls, "it would be very unfair on the black chap to put him through the difficulties of integrating at the point in time when integration wasn't on the cards."[236]

In June 1977, however, the Rhodesian Army commissioned its first black officers. Two former RSMs - Martin Tumbare (RSM, 1RAR) and Wurayayi Mutero (RSM, 2RAR) - were commissioned, and more black officers followed. According to the Regimental History, "on 25 August, [Tumbare] was presented with the late 'Kim' Rule's sword by Mrs. Rule. It had been Kim Rule's wish that his sword be presented to the first African to be commissioned in the Rhodesia Army. Fittingly, it was a member of the battalion he had commanded who received the honour."

Mrs. Rule, the widow of Lt Col. Kim Rule OBE, presents her late husband's sword to the first African to be commissioned, Lt N. M. Tumbare.

---

[235] Ibid.

[236] CE20110909R0001, former RAR officer, interview. The candidate in question commissioned into the Corps of Signals in 1978. He rose to the rank of Captain before the end of the war, and was believed to have retired from the Zimbabwe Army years later as a Lieutenant Colonel.

CHAPTER 7 - PHASE FIVE: APRIL 1979-APRIL 1981

On 30 January 1979, the (white) Rhodesian electorate went to the polls in a referendum on the majority-rule constitution. An overwhelming 85% voted 'yes' to black rule - probably one of the few times in history a people have willingly and deliberately voted themselves out of power. However, the British government declared the result irrelevant.
Alexandre Binda, Masodja: the History of the Rhodesian African Rifles
and its Forerunner, the Rhodesia Native Regiment

During the final phase of the war, Rhodesia voted itself into majority rule under its first black Prime Minister. Under the new government, and now called Zimbabwe-Rhodesia, the nation expected recognition from the British as well as an end to sanctions, having met all six conditions for recognition as laid out by the British government in 1965-6. However, ZANU and ZAPU refused to accept the arrangement, and instead intensified their military actions. The British declared the 1979 elections irrelevant, and the UN continued sanctions. In September 1979, the British hosted a conference in London, at Lancaster House, between the government of Zimbabwe-Rhodesia and the PF, along with representatives of the frontline states. In the subsequent election, Robert Mugabe and ZANU(PF) were voted into power. Zimbabwe was granted independence on 18 April 1980.[237]

The Army during this phase fought desperately to suppress ZANLA insurgents flooding the country, while striking at external targets in Zambia and Mozambique. The Third Battalion of RAR formed in October 1979, consolidating several of the racially integrated Independent Companies of the Rhodesian African Rifles (previously Rhodesia Regiment Independent Companies) under one headquarters. Once Mugabe took control of the country, the former RSF organizations began to break apart, and many of the white soldiers and officers chose to resign and leave the country.

The RAR, however, remained intact and began to integrate with its erstwhile enemies, ZANLA and ZIPRA. In consolidated holding camps, ZANLA and ZIPRA consolidated alongside each other and frequently clashed, most notably at a camp outside Bulawayo called Entumbane. Here, the RAR stood between ZIPRA and ZANLA to prevent the wholesale slaughter of one by the other and protect the civilian population from the two warring factions.[238]

APRIL 1979 ELECTIONS

1979 began with tremendous steps towards immediate majority rule in Rhodesia. The first step was a referendum among the white population to accept the majority rule constitution as drafted by the Interim Transition Government of Muzorewa, Smith, Sithole and Chirau. Placing their faith in the "black moderates", the white population of Rhodesia overwhelmingly voted in favor of black rule in their country. Subsequently, from 17-20 April, nearly 2 million black voters - about 64 percent of the country's eligible voters - went to the polls, and on the principal of "one man, one vote", elected Bishop Muzorewa's UANC into power, under the "Government of National Unity" between the various parties. This was a historic undertaking, and one which Rhodesians hoped would end the war. Several teams of international observers, including a British team led by Lord Boyd, reported that the elections were free and fair, by the strictest Western standards.[239]

---

[237] Binda, Masodja, 364, 383.

[238] Binda, Masodja, 389.

[239] Wood, War Diaries, 327-9. The vote was conducted at fixed and mobile polling stations across all eight electoral regions. Observed by a British Conservative Party team under Lord Boyd and several other international observers, 1,853,333 voters (63.9 percent of 2,900,000 eligible voters) went to the polls. Of these, 1,212,639 voted for Muzorewa's UANC (67.27 percent), 262,928 (14.58 percent) for Sithole's ZANU-PF, 194,446 (10.79 percent) for the United National Federal Party led by Chief Kayisa Ndiweni. Allocated by percentage of the vote, assembly seats awarded to each party were: 51 to UANC, 12 to ZANU-Sithole, and 9 seats to UNFP. The remaining 28 seats were reserved for the Rhodesian Front under Ian Smith to ensure that the sixth principal for recognition - that is, protection of the minority from the majority - was met.

From April to August 1979, Rhodesians waited for the Carter administration in the United States and the newly elected Conservative government of Margaret Thatcher in Britain to recognize Zimbabwe-Rhodesia. As the US and Britain delayed recognition of the new government, ZANLA and ZIPRA increased their operations, further taxing an already extremely stressed RSF.[240] From late 1978 to May 1979, officially recorded monthly incidents had nearly tripled, from under 600 to 1,706 as insurgent groups, primarily ZANLA, exacted revenge for local support given to the UANC. "By September 1979, the UANC popular base had vanished".[241]

Finally, instead of recognizing the new Zimbabwe-Rhodesia Government of National Unity, "on Monday, 6 August, at the Commonwealth conference in Lusaka, Margaret Thatcher reneged on her promise of recognition under pressure from Nigeria and Australia and set another course with a new commitment to an all-party conference in London".[242] This conference brought Nkomo and Mugabe back to the table with the Zimbabwe-Rhodesia government. In advising Muzorewa on attending the conference, Smith says:

> [W]hile I had previously resisted any thought of an all-party conference, believing that if we persisted we would gain recognition of our honest and straightforward effort, I was reconciling myself to a change of thought, and my close colleagues in the Rhodesian Front agreed. There were two main reasons I have mentioned.
>
> First, the terrorists were gaining support among the indigenous population, not through convincing argument and appeal, but by using the dreadful weapon of intimidation.
>
> Second, the Western leaders would not face up to making a decision which conflicted with the views of the OAU - 90 per cent of whose membership comprised countries governed by communist leaders.[243]

In September 1979, the British Foreign Secretary, Lord Peter Carrington, hosted a constitutional conference at Lancaster House in London, at which all parties, including Mugabe and Nkomo, were to resolve the problem of majority rule in Rhodesia.

LANCASTER HOUSE CONFERENCE

From 10 September to 23 December 1979, delegations led by Ian Smith, Robert Mugabe, Joshua Nkomo, and Abel Muzorewa attended the Lancaster House conference, along with delegations from the frontline states. The purpose of the conference was to develop an acceptable framework for the government and set a date for internationally supervised elections. Carrington's approach to settling the problem differed from previous attempts. Rather than negotiate primarily with the PF, his proposals "first were directed at Mozambique and Zambia as the countries serving as hosts to the insurgents. Both countries were economically desperate for an end to a war that was threatening to engulf them".[244] In fact, without pressure from Samora Machel of Mozambique, Mugabe would have left the conference and forfeited his stake in the British negotiations entirely.[245]

---

[240] Smith, 305-11.

[241] Cilliers, 55.

[242] Smith, 311; Wood, War Diaries, 355-8. Specifically, Nigeria nationalized British Petroleum holdings in its country and threatened further economic actions, including withdrawing from the Commonwealth, if Thatcher's government recognized Muzorewa's government and normalized relations with Zimbabwe-Rhodesia, as Thatcher stated she would do mere months before. Australian Prime Minister Malcolm Fraser supported Nigeria's action, as did Kenneth Kaunda of Zambia and Julius Nyerere of Tanzania. Their actions convinced Thatcher that recognition of Zimbabwe-Rhodesia would result in the downfall of the Commonwealth and severe economic (oil) pressure on Great Britain.

[243] Smith, 313.

[244] Cilliers, 55.

[245] Smith, 321. Mugabe believed that he had not gained sufficient concessions to ensure his victory in the election, and so he decided to register his protest by making a dramatic withdrawal from the conference. He had packed his bags and was making arrangements to fly out to the United States. Machel informed Mugabe that if he broke away from the conference, he would not be permitted to continue using Mozambique as a base for his operations. Mugabe, chastened, returned to the conference.

The results of the Lancaster House Conference were agreements to an immediate ceasefire, a Commonwealth Monitoring Force under General John Acland to supervise movement of belligerents into 16 assembly points, and an election to be held as soon as possible.

RAR ACTIONS

Fireforce actions continued, at an increasing pace for the RAR. In Operation Area Hurricane during November 1979, Support Company 1RAR planned an attack on a "liberated area" in a Tribal Trust Land, from which insurgents were routinely shooting at a Police Reserve Air Wing (PRAW) light aircraft. According to the plan, the PRAW pilot was to fly his normal route, with a 1RAR fireforce following about 15 miles behind. If the plane drew fire, the pilot was to drop a smoke marker on his way out of the area, and the fireforce would arrive directly behind to deal with the insurgents. The fireforce consisted of two K-Cars, four G-Cars (each with a four-man stop group), with a reserve of paratroops standing by at the airfield. There was also a land tail carrying more troops, ammunition and heavy weapons, driving a specific route to assist in any contact.[246]

On the morning of 14 November, the PRAW aircraft duly took off on his route, and the fireforce and land tail were shortly behind, following a preset pattern of rendezvous points while the helicopters flew just above the ground to avoid detection. At one such rendezvous point, the Company Sergeant Major (leading the land tail) reported spotting a group of 30 insurgents running into the hills 3 kilometers away. The fireforce immediately turned and deployed to engage the insurgents, with the K-Cars firing their 20mm cannon at the fleeing men. Shortly a Lynx dropped a frantan[247] canister near the top of a prominent *dwala*,[248] the stop groups on G-Cars landed at the top. After receiving reinforcements flown in from the land tail, two stop groups formed a sweep line and moved out to establish contact with the insurgents, now estimated at a strength of 40-50 men and hiding in a riverbed. The fireforce commander decided to use helicopters to cover the far exits of the riverbed as the sweep groups advanced.[249]

After advancing about thirty meters into their sweep, the RAR soldiers came under heavy fire, and remained in contact with this group of insurgents for the rest of the day and into the night, receiving reinforcements from the land tail through the afternoon. At one point, the commander of the first wave of troops, Lt. Lawless:

> I pulled my stop groups back from the cave, and called in an air strike from a Canberra armed with 200 Alpha bombs (small football shaped bombs which bounced, armed, then detonated at about waist-height), which had been scrambled from Salisbury and was orbiting the contact area. The first box of 50 bombs fell well short, the second landed beyond the target - and the third landed on my sweep line! Miraculously, nobody was hurt, and the Canberra pilot, obviously embarrassed by his performance so far, made no mistake with the fourth box, which landed short and bounced into the cave, shredding the luckless terrs inside.[250]

The RAR troops maintained contact through the night, engaging insurgents attempting to escape. In the morning, Lt. Lawless says:

> "I reported to my commanding officer that we had killed 26 terrs for the loss of one officer killed [Captain Jim Hardy, shot in the head during the initial sweep] and one wounded, and handed over command to him. By 1000, we were back at Mtoko [the

---

[246] Binda, Masodja, 371.

[247] Frangible tank munitions, or "frantan" were Rhodesian made napalm canisters.

[248] A *dwala* is a large rock formation, in chiShona.

[249] Binda, Masodja, 371-2.

[250] Binda, Masodja, 372.

fireforce base] . . . and by 1130 we were once again airborne en route to another terrorist sighting."[251]

OPERATION MUREX

Shortly after this fireforce action, in November 1979, Support Company 1RAR was selected for an external operation into Zambia. Selous Scouts had discovered and frustrated ZIPRA plans for a conventional invasion of Rhodesia. During operations in Zambia, Lieutenant Edward Piringondo of Selous Scouts discovered, mapped, and conducted reconnaissance on a ZIPRA brigade in a fortified base in the Kabanga Mission area (about 80 miles northeast of Livingstone). Support Company 1RAR and a troop of Selous Scouts were to attack the base and, if possible, capture the radios and message pads to decipher coded messages from a ZIPRA team operating in Rhodesia. The attack was coordinated to start at 1230 on the designated day, because at that time, ZIPRA soldiers were typically all cleaning their weapons.[252]

After detailed planning and rehearsals and a one-day weather delay, the operation was a "go", and it went "like clockwork". Seven Hunters, three Canberras and four K- Cars conducted preliminary air strikes, while two G-Cars, four Cheetahs,[253] and the Paradak all delivered troops to their objectives on time, receiving almost no ground-fire (because all of ZIPRA's weapons were disassembled for cleaning) in the process.

> After a short sharp contact with a few determined members of ZIPRA, we found and captured the radios and codes, which were immediately airlifted out by a Cheetah. A number of well-sited bunkers were located under trees among anthills, but the paras re-assembled ZIPRA's AA weapons (heavy Soviet 12.7 and 14.5mm machine guns) and blasted them. We found large food and ammunition supplies, which took several hours to clear. We killed 35 members of ZIPRA and captured five for the loss of one Selous Scout killed. One trooper and a pilot were injured by ground-fire while over-flying another large and hitherto unsuspected ZIPRA position as we withdrew.[254]

A few weeks later, the Rhodesian Army forces would withdraw back within its own borders as Lord Soames, the interim British governor, arrived to facilitate the peace settlement negotiated at Lancaster House.

The RAR in 1979 was busily engaged as a highly effective counterinsurgent force. Again, by this stage they were deployed constantly against ever-increasing numbers of ZANLA and ZIPRA, but they never wavered in their commitment, nor was recruiting a challenge. The soldiers remained absolutely loyal to the regiment, and the regiment remained true to the country.

3RAR

In September 1979, Army Headquarters announced that several of the independent companies of the Rhodesian African Rifles, now including conscripted black national servicemen, would form the Third Battalion RAR. Based in Umtali in eastern Rhodesia, 5 and 6 Independent Companies, along with 3 Independent Company in nearby Inyanga had rebadged into the RAR in December 1977. These companies had served with some distinction alongside the RAR and RLI in recent years, and they were well respected by both regiments. Senior NCOs from 1RAR and 2RAR came to the new battalion, and Depot RAR in Balla Balla ran several courses "to inculcate the values and traditions required of RAR soldiers into the Umtali and Inyanga troops".[255]

---

[251] Ibid.
[252] Binda, Masodja, 372-3.
[253] Bell UH-1 helicopters snuck into Rhodesia late in the war to replace the aging fleet of Alouettes were called "Cheetahs".
[254] Binda, Masodja, 374.
[255] Binda, Masodja, 365-6.

Lieutenant Colonel Terry Leaver was the first commander of the battalion, and by October 1979, 3RAR commenced operations. By this time, the Lancaster House Conference was ongoing, and the battalion's first missions were to prevent ZANLA infiltration across the Mozambique border during the conference. The battalion continued to operate on the eastern border throughout the transition of government. On 1 January 1981, 3RAR was designated 3:3 Infantry Battalion of the Zimbabwe Army under the command of Lieutenant Colonel Ron Marillier.

MUGABE ELECTED

By 6 January 1980, Lt. Gen. Acland's Commonwealth Monitoring Force - about 1,300 strong - had assembled 15,730 insurgents in assembly points. Within days, the number grew to 22,000, of which 16,500 were ZANLA and the remainder ZIPRA. RSF were restricted to their bases until elections were complete. Importantly, thousands of insurgents did not report to the Assembly Points; among these were the political commissars, key leaders, and "hard-core insurgents". Most of the population of the Assembly Point camps were mujiba, (local informants) and low-level recruits. Left among the population, these "hard-cores" would continue to intimidate and coerce the people to vote their way - for Mugabe.[256]

On 4 March 1980, the election results revealed that Mugabe had won 63 percent of the vote. On 18 April, he became the Prime Minister of an independent Zimbabwe, as Prince Charles and Lord Soames handed over the country and departed. 1RAR provided the guard of honor for the farewell ceremony.[257]

THE RAR IN THE ZIMBABWE ARMY

The three battalions of RAR continued to serve in the Zimbabwe Army, along with many of its officers. The three battalions of the regiment were designated 1:1, 4:2, and 3:3 Infantry Battalions of the Zimbabwe Army. While the rest of the army struggled to integrate factions of ZIPRA, ZANLA, and Rhodesian forces, the RAR remained as it was, and provided a model professional force for its sister units in the Zimbabwe Army.[258]

Other elements of the Rhodesian Army, however, did not survive the transition to Zimbabwe. The RLI disbanded on 17 October 1980. The SAS disbanded 31 December 1980. The Selous Scouts were integrated back into their parent regiments, and those who had only ever been Scouts consolidated into 4 (Holding Unit) RAR. "On 1 October 1980, 4 (HU) RAR ended its short life and became the 1st Zimbabwe Parachute Battalion". Many of the officers and men of the RLI, SAS, and even a few from the RAR went to South Africa and served in the South African Defense Force (SADF). In fact, a Pathfinder Company of SADF's 44 Paras, called "The Philistines", was made up entirely of ex-Rhodesians.[259]

For some time, the RAR remained untouched, retaining its distinctive badge, uniform, and shoulder patch (minus a "Rhodesia" insignia). In correspondence, the Battalion Commander, Lt Col. Mick McKenna, continued to refer to his unit as 1:1 Infantry Battalion (1RAR). The commanders and many officers continued to serve with the same men they had trained and fought beside throughout the war. There was some hope that this would remain so, and that the new Zimbabwe could form a professional force and transition into the peaceful, integrated society that had been the objective for so long.[260]

ENTUMBANE: "THE BATTLE FOR BULAWAYO"

The first Zimbabwe government was an uneasy union, under Prime Minister Robert Mugabe, of three factions - Mugabe's ZANU, Nkomo's ZAPU, and Smith's Rhodesian Front (in a much smaller capacity than before). The armies of these three factions were billeted together at various assembly points across the country as they waited for integration into the new national army. Old rivalries between ZANLA and ZIPRA dominated the camps, leading to several tense situations. The political and military situation was

---

[256] Wood, Counterstrike, 48.
[257] Binda, Masodja, 383; Martin, 330.
[258] CF20110920S0001, former RAR officer, interview.
[259] Binda, Masodja, 383; CE20110913M0001, former RAR officer, interview.
[260] CE20110913M0001, former RAR officer, interview.

not helped by constant ZANU(PF) propaganda distributed throughout the country, over television and radio broadcasts. The situation deteriorated rapidly when the newly appointed ZANU(PF) Minister of Finance, Mr. Enos Nkala, made a pair of speeches in November 1980 emphasizing the creation of a one-party state under the leadership of ZANU(PF).[261]

In response to Nkala's rhetoric and ZANU(PF) propaganda, ZIPRA forces near the township of Entumbane just outside Bulawayo began to move truckloads of reinforcements into their camp. The ZANLA soldiers quartered there noticed the increase, and someone started shooting. Police riot squads were unable to contain the ensuing four hour firefight, which spread into the town. Small arms fire, rocket grenades, mortars and machine guns inspired civilian supporters in the town to join the fray, adding to the chaos.[262]

Zimbabwe Army command therefore ordered 1RAR (now designated 1:1 Infantry Battalion, Zimbabwe Army) to stop the fighting.

D Company was first on the scene and deployed along the railway line at Mpopoma, thus cutting off the city centre to the now-mutinous warring factions. Support Company was positioned on D Company's right flank. The Zimbabwe Army 1:2 Battalion was also in support but proved to be more of a hindrance than a help. During the afternoon, A, B, and C companies arrived and took up positions to the right of D Company and Support Company.[263]

At nightfall, the fighting subsided, but ZIPRA had called to their nearby Gwaai River Mine assembly point for heavy weapons and vehicles to support their fight. In the morning, the reinforced ZIPRA forces attacked ZANLA's position, and the RAR swung into action. As the RAR initiated their assault on ZIPRA and ZANLA under the cover of Hawker Hunter aircraft, the mutineers reconsidered their options and called for a ceasefire. Brigadier Mike Shute, commander of 1 Brigade, Zimbabwe Army (and former commander of 1RAR), arranged for the mutineers to surrender their heavy weapons.

1RAR established an outpost at a beer hall overlooking the two camps, reinforced with mortars and a troop of armored cars to keep the peace. The battalion rotated a company at a time through observation duties at the beer hall in Entumbane.[264]

For the next few months, ZIPRA continued building strength in Matabeleland, apparently preparing for a coup. ZIPRA was concerned that they had no political future in Zimbabwe under Mugabe and ZANU(PF), and they had begun moving their vast stockpiles of Soviet equipment from Zambia into Zimbabwe. Equipped with T-34 tanks, armored cars, anti-aircraft guns, BTR 152 Armored Personnel Carriers, and about 6,000 soldiers, ZIPRA's forces were substantial. On 10 January, Mugabe fired Nkomo as Minister of Home Affairs. The RAR began planning for the imminent clash between ZIPRA and ZANLA.[265]

On 8 February, ZANLA soldiers attacked their ZIPRA colleagues in one of the assembly points, killing over 60 ZIPRA soldiers. When news of this incident reached the newly formed 13 Infantry Battalion - which was in training with a team of British instructors at another assembly point - the ZIPRA members of that battalion attacked their ZANLA colleagues, killing 12. Once again, D Company 1RAR drove into the camp to settle the issue. In the ensuing action, the RAR killed 40 ZIPRA soldiers, and much of the rest of the battalion was detained. "Arriving at work the following day, the British instructors were astonished to find the ZIPRA half of their trainees (minus the deceased and the escapees), clad only in underpants and squatting in neat silent rows under the watchful eyes of their RAR captors".[266]

The fighting continued over the next several days, during which a severely outnumbered 1RAR, reinforced with a troop of four armored cars[267] and supported by one Lynx aircraft, destroyed the better part of a motorized rifle battalion (equipped with Soviet BTR 152s). Of this action, the Lynx pilot explains:

---

[261] Binda, Masodja, 383-4; Moorcraft, 182.

[262] Binda, Masodja, 384.

[263] Ibid.

[264] Binda, Masodja, 384.

[265] Ibid., 385.

[266] Ibid., 385-6.

[267] The armored car used by the Rhodesian Army was the Eland 90 Mk9, a South African variant of the French-made AML Panhard. The Eland was a wheeled (4x4) vehicle armed primarily with a 90mm gun and a 60mm breech-loading mortar.

On the morning of the action [12 February 1981] I was dispatched as a first reaction singleton aircraft from the Thornhill base in Gwelo to Bulawayo to assist the RAR …My aircraft was armed with the standard two machine guns and SNEB rockets, which, because we were expecting to be marking for the Hunters were only smoke, not HE …[Once over the RAR's position] it was immediately apparent that he [Major Lionel Dyck] and his men were under considerable pressure and might be overrun. Lionel asked for a strike(s) on the position giving him the most problems …I then put in a strike firing the SNEB as a distraction and strafing with machine guns. After pulling out from this I seem to remember that Lionel was most appreciative but did mention that all the fire directed at him was now concentrated on me; something along the lines of all hell let loose. He then asked me for another strike and it was during this attack that I took damage. I was in the dive when I took a number of rounds through the cockpit which took out the front engine, destroyed the right side of the instrument panel, passed an inch or so in front of my nose and then out of the left side of the aircraft …I continued and strafed again but for lack of a front engine had to tell Lionel that I was off to Brady [airfield] but would be back as soon as I could. When I arrived I was greeted by a Wing Commander, who was a bit put out and it seemed to me at the time it was because I did not have the correct weapon load.[268]

According to the accounts in Masodja, when the commander of C Company 1RAR (Maj Lionel Dyck) called for air support, the request was denied. The pilot, however, heard the request, disobeyed orders and flew anyway, repeatedly striking targets in support of the RAR. His aircraft was repeatedly shot during his numerous gun and rocket runs. In Masodja, Maj. Dyck and Second Lieutenant John Hopkins (another officer involved the action) claim the pilot received or was recommended for a Silver Cross of Rhodesia. He did not receive any commendation, however, other than generous praise in subsequent correspondence between Dyck (1RAR), Brigadier Mike Shute (Commander, 1 Brigade), and Air Force Headquarters.[269]

On the evening of 12 February 1981, elements of the RAR battle group went to find the rest of ZIPRA's forces:

The armoured cars were sent down to Essexvale battle camp to deal with ZIPRA's armoured battle group but soon found that the enemy was prepared to surrender their ten T34s and remaining BTR 152 APCs, GSP bridging equipment, artillery and amphibious vehicles. On inspection, it was found that the T34s were fortunately unserviceable. These captured vehicles were subsequently removed to the battalion's concentration area on Brady Barracks Airfield where the RAR removed souvenirs and useful items.[270]

The official casualty figures listed 260 dissidents killed, but the RAR disagrees - the regiment accounted for over 400 dead on its own, without losing a man. After the Entumbane fight, massive ZIPRA factions deserted fearing retribution. Mugabe would never trust his Ndebele colleagues. He would eventually unleash a North Korean trained 5th Brigade of the Zimbabwe Army into Matabeleland in 1983 to massacre tens of thousands of Ndebele, accusing them of plotting against ZANU(PF).

The RAR's actions at Entumbane displayed - better than any other example - the loyalty and professional values of the regiment. By this point, everything had changed in Zimbabwe. The RAR's enemy had become its commander-in-chief. Its mission had gone from destroying two insurgent armies to integrating them. Outside of its own chain of command, the army around the RAR was a hollow shell of its former self. Lt. Gen. Walls stayed on briefly but had just resigned as the commander of the Zimbabwe Army, and nationalist faction leaders were filling the ranks of Army Headquarters. Fortunately, the headquarters of 1 Brigade, commanded by Brigadier (later Major General) Mike Shute remained largely intact, but the other units of the brigade and the army were beginning to degrade as a professional force - as 1:2 and 1:3 Infantry Battalions demonstrated during the actions in January and February 1981.

---

[268] CF20111116J0001, email correspondence with the author, 16 November 2011.
[269] Ibid.
[270] Binda, Masodja, 388-9. From a statement by 2nd Lt. John Hopkins, A Company 1RAR.

2RAR and 3RAR similarly remained intact, serving as model organizations within their respective brigades during similar ZANLA-ZIPRA confrontations in quieter areas of the country. Neither battalion had a large fight like 1RAR at Entumbane, however.[271]

So why would the RAR deliberately stop ZIPRA and ZANLA from killing each other? Why would white officers support the ZANU(PF) government, and why would black soldiers follow their white officers against black mutineers? As one officer involved in the fight said,

> My loyalties lay to my Brigade Commander (Mike Shute), my regiment, and to the country and its defenceless population. Insofar as the regiment was concerned, I believe their loyalty lay to their officers and, more importantly, to each other. ... There were no instances of a reluctance to obey orders or desertion as we fought without fear or favour against both ZIPRA and ZANLA and anyone else who got in our way as we carried out our duties.[272]

The actions of the RAR at Entumbane saved Mugabe's government from certain civil war against an enemy (ZIPRA) that was heavily armed, trained and supported by Soviet backers. Indeed, many outside Rhodesia believed that either Nkomo's ZIPRA or Walls' former RSF forces would execute a coup d'état against Mugabe, but no coup ever materialized. The end result of Entumbane was a final blow to the military might of ZIPRA, and most of its Soviet equipment was captured and redistributed among the rest of the Zimbabwe Army.[273]

RAR soldiers at Brady Barracks, February 1981
Source: Alexandre Binda, Masodja: The History of the Rhodesian African Rifles and its forerunner, the Rhodesia Native Regiment (Johannesburg: 30 Degrees South, 2007).

---

[271] CF20110920V0001, former RAR officer, interview.
[272] CE20110913M0001, former RAR officer, interview.
[273] Ibid.; CE20110920S001, former RAR officer, interview by author.

CONCLUSION

In the final phase of the Bush War, the RAR demonstrated its proficiency as a fighting force. The true nature of the loyalty and dedication of its soldiers to their regiment - never doubted during its history - was displayed one last time at Entumbane, where loyalty to anything else but the regiment would have faltered. The RAR by this point was an exemplary fighting force in its own right. The soldiers and leaders demonstrated tremendous learning and growth from Operation Nickel, where a company of RAR struggled against lightly armed, poorly trained insurgents in 1967, to Entumbane, where a battalion of RAR stood its ground against a motorized brigade, destroying a motorized battalion without losing a man.

In less than one year's time, the national government transitioned twice to majority rule - once to Bishop Muzorewa in April 1979, then to Robert Mugabe in March 1980. For the first time in its history, Rhodesia (as Zimbabwe-Rhodesia) pressed blacks into national service, leading to the formation of 3RAR and ending a long tradition of purely voluntary black service in the Rhodesian Army. Despite the tremendous pressure and volatile state of the country through its transition from Rhodesia to Zimbabwe, the RAR kept its tradition and culture alive and remained as a crucial element of stability in the new national army.

CHAPTER 8 - CONCLUSIONS

> Since the birth of the Regiment I have known it. Since its formation I have done what I could to teach these men of the Rhodesian African Rifles. I have seen the glorious results of that teaching of mine and of the officers of the Regiment.
>
> And today we all smile together. For have we not fought and risked our lives side by side to keep our land safe from the horrible things we have seen here? And the war being over, we feel that we may think of our fighting comrades and - having seen what war can cause to people and to lands - may humbly say Ishe Komborera Africa [God save Africa].
>
> RSM Stephen Machado, 1RAR, written after returning from Burma in 1945

This study of the RAR reveals several points about the Rhodesian Bush War that have been largely missed in previous accounts. Many of the existing histories of Rhodesia discount the important role of black soldiers in the Rhodesian Army - some flatly fail to acknowledge that, particularly towards the end of the war, most of the Rhodesian Security Forces were black. In the RAR, the Rhodesian government had a historical demonstration of blacks and whites working together - a true non-racial organization, and a model for cooperation across cultures. Many critiques of Rhodesia's transition to majority rule state that it was a case of "too little, too late". The tragic truth of this also applies to the RAR: throughout the war, there were not enough RAR battalions, and the realization that more black soldiers - and black officers - were needed occurred far too late in the war, despite early recommendations from the Rhodesian Army as early as 1963.

Throughout its history, and particularly during the Bush War, the soldiers of the RAR remained unquestioningly loyal and faithful to their regiment. The soldiers of the RAR were well trained, well-disciplined and feared by their enemy. They were respected by nearly every soldier who ever worked with them. They overcame precisely the same racial and tribal divisions that tore their country apart with an identity of their own - a regimental culture that demanded the best of its members, black and white.

WHY DID THE RAR FIGHT?

The RAR never suffered for recruits. By one officer's recollection, at the end of war, 1:1 Infantry Battalion (1RAR) was at full strength, with 1,505 soldiers, all the same soldiers who fought for Rhodesia.[274] The other battalions were similarly fully manned. The regiment never had to leave its base to conduct recruiting drives. They would simply announce what days they were open to recruits, and volunteers came to the depot in droves.

Young black men knew the regiment - their fathers served in it, as did their grandfathers. The pay and living arrangements, while far inferior to those of white soldiers, made the RAR a lucrative job for a black Rhodesian. The RAR uniform was something of which he could be justly proud. Once they arrived at the RAR for training, however, the traditions and mindset of the regiment began to manifest themselves in the actions of the young soldiers. Recruits were taught exactly what their predecessors had done, and what was expected of them, through traditions handed down from long-ago service with the British Army. This instruction built three basic values of the RAR soldier: loyalty, pride, and discipline. These values made the RAR a formidable force on the Rhodesian battlefield.

HOW DID THE RAR CHANGE THROUGH THE WAR?

At the beginning of the war, the RAR was still very linked to its past as a colonial British unit. That link never really faded. The badge, colors, uniform, and structure remained throughout the war. Even at Entumbane in 1981, the RAR still wore their Rhodesian patches and badge. However, over the course of the Bush War, some of the formalities of British African units fell away. Formal social gatherings were rare by the end of the Bush War, as officers spent more time training and deploying than socializing. Parades and drill instruction were not emphasized as heavily as marksmanship and patrolling.

---

[274] CE20110913M0001, former RAR officer, interview.

While the RAR conducted relatively few external raids, they showed that they were capable of doing so. Instead, the regiment tended to focus on internal operations - that is, operations within Rhodesia to locate and destroy insurgent networks in the *kraals* and tribal areas. The regiment could observe and engage the black population much more naturally and efficiently than their counterparts in the RLI.

Unfortunately, the Rhodesian Army could not act on its own advice in 1963 to form more battalions of RAR, or to equalize pay and commission black officers into the ranks. This would have been a welcome move for the army, but politics prevented it. 2RAR did not form until 1975, and 3RAR not until 1979. Had additional battalions formed earlier in the war - even as late as 1973 - the additional black troops might have accomplished the one critical task that Rhodesian strategy failed to address - they might have connected more of the black population with the government of Rhodesia.

The creation, late in the war, of Guard Force and Security Force Auxiliaries (*pfumo re vanhu*) indicate a belated attempt to secure the Protected Villages and tribal areas from insurgent infiltration. However, as the RAR well knew, properly trained forces took time to create. Earlier commitment of additional battalions of RAR to this task may have prevented the dismal failure of the PV program, and enabled the Rhodesian government to avoid the forced use of political militias such as the SFAs.

WHAT HAPPENED TO THE RAR?

When the regiment disbanded, most of the RAR soldiers stayed in Zimbabwe. They had nowhere else to go, and most lacked the means to move. Some white officers, committed to helping their new country, also stayed. Most of the white officers, seeing no hope for their future in Zimbabwe, either left for South Africa or Great Britain.

Some of the black soldiers, NCOs and officers who stayed in Zimbabwe continued to serve in the Zimbabwe Army - one former RAR soldier is reported to have become a Lieutenant Colonel, eventually commanding 1:1 Infantry Battalion (formerly 1RAR).[275] In 2007, four former RAR soldiers came to London for the release of the Regimental History, Masodja. When reunited with their former officers, these men were overcome with emotion, as were the officers. There was no hatred or anger between these men and the whites who left.[276]

In the end, the legacy of the RAR is the creation of a multicultural organization that stood the test of tremendous pressure as the nation it served changed, struggled, and ultimately collapsed. Despite the violent changes in the world around it, the regiment stood until it was forced to abandon its link to past traditions and merge into the ranks of the Zimbabwe Army.

WHAT DOES THIS MEAN?

As of the writing of this paper the U.S. military is involved in developing military organizations to build and maintain stability in Iraq and Afghanistan. The role of the U.S. military in developing and assisting African militaries is also increasing, after the 2008 establishment of U.S. Africa Command. These examples share the challenges that the RAR successfully overcame. The challenges of creating a national army out of Tajik, Pashtu, and Dari cultures, or Sunni and Shia tribes in Iraq, or any number of tribes in any African country, is not unlike the RAR's challenge of uniting its white, Ndebele, and Shona cultures into a cohesive and effective unit. The success of the RAR resided in its creation of an overriding concept - the regiment - to which every soldier bound himself above all other divisive elements of his background. Properly developed and maintained, military culture, based on loyalty to the regiment, can be a catalyst to unite disparate cultural groups of soldiers.

---

[275] CF20110920S0001, former RAR officer, interview.
[276] CF20110920H0001, former RAR officer, interview.

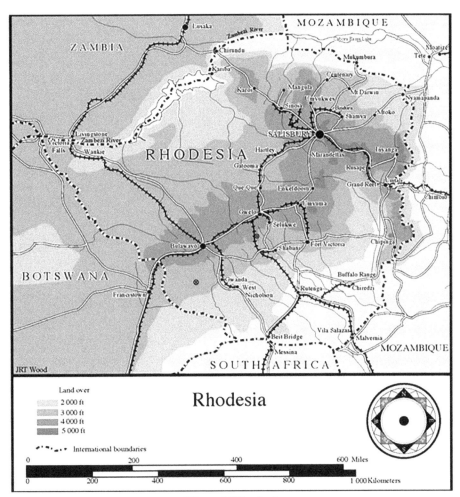

Map of Rhodesia
Source: Courtesy of Dr. J. R. T. Wood.

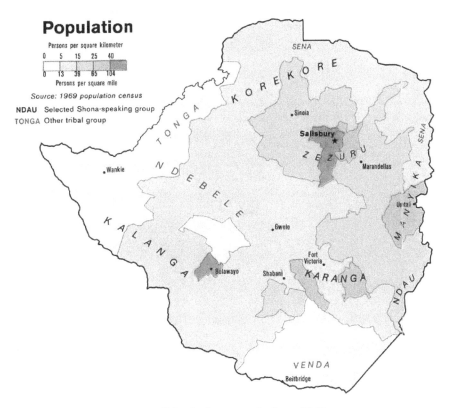

Rhodesian population, 1969
Source: 1969 Census data, as found at: http://mappery.com/South-
Rhodesia-Population- Map (accessed 10 October 2011).

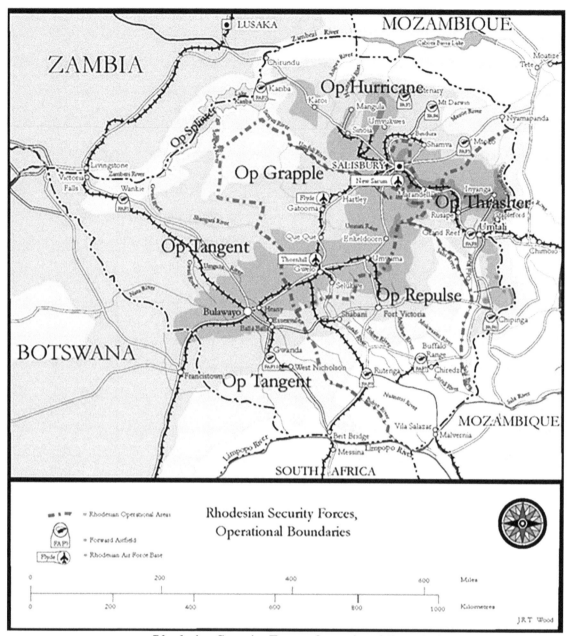

Rhodesian Security Forces Operational Boundaries
Source: Courtesy of Dr. J. R. T. Wood

BIBLIOGRAPHY

Primary Sources

Interviews

Command and General Staff College (CGSC) Scholars Program 2011. Scholars Program Art of War Research Study 2011. Research Study, Fort Leavenworth, KS: Ike Skelton Chair in the Art of War, 2011. This study included interviews of counterinsurgency practitioners and policy professionals from the United States, United Kingdom, and South Africa. Each interview was executed as an oral history interview and adhered to Army policies of informed consent in compliance with federal law. Finally, each interview was coordinated through the Ike Skelton Chair in the Art of War, CGSC Fort Leavenworth, KS.

Johannesburg, Republic of South Africa

CE20110908G0001. Former RAR officer. Interview by author, 8 September 2011.
CE20110908W0001. Former RAR and SAS officer. Interview by author, 8 September 2011.
CE20110908M0001. Former RAR officer. Interview by author, 8 September 2011.
CE20110909R0001. Former RAR officer. Interview by author, 9 September 2011.
CE20110910T0001. Former RAR officer. Interview by author, 9 September 2011.
CE20110910H0001. Former NRR and RAR officer. Interview by author, 10 September 2011.

Durban, Republic of South Africa

CE20110910W0001. Former RR NCO and officer. Interview by author, 10 September 2011.
CE20110912A0001. Former RLI officer. Interview by author, 12 September 2011.
CE20110912G0001. Former Royal Gurkha Rifles and RAR officer. Interview by author, 12 September 2011.
CE20110912G0001. Former BSAP, RRR and RAR officer. Interview by author, 12 September 2011.
CE20110913B0001. Former RAR officer. Interview by author, 13 September 2011.
CE20110913M0001. Former KAR, RAR and Grey's Scouts officer. Interview by author, 13 September 2011.

Cape Town, Republic of South Africa

CE20110913R0001. Former RAR and SAS officer. Interview by author, 13 September 2011.
CE20110914B0001. Former KAR, RLI, and RAR officer. Interview by author, 14 September 2011.
CE20110914H0001. Former RAR Warrant Officer. Interview by author, 14 September 2011.
CE20110915C0001. Former RAR, Royal Gurkha Rifles, and SAS officer. Interview by author, 15 September 2011.
CE20110915B0001. Former RAR and SAS officer. Interview by author, 15 September 2011.
CE20110916G0001. Former RAR officer. Interview by author, 16 September 2011.
CE20110916M0001. Former RAR and SAS officer. Interview by author, 16 September 2011.

Aylesford, England

CF20110919C0001. Former RAR officer. Interview by author, 19 September 2011.
CF20110919H0001. Former RRR, RAR, and Rhodesian Army Education Corps officer. Interview by author, 19 September 2011.
CF20110919W0001. Former RLI and RAR officer. Interview by author, 19 September 2011.

London, England

CF20110920H0001. Former RAR officer. Interview by author, 20 September 2011.
CF20110920S0001. Former KAR, RAR officer. Interview by author, 20 September 2011.
CF20110920V0001. Former RAR officer. Interview by author, 20 September 2011.

Reading, England

CF20110922L0001. Former British Army, RAR officer. Interview by author, 22 September 2011.
CF20110922L0002. Former RAR, British Army officer. Interview by author, 22 September 2011.
CF20110922M0001. Former RAR, SAS officer. Interview by author, 22 September 2011.

Portland, Oregon

CG20110927S0001. Former U.S. Special Forces, RAR officer. Interview by author, 27 September 2011.

Fort Leavenworth, Kansas

CB20111110S0001. Former Selous Scouts officer. Interview by author, 10 November 2011.

Personal Accounts

Croukamp, Dennis. The Bush War in Rhodesia: An Extraordinary Combat Memoir of a Rhodesian Reconnaissance Specialist. Boulder, CO: Paladin Press, 2007.
Cox, Chris. Fireforce: One Man's War in the Rhodesian Light Infantry. Johannesburg: 30 Degrees South, 2006.
Essex-Clark, John. Maverick Soldier: An Infantryman's Story. Carlton: Melbourne University Press, 1991.
Lemon, David. Never Quite a Soldier: A Rhodesian Policeman's War 1971-1982. Alberton: Galago, 2006.
Mills, Greg, and Grahame Wilson. "Who Dares Loses? Assessing Rhodesia's Counter- Insurgency Experience". RUSI 152, no. 6 (December 2007): 22-31.
Smith, Ian Douglas. The Great Betrayal: The Memoirs of Ian Douglas Smith. London: Blake, 1997.
Warren, Charlie. Stick Leader: RLI. South Africa: Just Done Productions, 2007.
Wood, J. R. T. The War Diaries of André Dennison. Gibraltar: Ashanti, 1989.

Documents

DesFountain, Trevor. Summary and Background of 1979 Rhodesian Strategy Revision Conference.
Essex-Clark, John. "The Incorrigible Trio - A Subaltern's View: A Controversial Essay in Bonding, Leadership, and Morale".
National Security Council. Study In Response to National Security Study Memorandum 39: Southern Africa. Washington, DC, 9 December 1969.
Redfern, John "Racial Discrimination in the Rhodesia and Nyasaland Army". Rhodesian Army memorandum, October 1962.
——— "The Requirement for a Non-Racial Army in Southern Rhodesia". Rhodesian Army memorandum, October 1963.

Doctrinal References

Department of the Army. FM 3-24, Counterinsurgency. Washington DC: Government Printing Office, 2006.
Rhodesian Army. COIN Manual, Part II - ATOPS [Anti-Terrorist Operations]. Salisbury, 1975.

Secondary Sources

Andrade, Dale. "Westmoreland was right: Learning the wrong lessons from the Vietnam War". Small Wars and Insurgencies 19, no. 2 (June 2008): 145-181.

Bergerud, Eric. The Dynamics of Defeat: The Vietnam War in Hau Nghia Province. Oxford: Westview Press, 1991.

Binda, Alexandre. Masodja: The History of the Rhodesian African Rifles and its forerunner, the Rhodesia Native Regiment. Johannesburg: 30 Degrees South, 2007.

Bridgland, Fred. "Angola and the West". In Challenge: Southern Africa within the African Revolutionary context, edited by Al J. Ventner, 117-145. Gibraltar: Ashanti, 1989.

Burton, Brian, and John Nagl. "Learning as we go: the US Army adapts to COIN in Iraq". Small Wars and Insurgencies 19, no. 3 (September 2008): 303-327.

Cann, John P. Counterinsurgency in Africa: The Portuguese Way of War, 1961-1974. Westport, CT: Greenwood Press, 1997.

Cilliers, J. K. Counter-insurgency in Rhodesia. London: Croom Helm, 1985.

Clayton, Anthony. Counterinsurgency in Kenya: A study of military operations against the Mau Mau, 1952-1960. Manhattan, KS: Sunflower University Press, 1976.

Coates, John Suppressing Insurgency. Boulder, CO: Westview Press, 1992.

Cocks, Chris; Bone, Craig; Binda Alexandre. The Saints: The Rhodesian Light Infantry. Johannesburg: 30 Degrees South, 2007.

Cole, Barbara. The Elite: The story of the Rhodesian Special Air Service. South Africa: 1985.

Comber, Leon. Malaya's Secret Police 1945-1960: The Role of the Special Branch in the Malayan Emergency. Melbourne: Monash University Press, 2009.

Corum, James. "Training Indigenous Forces in Counterinsurgency: A Tale of Two Insurgencies". March 2006. http://www.strategicstudiesinstitute.army.mil/ pubs/display.cfm?PubID=648 (accessed 20 June 2011).

Dobbins, James, Seth G. Jones, Keith Crane, Andrew Rathnell, Brett Steele, Richard Teltshik, and Anga Timilsina. The UN's Role in Nation-Building: From the Congo to Iraq. Santa Monica, CA: RAND, 2005.

Dornan Jr., James E., ed. Rhodesia Alone. Washington, DC: Council on American Affairs, 1977.

Downie, Nick, and Lord Richard Cecil. Frontline Rhodesia. DVD. Johannesburg: 30 Degrees South, 2007.

Farwell, Byron. Mr. Kipling's Army. New York: W. W. Norton, 1981.

Gann, Lewis H., and Thomas H. Henriksen. The Struggle for Zimbabwe: Battle in the Bush. New York: Praeger, 1981.

Galula, David. Counterinsurgency Warfare: Theory and Practice. London: Praeger Security International, 1964, 2006.

———. Pacification in Algeria 1956-1958. Santa Monica, CA: RAND, 2006. Gentile, Gian. "A strategy of tactics: population centric COIN and the Army". Parameters (Autumn 2009): 5-17.

Green, T. N. The Guerilla - Selections from the Marine Corps Gazette. New York: Praeger. Hack, Karl. "The Malayan Emergency as a Counter-Insurgency Paradigm". The Journal of Strategic Studies 32, no. 3 (June 2009): 383-414.

Hammes, Thomas X. The Sling and the Stone: On War in the 21st Century. St. Paul, MN: Zenith Press, 2006.

Henniker, M. C. A. Red Shadow Over Malaya. London: William Blackwood and Sons, 1955.

Hoffman, Bruce. Lessons for Contemporary Counterinsurgencies: The Rhodesian Experience. Santa Monica : RAND, 1992.

Hoffman, Frank. "Neo-Classical Counterinsurgency?" Parameters (Summer 2007): 71- 87.

Hoffman, Frank, Jennifer M. Taw, and David Arnold. Lessons for Contemporary Counterinsurgencies: The Rhodesian Experience. Santa Monica, CA: RAND, 1991.

Hopkinson, Michael. The Irish War of Independence. Montreal: McGill-Queen's University Press, 2002.

Horne, Alistair. "The French Army and the Algerian War 1954-62". In Regular Armies and Insurgency, edited by Ronald Haycock, 69-83. London: Croom Helm, 1979.

Hunt, Richard. Pacification: The American Struggle for Vietnam's Hearts and Minds. Boulder, CO: Westview Press, 1995.

Hyam, Ronald. Britain's Declining Empire: The Road to Decolonisation, 1918-1968. Cambridge: Cambridge University Press, 2006.

Jeudwine, Hugh. "A Record of the Rebellion in Ireland in 1920-1, and the Part Played by the Army in Dealing with it (Intelligence)". In British Intelligence in Ireland: The Final Reports, edited by Peter Hart, 17-60. Cork: Cork University Press, 2002.

Kempton, Daniel R. Soviet Strategy Toward Southern Africa: The National Liberation Movement Connection. New York: Praeger, 1989.

Kilcullen, David J. The Accidental Guerilla: Fighting Small Wars in the Midst of a Big One. Oxford: Oxford University Press, 2009.

———. Counterinsurgency. Oxford: Oxford University Press, 2010. Kitson, Frank. Bunch of Five. London: Faber and Faber, 1977.

Komer, Robert. Bureaucracy at War: U.S. Performance in the Vietnam Conflict. Boulder, CO: Westview Press, 1986.

———. The Malayan Emergency in Retrospect: Organization of a Successful Counterinsurgency Effort. Santa Monica, CA: RAND, 1972.

Krepinevich, Andrew. The Army and Vietnam. Baltimore, MD: Johns Hopkins University Press, 1986.

Kriger, Norma. Zimbabwe's Guerilla War: Peasant Voices. Cambridge: Cambridge University Press, 1992.

Lockhart, J. G., and The Hon. C. M. Woodhouse. Cecil Rhodes: The Colossus of Southern Africa. New York: Macmillan, 1963.

Lunt, James. Imperial Sunset: Frontier Soldiering in the 20th Century. London: Macdonald Futura, 1981.l

MacKinlay, John "Rethinking Counterinsurgency". RAND Counterinsurgency Study, Volume 5, 2008.

———. The Insurgent Archipelago. London: C Hurst and Co Publishers Ltd., 2009. Malkasian, Carter, and Daniel Marston, eds. Counterinsurgency in Modern Warfare. Oxford: Osprey Publishing, 2010.

Martin, David, and Phyllis Johnson. The Struggle for Zimbabwe: The Chimurenga War.
London: Faber and Faber, 1981.

McCuen, John. The Art of Counter-Revolutionary War. Harrisburg, PA: Stockpole Books, 1966.

Miers, Richard. Shoot to Kill. London: Faber and Faber, 1959.

Minford, John Sun Tzu The Art of War: The Essential Translation of the Classic Book of Life. New York: Penguin Press, 2002.

Moorcraft, Paul L., and Peter McLaughlin. The Rhodesian War: A Military History. Johannesburg: Jonathan Ball, 1982.

Nagl, John. Counterinsurgency Lessons from Malaya and Vietnam: Learning to Eat Soup with a Knife. Westport, CT: Praeger, 2002.

Nyangoni, Wellington W. African Nationalism in Zimbabwe (Rhodesia). Washington, DC: University Press of America, 1977.

O'Meara, Patrick. Rhodesia: Racial Conflict or Coexistence? Ithaca: Cornell University Press, 1975.

Owen, Christopher. The Rhodesian African Rifles. Edited by Lt.-General Sir Brian Horrocks. London: Leo Cooper, 1970.

Paret, Peter. French Revolutionary Warfare from Indochina to Algeria: The Analysis of a Political and Military Doctrine. London: Pall Mall Press, 1964.

Phillips, Rufus. Why Vietnam Matters: An Eyewitness Account of lessons not learned. Annapolis, MD: Naval Institute Press, 2008. Porch, Douglas. "Bugeaud, Gallieni, Lyautey: The Development of French Colonial Warfare". In Makers of Modern Strategy, edited by Peter Paret, 376-407. Princeton, NJ: Princeton University Press, 1986.

———. "French Imperial Warfare 1945-62". In Counterinsurgency in Modern Warfare, edited by Daniel Marston and Carter Malkasian, 87-101. Oxford: Osprey Publishing, 2010.

Race, Jeffrey. War Comes to Long An. California: UC Press, 1972.

Ramsey, Robert. Savage Wars of Peace: Case Studies of Pacification in the Philippines, 1900-1902. Fort Leavenworth, KS: Combat Studies Institute, 2007.

Reed, Douglas. The Battle for Rhodesia. New York: Devin-Adair, 1967.

Reid-Daly, Ron. Selous Scouts: Top Secret War. Cape Town: Galago, 1983.

———. "War in Rhodesia - Cross-Border Operations." In Challenge: Southern Africa within the African Revolutionary context, edited by Al J. Ventner, 146-182. Gibraltar: Ashanti, 1989.

Scully, Pat. Exit Rhodesia. Ladysmith: Cottswold Press, 1984.

Shy, John and Thomas Collier. "Revolutionary War." In Makers of Modern Strategy, edited by Peter Paret, 815-862. Princeton, NJ: Princeton University Press, 1986.

Sibanda, Eliakim M. The Zimbabwe African People's Union 1961-87: A Political History of Insurgency in Southern Rhodesia. Trenton: Africa World Press, 2005.

Smith, Simon. "General Templer and Counter-insurgency in Malaya: Hearts and Minds, intelligence, and propaganda." Intelligence and National Security 16, no. 3: 60- 78.

Sobel, Lester A., ed. Rhodesia / Zimbabwe 1971-77. New York: Facts On File, 1978.

Stiff, Peter. Cry Zimbabwe: Independence - Twenty Years On. Alberton: Galago, 2000.

Stubbs, Richard. "From Search and Destroy to Hearts and Minds: The Evolution of British Strategy in Malaya 1948-1960". In Counterinsurgency in Modern Warfare, edited by Daniel Marston and Carter Malkasian, 101-118. Oxford: Osprey Publishing, 2010.

Sutherland, Riley. Army Operations in Malaya, 1947-1960. Santa Monica CA: RAND, 1964.

Thompson, Robert. Defeating Communist Insurgency. London: Chatto and Windhus, 1966.Thompson, W. Scott, and Donaldson Frizzell, eds. The Lessons of Vietnam. New York: Crane, Russak and Company, 1977.

Trinquier, Roger. Modern Warfare: A French View of Counterinsurgency. Fort Leavenworth, KS: CSI, 1985.

Tse-Tung, Mao. On Guerilla Warfare. New York: Dover Publications, 2005.

Ucko, David. The New Counterinsurgency Era: Transforming the US Military for Modern Wars. Washington, DC: Georgetown University Press, 2009.

Ventner, Al J. ed. Challenge: Southern Africa within the African Revolutionary context. Gibraltar: Ashanti, 1989.

———. The Chopper Boys: Helicopter Warfare in Africa. London: Greenhill, 1994.

Willbanks, James. Abandoning Vietnam. Lawrence, KS: University of Kansas Press, 2004.

Wood, J. R. T. "Countering the CHIMURENGA: The Rhodesian Counterinsurgency Campaign." In Counterinsurgency in Modern Warfare, edited by Daniel Marston and Carter Malkasian, 191-208. Oxford: Osprey Publishing, 2010.

———. Counterstrike From the Sky: The Rhodesian All-Arms Fireforce in the War in the Bush 1974-1980. South Africa: 30 Degrees South Publishers, 2009.

———. "Counter-punching on the Mudzi: D Company, 1st Rhodesian African Rifles, on operation 'Mardon' 1 November 1976." Small Wars and Insurgencies 9, no. 2 (Autumn 1998): 64-82.

ENTUMBANE I AND II TIMELINE
Nov 1980 and Feb 1981

Please refer to the map on the back endpapers.

Note: Troop movements during Entumbane I are shown with dashed lines. Troop movements during Entumbane II are shown with solid lines.

ENTUMBANE I

Sep/Oct 1980: A ZIPRA Motorized Infantry Brigade arrives from Zambia and is based at Assembly Point (AP) Mike/Gwaai River Mine and comprises 800-1000 men (5000 according to ZAPU leader Joshua Nkomo). Equipped with Land-Rovers, Zil and Gaz trucks, BTR 152 APCs.

16 Oct 1980: First clash in an urban area between ZIPRA and ZANLA (ex-combatants awaiting integration into the ZNA) in Chitungwiza near Salisbury. 3000 ZANLA exchange fire with 1200 ZIPRA. Mugabe accuses ZIPRA of firing on civilians.

29 Oct 1980: Four ZANU PF supporters are killed, 16 injured by a grenade and small arms attach in the west of Salisbury. The next day ZANLA and ZIPRA start shooting wildly in Chitungwiza, One man is killed.

5 civilians killed.
16 civilians injured.

Early Nov 1980: Three trains comprising 49 wagons cross the Vic Falls bridge, carrying 2000 tonnes of ZIPRA weaponry and two armoured vehicles. The cargo is consigned to Brady Barracks, Bulawayo, but two of the trains are diverted to Impofu Siding, south of Dete, and taken to AP Mike/Gwaai River Mine. The third is intercepted by elements of 1RAR and removed to Methuen Barracks.

8 Nov 1980: Minister of Finance Enos Nkala, addressing the first day of a two-day ZANU PF local election rally at White City Stadium in Bulawayo threatens the imposition of a one-party ZANU PF state in Zimbabwe.

9 Nov 1980: Addressing the second day at White City, Nkala's address is met by a jeering and stone-throwing crowd and spills out into a riot. 34 are injured and one man is killed. The violence spreads from the Stadium.

1 civilian killed
34 civilians injured

At 17h15 that afternoon, fighting erupts between 3000 ZANLA and ZIPRA ex-combatants in holding camps 1 and 4 at Entumbane, and soon spreads to the ZANLA Camp 2 and the ZIPRA camp 3. ZRP Support Unit and other police are deployed from bases at Ross Camp. the Drill Hall, the Plumtree Road Water Works and Bembezi. The violence continues, and supporters of ZANU PF and ZAPU roam the streets attacking perceived supporters of the other party. By 21h30 the ZRP and ZRP Support Unit companies have suppressed the fighting and rioting. Overnight, ZIPRA and ZANLA dig in and turn their camps into defensive positions. Civilians are evicted from the areas around the two Entumbane camps at gun-point by ZIPRA. Four civilian men not carrying ZAPU cards are murdered.

4 civilians killed.

ZIPRA, having come off worst during the day's fighting, radios the ZIPRA base at AP Mike/Gwaai River Mine and ask for support. A ZIPRA relief column drives into Bulawayo establishes road blocks around the western suburbs, and reinforces the ZIPRA camp at Entumbane. A security officer, Patrick LENNON, is fatally wounded at one of these road blocks.

1 civilian killed.

The 1RAR Battle Group moves to Brady Barracks from Methuen Barracks.

Three off-duty RAR men in civilian clothes – Pte George Chiwanza, L/Cpl Robson Kujinga and Pte Matthew Siziba - are murdered at a ZIPRA road block at Magwegwe Cemetery.

3 RAR Murdered: Pte CHIWANZA; L/Cpl KUJINGA; Pte SIZIBA

10 Nov 1980: A cordon is thrown around the north western suburbs.

D Coy, 1RAR deploys first, along the railway line north of the Luveve Bridge.

Elements of Sp Coy with 75mm RCLs and 81mm mortars deploys on the Falls Road.

A, B and C Coys drive further up the Falls Road to a point just south of the tented camp of ZNA 1:3 Bn at Glenville, then walk south to the railway line just west of Camps 1 and 4. Elements of Sp Coy with 60mm mortars and a Vickers HMG deploy near the railway line north of Camp 1. The plan is to deal with Camp 1 (ZANLA), then Camps 4 (ZIPRA), 2 (ZANLA) and 3 (ZIPRA) in turn.

The newly formed ZNA 1:2 Bn arrives from Ntabazinduna to reinforce the cordon.

ZIPRA attacks the ZANLA camp at dawn. Fighting continues all day between the two factions. An RAR position comes under fire but fire is not returned. A delegation of senior ZIPRA and ZANLA officers arrives in Entumbane to negotiate a ceasefire but is met with gunfire and two of their number are wounded. A "skyshout" aircraft is sent over the camps in the afternoon demanding a ceasefire, but it too is driven off by gunfire.

A and B Coys in the lead, with C Coy in reserve, advance in extended line towards the Camps. Air Force Hunters scream low over the camps as they advance. After ineffective fire at the advancing troops, both the ZIPRA and ZANLA camps call for a ceasefire.

Dumiso Dabengwa (ZIPRA), and Rex Nhongo (aka Solomon Mujuru, ZANLA) meet Brigadier Mike Shute (Commander, 1 Bde). Shute, Dabengwa and Nhongo enter Entumbane and persuade both factions to give up their heavy weapons. The ZIPRA relief column returns to AP Mike/Gwaai River Mine. The official death toll is 58 – 15 of which are ZIPRA and ZANLA – and over 500 wounded. Other reports claim 190 civilians have been killed. Apart from the three murdered RAR men, there are no Army casualties. Not one shot was fired by Army personnel.

15 ZIPRA/ZANLA KIA
Between 15 and 190 civilians killed
500+ civilians wounded

As the fighting in Entumbane subsides, three ZIPRA men are abducted in Chitungwiza. One is found dead, two missing. The bodies of three ZANLA men are found in the area. Problems begin at 2:2 Bn in Mtoko. Six ex-ZIPRA men are abducted. Three escape. One is killed and two are badly injured.

4 ZIPRA/3 ZANLA murdered. 2 ZIPRA missing
2 ZIPRA badly injured

27 Nov 1980: Three off-duty ex-ZIPRA from 3:1 Bn are abducted by ZANLA from AP Foxtrot at Dzapasi in Buhera. One escapes, one is missing believed dead, one is killed.

1 ZIPRA murdered. 1 ZIPRA missing believed murdered

29 Nov 1980: A group of ex- ZIPRA are attacked on a train in Umtali. At a rally in Gutu attended by Mugabe, an assassination attempt against him is staged. A ZANLA man fires, and two ZIPRA men are forced to run through the crowd as "culprits" One is wounded but escapes. The other is shot 17 times and a rifle is thrust into his dead hands. As a result, all ex-ZIPRA from 4:3 Bn, except for twelve, abscond.

1 ZIPRA murdered
1 ZIPRA wounded

Dec 1980: RAR Coys continue to fortify and occupy Entumbane beerhall in rotation. A platoon of Sp Coy 81mm mortars on Scorpion mortar carriers are also stationed there for tours of a week. Vehicles are positioned against the interior of the walls of the beerhall to allow troops to fire over the top. Two names are proposed for the base – Rorke's Drift, a victory for the South Wales Borderers (proposed by 2 Lt John Hopkins, of Welsh heritage) and The Alamo (proposed by Lt Fleetwood, an American). The Alamo wins.

Four Eland 90 armoured cars from the Zimbabwe Armoured Regiment – manned by national servicemen and under the command of Sgt Stephen Devine - are brought to Methuen Barracks to bolster the 1RAR battlegroup.

The ZIPRA force at AP Mike/Gwaai River Mine has been swollen by deserters from collapsing ZNA battalions, and is now thought to comprise 6000 men, with T34 tanks, BRDM2 armoured cars, BTR 152 APCs, D30 artillery, PT-SM amphibious cargo carriers, GSP bridging equipment, various and assorted anti-aircraft weapons which could be used in the ground role, including various trucks and equipment – all dug in around hill features. The large ZIPRA force at the 1 Bde Battle Camp at Essexvale has ten T34 tanks and numbers of BTR 152 APCs and other vehicles.

Over the Christmas break, 300 ZIPRA men go AWOL from 4:3 and 3:1 Bns alone, and make their way to Entumbane and Gwaai River Mine. In early January there are further murders in Chitungwiza.

5 Jan 1981: ZIPRA at Chitungwiza and Entumbane, fearing for their safety, refuse to take part in an accelerated integration process into the ZNA. 100 ZANLA are moved to Entumbane from AP Foxtrot. ZIPRA from Chitungwiza are moved to Silalabuhwa and Gwaai River Mine.

ENTUMBANE II

Jan 1981: Four-man RAR early-warning OPs are established on the routes into Bulawayo, in particular at the Umguza River Bridge on the Vic Falls Road towards AP Mike/Gwaai River Mine to the north west, and in the Blue Hills on the Jo'burg road towards the 1 Bde Essexvale Battle Camp at Essexvale to the south east. Anti-tank hunter killer teams (4 man sticks) are trained up with RPG7s and 75mm RCLs, to be deployed well forward by helicopters to intercept and ambush any ZIPRA armoured vehicles trying to move towards Bulawayo.

11 Jan 1981: Mugabe demotes Joshua Nkomo from Home Affairs Minister to Public Services Minister.

13 Jan 1981: There are three separate incidents of exchanges of fire between ZIPRA men and patrolling ZNA soldiers in Chitungwiza, Salisbury.

8 Feb 1981: Full-scale fighting starts between former ZIPRA and ZANLA members of the newly-formed ZNA 4:1 Bn, at Connemara Barracks between Gwelo and Que Que. Former ZIPRA men gain control of the arsenal and shoot at their ex-ZANLA comrades. The former ZANLA men escape into the surrounding bush. The mutiny is defused by senior officers from 4 Bde. (The mutineers on both sides are eventually fired from the ZNA.)

10 Feb 1981: Fighting erupts at the newly formed ZNA 1:3 Bn in Glenville near the Bulawayo Motor Racing Circuit on the Vic Falls Road. There is a rush for the arsenal. ZIPRA win again, and the ZANLA men scatter into the surrounding bush, leaving twelve dead behind them. Around 70 former ZANLA men flee to a nearby secretarial college owned by Nkomo, harassing students there for several days.

12 ZIPRA/ZANLA KIA

At 20h00 Lt Col Mick McKenna of 1RAR gets a call at Methuen Barracks telling him about the events at Glenville. He dispatches the four Eland 90s with D Coy in support. In line abreast they storm the camp, straight through the tents, encountering no resistance. The troops are accompanied by Brigadier Mike Shute and ZIPRA and ZANLA Liaison Officers in a bid to restore discipline and order. Two ex-ZIPRA captains of 1:3 Bn hiding under their beds in their tents are run over by the armoured cars and injured. The BMATT team arrives the next morning to find the ex-ZIPRA members of the battalion squatting in rows in their underpants. "While you were away, your battalion fell apart", they are told.

Unknown number of ZIPRA KIA and wounded

11 Feb 1981: The day is spent sorting out the mess at Glenville, and the RAR soldiers then return to Brady Barracks.

In the evening fighting breaks out at the newly formed 1:2 Bn at Ntabazinduna, outside Bulawayo. This time it is former ZANLA men who gain control. (1:2 Bn had been deployed with other government units to deal with the Entumbane fighting in November 1980, its conduct then being taken as evidence of successful integration of both ZIPRA and ZANLA ex-combatants into the new ZNA.) ZIPRA men working on an agricultural project at Silalabuhwa Dam, south east of Bulawayo join the mutiny, and set up road blocks on the main road between Filabusi and Balla Balla.

Unknown number of ZIPRA/ZANLA KIA and wounded

20h00: A three-way battle breaks out in Entumbane, with ZIPRA and ZANLA firing at each other and both firing at C Coy under Maj Lionel Dyck at The Alamo. C/Sgt Huni, C Coy's CQMS, is struck by shrapnel from an RPG7, sustaining severe wounds to his arm and shoulder. The 1RAR battlegroup and the Eland 90s move to HQ 1 Bde at Brady in Bulawayo. Four T54 tanks from E Sqn ZAR, and a troop of three 25-Pdr field guns from the Artillery, are brought to Brady from Salisbury.

D Coy are sent to cordon off the western suburbs from the city centre. They are attacked by a large ZIPRA force, but, supported by the 81mm mortars of Sp Coy on the Luveve Bridge, they manage to seize high ground - Lurker's Ridge – just west of the Luveve Bridge.

Another section of 81mm mortars is positioned at Mpilo Hospital, with an OP on the roof. (The mortarmen are treated <u>very</u> well by the nurses…)

A radio message is received by the OP in the Blue Hills south east of Bulawayo saying an armoured column is on its way from Essexvale on the Gwanda Road, comprising BTR 152 APC and T34 tanks. The Eland 90s are sent from Brady to destroy the column, with supporting troops from Sp Coy and 1 Pl, A Coy.

M At the intersection of George Avenue and Selborne Avenue, the Eland 90s halt at a red traffic light, intending to turn left onto Selborne Avenue (now Leopold Takawira Avenue), which becomes the Gwanda Road. A BTR 152 passes in front of the lead Eland 90, travelling into the centre of Bulawayo. It is completely destroyed by a round from the 90mm cannon of the armoured car.

Unknown number of ZIPRA KIA

On the assumption that this BTR 152 is the lead vehicle – and not the final vehicle - of the Essexvale armoured column, the Eland 90s and RAR troops turn left and travel out on the Gwanda Road until just before a slight right hand bend in the road at the top of a hill, just past the Hill Top Motel and near the Skyview Drive-In Cinema, where they lie in ambush.

M1 It later transpires that the vehicle destroyed by the Eland 90 was not the lead vehicle after all. Another BTR 152 is found the next morning, smashed into a tree further into the centre of Bulawayo up Selbourne Avenue, near the fountain on the southern side – the ZIPRA driver having apparently lost control.

N **12 Feb 1981:** At 01h15 in the early morning, picquets sent forward report that two BTR 152s are on their way. As they crest the hill ahead of Eland 90s they are destroyed. Two BTR 152s surrender. Another BTR 152 escapes into the side roads and is rammed by a police vehicle. On a nearby road, 2 Pl, A Coy ambush a Peugeot station wagon ZIPRA staff car, destroying it with machinegun fire.

Unknown number of ZIPRA KIA

O At the same time, a brand new Toyota Land Cruiser is stopped on the Old Essexvale Road into Bulawayo by a 3Pl of A Coy. Six ZIPRA officers are captured and relieved of their Tokarev pistols. Focus now shifts to the other side of town, where C Coy in The Alamo at Entumbane are under pressure and running out of ammunition.

Six ZIPRA captured

P D Const. Moraka Chinzi and PO Alistair Taylor, both plain-clothes CID officers, are in a vehicle in Luveve when they are stopped by an armed gang. They are pulled from their vehicle and assaulted. Taylor is shot dead. Chinzi is told to return to his station and is shot as he walks away. A sub-machine gun, a revolver and four radios are stolen.

At midday a column of twelve BTR 152s and BRDM2 APCs leaves AP Mike/Gwaai River Mine and heads for Bulawayo.

Q Replaced by A Coy, an armoured column of D Coy and the Eland 90s commanded by Maj Husher leaves to relieve The Alamo, working their way through Mpopoma and Mabutweni towards Entumbane. A Lynx aircraft takes off from Brady airfield in support of the RAR troops at The Alamo. Despite coming under voluminous fire from the ground, the pilot, Fl Lt Colin James, puts in several strikes at ZIPRA positions, including the destruction of a Zil heavy transporter filled with ZIPRA men. At 13h00 on 12 Feb The Alamo is finally relieved. C/Sgt Huni is brought out by vehicle to an Alouette waiting near the Luveve Bridge. He is casevaced to hospital.

2 ZRP CID murdered: D Const Chinzi; PO Taylor (Bronze Baton)
4 RAR wounded, including CQMS C/Sgt Huni who is severely injured.
Unknown number of ZIPRA/ZANLA KIA and wounded

An O-group is held by Lt Col Mick McKenna at Brady, outlining the plan to deal with the ZIPRA position at AP Mike/Gwaai River Mine. The operation would begin with a preliminary bombardment by the artillery, with the T54s moving in from the south with supporting RAR troops as the main thrust to clear the position. Other elements would take up stop positions to block any withdrawal.

One of the companies of 4:2 Bn (formerly 2RAR) is sent up the Vic Falls Road to set up an ambush for the ZIPRA column at the Umguza Bridge. A senior ZIPRA officer is sent forward from there to stop the column. The column is buzzed by two Air Force of Zimbabwe Hunters, who are patrolling up and down the Vic Falls Road. It halts as darkness falls and then turns off the main road into a dirt road at Kenmaur. It travels no further towards Bulawayo and camouflages itself in the bush, disappearing from view.

13 Feb 1981: A column of Eland 90s and supporting RAR troops are sent to Essexvale. En route they encounter an abandoned T34, which is driven back to Brady. At the Essexvale Battle Camp, ZIPRA is persuaded to surrender its remaining tanks, APCs and heavy weapons.

14 Feb 1981: There is scattered fighting. Western Commonage Police Station is attacked, then Mabutweni Police Station, right next to where the whole thing started at White City Stadium on 9 November, three months previously. But the second battle for Bulawayo is over, with over 400 dead, none of which are from the RAR battle group. Armoured vehicles and heavy weaponry at Gwaai River Mine and Essexvale Battle Camo are surrendered by ZIPRA and removed to Brady Barracks. ZIPRA's conventional military capability is destroyed.

The following men were decorated for their actions at Entumbane – among the first tranche of decorations awarded under the then-new Zimbabwe Honours system:

Silver Cross of Zimbabwe	Maj Lionel Dyck.
Bronze Cross of Zimbabwe	Sgt Stephen Devine
	Lt David Hill
	Maj Anthony Husher
	WO2 Stephen Ncube
Zimbabwe Commendation Medal	2 Lt Max Chinyanganya
	Fl Lt Colin James

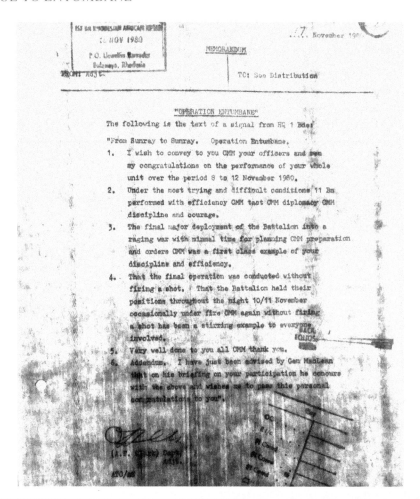

SOLDIER A: RECOLLECTIONS 19 YEARS ON
(transcribed from the handwritten original)

This report is incomplete without the findings of the causes of the conflicts that took place between ex ZIPRA and ZANLA guerrillas during the early stages of Zimbabwean independence. Below is the piece story of the heavy battle that took place between the above warring functions leading to the involvement of C Coy 1:1 Inf Bn in a bid to stop the fighting of the two different parties.

On --- February 1981 C Coy 1:1 Inf Bn under the command of Col L. Dyck who was the OC had been deployed to monitor the movement and behavior of the ZIPRA and ZANLA combatants who had just been translocated into camps of ENTUMBANE Western Suburbs awaiting integration into the then newly formed Zimbabwe National Army.

A week after C Coy's deployment at a beerhall situated in the middle of Entumbane Suburbs spotted on top of a small high ground tactical enough to observe all the camps to the east, south north and western directions manned by ZIPRA cadres on the west and north, ZANLA on the east. No camp was established on the southern part of C Coy's central position since the area had been earmarked for the establishment of a police post which is now existing.

On the day of the event, C Coy troops started to observe unusual movements of the ZIPRA force who were busy organising ammunition and weapons during the day up to 4 pm. Their motors were mounted facing C Coy's position. This made the C Coy troops to be suspicious.

At around 1800 hrs a truck with ZIPRA members was driven towards ZANLA camps, a long burst of fire was heard coming from said truck. Firing at ZANLAs and drove away towards the Gwaai Rover ZIPRA's main Assembly Point.

An hour later, around 1900 hrs, heavy motor and small arms fire was started from the western camp landing at C Company position and ZANLA camps. Firstly C Coy troops took up fire positions and were ordered to remain in positions without firing back. Eventually the fire erupted from all directions targeted at C Coy's post and also on the hearing of ZIPRA's skirmishing towards our object we started to strongly fire back causing them to withdraw back. The attempt by ZIPRAs to take over C Coy's position continued for the whole night but failed due to C Coy troops firm positions of defending themselves. During the first light C Coy troops had very little ammo left in the individual members' magazines since no resupply could be carried out during the previous all night war. At around 6:30 the following morning, the resupply was brought in by Armoured cars and helicopters this facilitated by C Coy troops from their stronghold position.

The remaining companies of 1:1 Infantry Bn were assigned to go and rescue C Coy the previous night of the battle but were pinned down as they approached the Nguoyenja flyover bridge hence, they remained firing from those positions until the following morning when they managed to maneover through with the help of Zimbabwe Armoured Cars and finally got to C Coy's at around 11 hrs the following morning. This time the fire was a bit calm except some sporadic bursts of fire coming from the surrounding areas. However, before the arrival of the reinforcement, heavy and small arms lodged at C Coy's position from the northern camp resulting in the slight injuries of the then Maj Dyck, his dog, CSM and one Pte who all received some fragments in their legs from a bomb which landed few metres from them. Treatment was carried out at the CAP and the members continued with their battle chores.

Also injured seriously was the company CQMS whose right hand was ripped off by a rocket fired from 300m north of the Coy position and exploded few metres in front of his trench. He was then immediately evacuated to Mpilo General hospital where he was treated and discharged after a long time and his hand is permanently paralysed.

It was during the following day in the morning hours of pandemonium when the Army Comdr. Two functions' top comders flew over the area announcing that the soldiers should stop firing and lay their guns down or they could risk serious action from the Formal Forces. The fire eventually ceased at approximately midday of the 2nd day (D+1). The ceasefire was also necessitated by a large number of casualties they had suffered and also a large number of ZANLA and ZIPRA troops had in the early morning hours abandon their positions with some running and gather up at 1 Bde HQ, 1:1 Inf Bn and at Llewellin Brks for protection as armed refugees.

1:1 Bn suffered no deaths, one seriously injured, and three minor injuries including the OC's dog. The two insurgent sides suffered an undisclosed large number of deaths and injuries. This report is not complete if we don't mention the heavily armed and equipped battalions of the ZIPRA force who had

Armoured cars and heavy weapons at Gwaai Assemble point and essexvale assy pt. They had also attempted a fierce advance in order to come and reinforce their troops but their advance did not succeed thanks to our formal Armoured Car Regt who blocked and destroyed their Armoured cars from the two directions and were finally asked to surrender.

The source of these reactions may be concluded from the layman's point of view as that the other function was not pleased by the leadership of the other function hence triggered the short lived battle that involved all the players mentioned above and the OC's lovely dog.

This report in not in its widest spectrum since the writer is only focussing on the events that took place in his closer proximities.

AN RAR SCRAPBOOK

Border Control, Chete Island, Kariba, 1963.

Border Control, Kariba shore, 1963.

Ptes Titus and Zangayi, Border Control, Sengwe, 1963.
Tattered uniforms after four weeks in the bush. During Op Nickel the
RAR troops got through 150 pairs of boots.

1RAR, Op Nickel, northern Matabeleland, August 1967.

Above, left and below:
C Coy 1RAR, Op Cosmic, northern Matabeleland, April 1968.

Above and below right: captures, Op Mansion, northern Matabeleland, July 1968.

Northern Matabeleland, Op Mansion, July 1968. Crossing a bridge made by the Engineers.

Retirement party for RSM Matambo ICD BEM, 1968. He was later brought out of retirement to be FSM of Guard Force. He was murdered at his house in Gwelo in 1981 by ZANU thugs.

Binga, northern Matabeleland, 1969. C Coy 1RAR hosts the President, Clifford Dupont.

Methuen Barracks. A Coy 1RAR marks Inyantue Day, 13 August 1969.

1RAR Mortar Section 1968.

1RAR Mortar Section 1970.

Bush hats for some … (Tanlwe Chaung Day, 1969).

…Bush hats for all. (Tanlwe Chaung Day 1971).

With drums beating, and bayonets fixed... 1RAR on parade, marking
Tanlwe Chaung Day 1972 at Methuen Barracks.

JOC Sipolilo 1973/74. Capt Terry Hammond, Adjt (Seagull)
1RAR gives his warning. He was later CO 2RAR.

Ops Room, JOC Sipolilo 1973/74.

Kotwa, near Mtoko, Op Hurricane. Brian Lennon-Smith leads a patrol, MAG gunner Cpl Mugwagwa immediately behind him, Lt Ian Gillespie at the rear.

'Hobo' Hobson MMM JCD and Dave Padbury with the juju men of D Coy 1RAR.

1RAR move to JOC Mtoko, Op Hurricane, 1975.

Pte Newani, L/Cpl Nyangi, Cpl Ncube, A Coy 2RAR.

Pte Chipika, A Coy 2RAR.

L/Cpl Moswa, A Coy 2RAR.

Maj Andre Dennison MLM BCR (MFC (Ops)), OC A Coy 2RAR.

Up...

...Over...

... and Down.
Depot RAR, Shaw Barracks. Balla Balla, 1976.

Range practice, Depot RAR.

Hup, Two, Three…

Maj Peter Morris DMM, Commandant Depot RAR.

WO1 Julius Vakisayi Manunure DMM, RSM Depot RAR.

B Coy 1RAR, 1976. Lt Bill Liversidge, second row, fifth from the right. B Coy were the first RAR company to man a fireforce.

Regular RAR men attached to C Coy 6RR at Essexvale Battle Camp, Op Tangent.

Above and below: Regular RAR men attached to an RR battalion at Essexvale Battle Camp, Op Tangent.

Regular RAR men and Territorial Rhodesia Regiment men, both of C Coy 6RR, leave Essexvale Battle Camp for a six week call-up.

BASIC STATIC LINE PARACHUTE COURSES

Combat uniform wings

Dress uniform wings

An airborne Chronicle photographer captured the perfect dressing displayed by the men of Depot Rhodesia Regiment as they marched up Selborne Avenue, Bulawayo yesterday. (Story, pictures — Page 9) 1/12/77

The Passing-Out Parade of the first integrated draft to the newly rebadged Independent Companies on 30 November 1977. Intakes 158 and 159 from Depot RR Llewellin Barracks march together with men from Depot RAR Shaw Barracks after a phase of training together. The RAR Band is at the centre.

Maj Ian Moore leads the parade at left. WO2 T. McChlery, later CSM 5 (Indep) Coy RAR, at centre in SAS beret.

Maj Don Price BCR with Chaka, the 1 (Indep) mascot, in the 'hit cab'. Victoria Falls, 1977.

Together at last: 1 (Independent) Coy RAR, Victoria Falls, 1977.

Cpl Victor Carl Meyer KOAS. Died while saving his platoon commander from drowning.

Wrecked 2.5, Old Kazangula Road, Op Tangent, Sgt Colin Rhodes, Cpl Fin O'Donaghue and Sgt Theo Nel BCR. Vic Anderson's leg was broken by the landmine blast.

Swimming pool at the 1 (Indep) camp at Beitbridge. Suntan lotion was equal parts vinegar, Olivine and brake-fluid.

Beitbridge. The B-10 82mm recoilless rifle on the back was abandoned by ZIPRA after an attack on the Sprayview Hotel in 1977.

Pando (Liebig's Ranch tracker) and Capt Andy Barrett.

25-pounder at Beitbridge Airfield

1 (Indep) personnel teaching fireforce to the South Africans. Pumas and Alouettes of an SAAF Jumbo Fireforce, Madimbo, east of Messina, South Africa, May-June 1979.

Beitbridge-Rutenga rail line, late 1978. ZANLA had blown the line in 47 places.

Beitbridge-Bulawayo road, May 1979. Fuel tanker torched by ZANLA.

Bubye River Bridge, Op Tangent. l-r Pte Moyo, Saed (Liebig's Ranch tracker), Pte Rapson Murindi.

Canberra strike on a ZANLA transit camp, north of Tshiturapadsi village, Chipisi TTL, Beitbridge East, Op Tangent, November 1978.

Hunter strike on a ZANLA transit camp north of Tshiturapadsi village, March 1978.

PRAW pilot Robin Watson with his Beechcraft at Makado Ranch, West Nicholson. He was awarded a DFC flying Boston bombers over Italy in WW2. The plane has .303 Brownings mounted under the wings.

Sgt 'Mortar Mike' Whittstock, a TF member of 1 (Indep), with his wife Lynette. Their daughter Charlene, an Olympic swimmer, married Prince Albert II of Monaco in 2011.

1 (Indep) Beitbridge from the air, January 1979.

Pte John Ncube and Sgt Roy Amm, 2 (Indep) mortar section, Kariba (above left). Pte John Ncube marching in the 30 November 1977 Passing Out Parade, Bulawayo (above right).

2 (Indep), Kariba. The view from the upper parking lot.

2 (Indep)'s patch. The Zambezi below Kariba (above right) and the Zambezi Valley at Chirundu (below), Op Hurricane.

Ian Wood (right) and others, Intake 158, 2 (Indep), Kariba.

Eland 90 at Kariba…

2.5 with Russian 12.7mm DShK mounted, Chirundu.

…and a Ferret.

Sgt Jo Amos catching those beneficial rays.

Another day at the office.

Catch of the Day. Pte Tembo, Cpl Andrew Krajewski and Pte Vincent Ngwenya of c/s 22B.

Rocky Jordaan (left), Mark Marillier (right) with their sticks. At the rear of Jordaan's stick is Tunha, formerly of ZIPRA.

Jo Amos and Johnny Mauvis demonstrate the .50 cal at Chirundu.

Chirundu camp.

Pte 'Stretch' Luginga and friend, 2 (Indep).

Clive Hooper (right), 3 (Indep), and father.

Rod Sinclaire (left) and Peter Gill, 3 (Indep), Inyanga Barracks, Op Thrasher.

The bombed-out hospital at Nyamaropa. Op Thrasher.

If the cap fits… a member of 3 (Indep) wearing a borrowed British Police election monitor's helmet, Nyamaropa, February 1980.

Air Botswana drops in to Nyamaropa to transfer full ballot boxes.

"The coldest place on earth." Ian Clarke, Mark Sasman, Oscar Alpha 4 Relay, Mt Inyangombe, Op Thrasher, 1978.

3 (Indep) pub, Inyanga Barracks.

Taking advantage of the sun, 3 (Indep), Inyanga Barracks.

l-r Andy Smith, Peter Colbourne, Tony Carroll (KIA), Mark Sasman, Anders Elias. 3 (Indep).

Climb every mountain. l-r Norman Pieterse, Rob Cook, Charlie Parker.

Above and below, left and right. 4 (Indep) at the Zambezi above the Falls. Bruce Greetham second from right (at left, below) and at left (below).

1 Pl, 5 (Indep) embus for a week in Fern Valley, Umtali, 1979. Harry Linneveldt with his back to camera.

Nick Mullen, Benny Basson, Al Myburgh, Jan Kirstein, Russell Howden, Fern Valley, 1979

5 (Indep) convoy for the April 1979 elections forms up at Addams Barracks.

5 (Indep) convoy at Derowa Mine en route to Buhera, Op Thrasher, April 1979 elections.

One of two 1 Pl, 5 (Indep) vehicles (plus a Mobile Surgical Unit) wrecked by landmines between Derowa and Buhera in one morning. No casualties.

l-r Mike Greer, Macky Horsfield, Harry Linneveldt, Nick Holmes, Andre Barlow, Lionel Batty, Mark Coombes.

Collective punishment for some heinous crime or other: testing the gasmasks with tear gas in the trenches at Addams Barracks. Alan Doyle just emerged at right, above.

5 (Indep) NCOs at the forming-up point to walk into Ngorima, Op Thrasher.

l-r Harry Linneveldt, Mark Coombes, Seb Prinsloo in the forest north of the Ngorima Valley, Seb Prinsloo is a South African who opted to do his national service in Rhodesia.

The long and the short and the tall. c/s 51C, June 1979.

On an errand to Inyanga on the day before demob, 29 June 1979. Back: Alan Doyle, Lionel Batty, Si Osborne. Front: Nick Holmes, Chris Ferreira, Rob Sivertsen.

Ralph Cant, 6 (Indep), Cashel, Op Thrasher.

Jonah, Dube and others, 6 (Indep), Cashel, Op Thrasher.

Anthony Manning, 6 (Indep), Addams Barracks, 1979.

Back: Keith Jackson, John Godfrey, Nick Watson. Front: Mickey Wilson. 6 (Iindep), Addams Barracks, 1979.

2 Lt Johan Pretorius and Lt Col Terry Leaver at the grave of Sgt Piet Nel, 6 (Indep), KOAS. Lt Col Leaver was the first CO of 3RAR, having been OC of 6 (Indep).

Not quite horseplay …

"Pick up your feet there, you!" An integrated squad from Intake 163, the first to include black national servicemen, doubling along a road through Llewellin Barracks yesterday.

National Service Intake 163 – the first to include African school-leavers - was called up on 10 January 1979. In contrast to the over-supply of volunteers for training as regular members of the RAR, many African school-leavers did not respond to their conscription papers. (Peter Gill, later of 3 (Indep), leading the squad.)

Pretend you're breaking out of prison. Intake 163 on the assault course at Llewellin.

2RAR RSO Lt Taffy Machiridza, entering the telex room at 2RAR Tac HQ.

137

2RAR Tac HQ, Bolo Ranch, Op Repulse, 1978. The retractable telex mast is visible above the trees at right.

Bolo Ranch. FF Charlie taxis past a 2RAR mortar pit.

FF Charlie. All tanked up and ready for the call.

Acres and acres of scrim. 2RAR Tac HQ Glenlivet, Op Repulse.

'Biltong trees' of scrim. Signallers outside the telex room.

Above and left: B Coy 1RAR at Mtoko, Op Hurricane, December 1978.

"Welcome to Ulcer Gulch"says the sign at the RDR guardpost at Rutenga, Op Repulse.

2RAR Tac HQ. Digging-in at Glenlivet, Op Repulse, 1978.

The Queen Mother's Christmas card to 1RAR, December 1978.

The view from the Glenlivet Relay.

FF Charlie coming back in. 2RAR Tac HQ, Mashaba, Op Repulse, 1978.

Lt Col Ian Pullar, CO 2RAR, 1978.

Maj Noel Morgan-Davies and CSM Vanhuvavone Rashayi BCR of Sp Coy 2RAR. Maj John Pritchard, Bn 2 i/c in the 2.5. Maj Morgan Davies was later the first CO of 4:2 Bn.

2RAR Tac HQ defence.

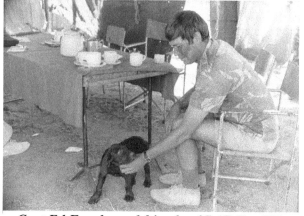

Capt Ed Fouche and friend at 2RAR Tac HQ.

Maj John Irvine (RMO), WO2 T. Mufanebadza, Maj Gen Sandy Maclean OLM DCD – Army Commander, WO2 M. Hamandishe (MFC (Ops)), Capt Alf Logan, WO2 Athol Pirie, 1979. All 2RAR and just received their DMMs from Maj Gen Maclean, who was once CO of 1RAR.

Above, and below left: The RAR Band plays farewell to their Director of Music, Maj Ken 'Bandy' MacDonald at Bulawayo Airport on his retirement, May 1979.

Brig David Heppenstall, Alderman Bill Kinleyside OLM, Maj Ken MacDonald MLM LRAM at his leaving drinks.

2RAR receive the Freedom of Fort Victoria, Oct 1979. Maj Sean von Stranz (with medals shining) leads A Coy. He served with 1/2 Gurkha Rifles in Borneo in 1965/66.

A Coy 2RAR vs the Blue Jobs, 1978. Cpl M'Qwayi receiving the ball.

60mm Mortar Pl, Sp Coy, 1RAR (minus two sections – 16 men – detached on ops under Cpls Benjamin Horayi and Jack.). Cpl Ernest Rashamira BCR (third row, third from left); Pte Frederick Nyamayabo KOAS (third row, second from right); Pte Isaac Nemanwa KOAS (second row, second from left); L/Cpl Ndlovu, MAG gunner (second row, third from right); L/Cpl Stanley Matize (second row, at right); WO2 (PWO) Francis Charamba (MFC (Ops)) (first row, on left); C/Sgt Runesu Obert Mbau (first row, second from right); Lt Pat Lawless SCR (first row, centre).

Display jump onto Ascot Racecourse, Bulawayo, Tanlwe Chaung celebrations, April 1979. Cpl Benjamin Horayi (left, Lt Pat Lawless (centre), L/Cpl Ndlovu (right). Note Ndlovu's MAG bipod has been deployed by the shock of the static line. Not helpful in the roll on landing, where Ndlovu hurt himself.

Pte Raphael, 2RAR Open Day, October 1979.

B Coy 2RAR at Nuanetsi, Op Repulse, Aug 1979.

Stand in the door! 2 Lt Mike Matthews, A Coy 1RAR.

3RAR, Mt Selinda, Op Thrasher, 1980. Pte Kufakurumbe at right.

3RAR, Mt Selinda, Op Thrasher, 1980.

D Coy 3RAR on parade, 1980.

Part of the country's "collection of vintage aircraft."

Capt Trevor McEnery (LO), 2RAR Tac HQ Ops Room, Chiredzi.

A Coy 2RAR para.

2RAR Tac HQ defence platoon, Chiredzi, Op Repulse, Dec-Jan 1979/80.

Fireforce – waiting for the order to emplane.

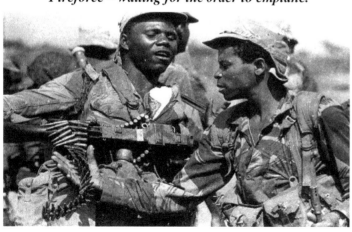

Lt Edward Piringondo SCR, KOAS while a member of 4 (HU) RAR.

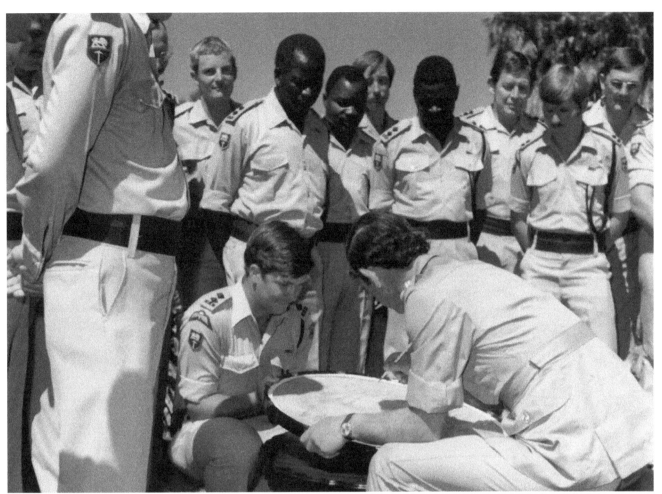

Prince Charles adds his signature to the regimental drumskin on a visit to 1RAR, April 1980.

From left: Maj Lionel Dyck SCZ; Capt John Heggart; Maj Glenn Reid; 2 Lt Dave Grant; Lt Graham Swart; Lt David Hill BCZ; Lt Giles Chinyenze, RSO; 2 Lt Andy Todd; Lt Rufu Mutandwa; HRH Prince Charles; Capt Ron Revell (MFC (Ops)); Lt Percy Chiyanike; Capt Tony Hagelthorn; Ian Macdonald; Brig Mike Shute OLM; Capt N.A. Cosgrave (MFC (Non-Ops)), Paymaster; Lt Willard Fleetwood; a member of the neighbouring Llewellin Barracks Mess; 2 Lt Graham Watson-Smith; Capt Mike Jones; Capt Trevor Jones; Capt Anthony Husher BCZ.

Brigadier Mike Shute visiting AP Mike/Gwaai River Mine, 1980. He is flanked by Lt Gen Lookout Masuku, ZIPRA commander, and Lt Col D Drysdale RM, ZIPRA Liaison Officer with the Commonwealth Monitoring Force. Maj Andrew Parker Bowles (first husband of the Duchess of Cornwall) peers over Brig Shute's right shoulder. He was Senior Military Liaison Officer to Lord Soames. (Captain Iain Duncan Smith, later leader of the British Conservative Party, was also part of the CMF, as aide-de-camp to Maj Gen Acland.)

Brig Shute with Joshua Nkomo at AP Mike. Brig Shute is a former CO of 1RAR.

ZIPRA Commander-in-Chief.

An Entumbane holding camp, simmering in the heat.

Slow and fragile integration of ZIPRA and ZANLA into ZNA battalions.

A Coy 1RAR vehicles at HQ 1 Bde, Brady Barracks.

The mess tent at Brady. Foreground: 2 Lts John Hopkins, Tex Chinyani, Des Gijima.

149

The gate to The Alamo.

Keeping tabs on the holding camps.

A higher vantage point.

Sgt Tumla Pilat, 3Pl, A Coy.

WO2 Januari, CSM, A Coy 1RAR

Artist-in-Residence: John Hopkins

The 81s of Sp Coy at The Alamo.

3 Pl, A Coy in The Alamo.

75mm RCL anti-tank team, above. RPG7 anti-tank team, below.

John Hopkins' take on Alamo life.

C Coy Shark.

1RAR MAG gunner on the Luveve Bridge, looking towards The Alamo and the holding camps.

T54 of the Zimbabwe Armoured Regiment at Brady.

Eland 90 of the Zimbabwe Armoured Regiment. Sgt Stephen Devine BCZ standing.

Armoured column gathering at Brady.

Zimbabwe Armoured Regiment T54s at Brady.

Hungry troops to feed. Field kitchen at Brady.

Scorpion of Sp Coy.

A Coy command post at Brady.

Deserted. The ZNA 1:3 Bn camp at Glenville the morning after.

Wrecked car in Entumbane, caught in the crossfire.

ZIPRA staff car destroyed by 2Pl near the Hilltop Motel.

Above and below: BTRs destroyed near the Hilltop Motel.

BTR destroyed at the George Avenue/Selborne Avenue intersection.

C/Sgt Huni is casevaced to hospital. He was the C Coy CQMS in The Alamo and was badly injured by RPG7 shrapnel. He was brought out in a relief column vehicle to a waiting helicopter.

Hurry up and wait. 1RAR troops on standby in Entumbane.

Elements A Coy HQ screening the Luveve Bridge area: Back l-r Capt Trevor Jones; Lt Willard Fleetwood; 2 Lt John Hopkins. Front l-r WO2 Tarcisious; WO2 J. Gwara; WO2 J. Manuki.

Max Chinyanganya and Rex with a ZIPRA BTR 152 surrendered intact.

155

Proud new owners. ZIPRA T34.

Captured BTR 152s.

Captured and surrendered ZIPRA equipment at Brady. GSP pontoon carrier above left, T34s above right. BRDM2 Armoured car and BTR 152 APC on a Muppet low-loader below left, small arms below right.

1RAR troop carriers wait on the Luveve Road to move ZIPRA and ZANLA out of Entumbane.

ZIPRA leaves Entumbane, cheered by the crowds. "ZIPRA also deserves publicity on radio."

Above and left: Gen Sandy Maclean reviews the 1RAR Victory Parade at Brady Barracks. Brig Mike Shute stands behind him.

Lt Col Mick McKenna, last CO of 1RAR.

The last parade of 3RAR, marking Tanlwe Chaung Day, 1981, at the Show Grounds in Umtali. Lt Col Ron Marillier BCR, second, and last, CO of 3RAR, is at extreme left.

The last gathering of 1RAR officers in RAR No1 uniform.

*The RNR/RAR Memorial at the National Memorial
Arboretum, Alrewas, Staffordshire, United Kingdom.*

ROLL OF HONOUR

Rolls of Honour are never quite finished. Flanders' fields are still offering up evidence for the memorials on the Western Front. In our case, the evidence is documentary rather than ploughed up from the mud, but, more frequently than you might imagine, a name, or a date, or a photograph comes to light which helps to fill in the gaps. These snippets of information are important, given the political and geographical constraints on access to official records relating to southern African conflicts.

By way of example: there are three possible locations for the dam wall where members of the RAR Band were drowned in 1972. Also, an RAR soldier was shot by accident during the integration training phase with national servicemen in late 1977. The incident itself is well documented. However, the name of that RAR man is not known, and can only be guessed at until evidence comes forward.

You will see that there are occasional names without details as to how they died. Some RAR soldiers, particularly in the earlier years, have no family name or first name recorded, or no service number. No doubt that information exists somewhere, but it hasn't been found yet. We live in hope, and keep digging. But things are as they are, and the Roll of Honour for the RAR in the Bush War period on the following pages is, I hope, getting close to the full story.

The Roll uses a simple categorization: KIA for all those who died as the direct result of enemy action, whether "in action" or "died of wounds"; KOAS for deaths resulting from avoidable accidents, including "blue-on-blue" incidents; and DOAS for all others. Medals entitling the bearer to post-nominals are shown as such. Decorations not carrying post-nominals are shown in parentheses. The names are of those who died serving in the various units of the RAR, or who lost their lives, badged as RAR, serving on attachment to other units. In particular, this means the RAR men who served in the eight TF Rhodesia Regiment battalions from late 1977 onwards.

The foundations for this Roll of Honour are the records built and maintained by Craig Fourie, Adrian Haggett and Dr Richard Wood. I am very grateful for their generous and cheerful help.

A short note about dates:

1RNR	Established 20 Apr 1916.
2RNR	Established mid-1917.
RNR	Disbanded from Jan 1919.
1RAR	Established early May 1940.
2RAR	Established Feb 1975.
Depot RAR	Established 1 Jan 1976.
TF RR Bns	RAR soldiers began attachment to TF Rhodesia Regiment battalions from late 1977.
RAR (Indep) Coys	Six Rhodesia Regiment Independent Companies rebadged as RAR 1 Dec 1977.
African NS	National Service for African school-leavers began with Intake 163 on 10 Jan 1979.
3RAR	Formed around the nucleus of 3 (Indep), 5 (Indep) and 6 (Indep) Coys RAR in Oct 1979. 1, 2 and 4 (Indep) Coys also lost their independent status and came under the control of the other RAR battalions, rather than, as previously, answering directly to the Brigade to which they belonged.
End of NS	National Service for all school-leavers ended with Intake 168 which began training in Apr 1980 and stood down in Mar 1981.
4 (HU) RAR	Formed 23 Apr 1980. Became 1 Zimbabwe Parachute Regiment on 1 Oct 1980
2RAR	Ceased wearing RAR insignia (as ZNA 4:2 Bn) in Apr 1981.
3RAR	Ceased wearing RAR insignia (as ZNA 3:3 Bn) in Apr 1981 after marking a final Tanlwe Chaung Day.
1RAR	Ceased wearing RAR insignia (as ZNA 1:1 Bn) in Apr 1981 after marking a final Tanlwe Chaung Day.

Alan Doyle

Pte MUYUNDA	R40574	1RAR	DOAS 3 Aug 1961	Died aged 34 from a cerebral haemorrhage in Mpilo Hospital, Bulawayo. Buried in Bulawayo
L/Cpl MUGWAGWA	R4640	1RAR	DOAS 3 Oct 1961	Died of natural causes.
Pte Grason NAKUNGWA	R40802	1RAR	DOAS 14 Jun 1962	Died aged 29 of cancer in Mpilo Hospital, Bulawayo. Buried in Bulawayo
WO1 Samuel MORUDU BEM	R9	1RAR	DOAS 31 Jan 1963	Died aged 51 from a cerebral thrombosis. WO1 Morudu was the Battalion's well respected Orderly Room Warrant Officer. (Note: There are two headstones in Lady Stanley Avenue Cemetery, Bulawayo with his name on them.)
Pte SWONDO	R43928	1RAR	KOAS 17 May 1967	Killed in a vehicle accident.
Pte Dennis NCUBE	R44158	1RAR	KOAS 3 Jul 1967	Buried in Luveve Cemetery, Bulawayo.
Pte Koroni KAMBANTE	R43593	A Coy 1RAR	KIA 13 Aug 1967	Killed aged 21 in a contact during Op Nickel near Inyantue, northern Matabeleland. His unit engaged a gang of 21 CTs comprising ZAPU and the SAANC from the Lobengula Group. Buried in Vunga African Purchase Area, Lower Gwelo.
Cpl Davison MUKOMBO	R41628	A Coy 1RAR	KIA 13 Aug 1967	Killed in a contact during Op Nickel near Inyantue, northern Matabeleland. His unit engaged a gang of 21 CTs comprising ZAPU and the SAANC from the Lobengula Group.
Lt Nicholas John SMITH	590	A Coy 1RAR	KIA 22 Aug 1967	Killed aged 23 in a contact during Op Nickel, Tjolotjo TTL, northern Matabeleland. Went to the aid of WO2 Timitiya, who had been fatally injured, and was himself shot. Buried in Warren Hills Cemetery, Harare.
WO2 Havahli TIMITIYA	R3063	A Coy 1RAR	KIA 22 Aug 1967	Killed aged 42 in a contact during Op Nickel, Tjolotjo TTL, northern Matabeleland. He was standing behind a tree firing an MAG when hit. Lt Smith was killed a moment later when he came across to Timitiya. He saw active service in Malaya. Buried in Masvingo.
Cpl Cosmos MUSHURE	R43721	E Coy 1RAR	KIA 23 Aug 1967	Killed aged 26 in a contact during Op Nickel, northern Matabeleland. His platoon were getting ready to spend the night near a CT camp when they were fired on. PO Spencer Thomas of the BSAP was killed at the same time. Buried in the Enkeldoorn area.
Lt Kenneth PEIRSON	531	E Coy 1RAR	KOAS 23 Aug 1967	Killed by friendly fire in the Tjolotjo area, Op Nickel. He was commanding several ambushes for the Lithuli Group, but left his position during the evening to investigate an attack on RAR vehicles parked a short distance away and was mistaken for the enemy on his return.

Pte Nyika MUCHAZOREGA	R42580	D Coy 1RAR	KIA 4 Sep 1967	Killed aged 25 in a contact at Intundhla Siding, Lupane District, in the final mopping-up of the ZIPRA Lithuli Group towards the end of Op Nickel. Elements of 10 Platoon under Lt Noble had been following the tracks of 5 CTs since early on the morning of 4 September. Contact was made 20 miles south west of Intundhla Siding at 1300 when a CT was killed and another wounded. The wounded man threw a grenade killing Muchazorega and wounding Pte Pedzisayi.
Cpl Erisha CHIKUDZA	R40349	E Coy 1RAR	KIA 18 Mar 1968	Killed aged 30 in a contact during Op Cauldron, Urungwe TTL. Buried in Buhera District.
Doda SIZIWA		1RAR	KOAS 2 May 1969	Died aged 45 from anoxia at the Methuen Barracks. Buried in Buhera.
Pte Ignasio Mungani ANASI	R43702	C Coy 1RAR	KIA 22 Jan 1970	Killed in a contact during Op Teak south of Victoria Falls, aged 29. Buried in Bikita District.
Capt Peter Noel SMEE	564	1RAR	DOAS 10 Oct 1970	Died aged 44 in Hendrik Verwoerd Hospital, Pretoria, after treatment for leukaemia.
Lt Thomas Hart BENNETT	755	1RAR	KOAS 20 Nov 1970	Killed aged 23 in a vehicle accident on the Salisbury-Bulawayo road. Cremated at West Park.
Pte Never MUTENGIZANWA	R44047	1RAR	KOAS 21 Nov 1970	Died aged 25 from multiple injuries sustained in a vehicle accident in Grey Street, Bulawayo. Buried in Kadoma.
Sgt Cosmas MUSUNGO	R4721	1RAR	DOAS 26 Jan 1971	Died aged 44 of aortic incompetence. Buried in Kwe Kwe.
Pte Siabuwa SIASUMPA		Regtl Band, 1RAR	KOAS 13 Mar 1971	Died aged 46 of asphyxia at Methuen Barracks. A member of the Regimental Band. Buried in Binga District.
Pte Newton MAKOFI	R44159	1RAR	KOAS 8 Aug 1971	Died aged 24 at Methuen Barracks of haemorrhaging. He was based at Brady Barracks, Bulawayo. Buried in Urungwe TTL.
Pte Fanuel Nharo CHAUSINA	R44526	C Coy 1RAR	KOAS 5 Apr 1972	Drowned aged 23 on Kariba whilst on border patrol in the Deka area, northern Matabeleland. They had been picked up at the end of a patrol by a small boat with a powerful outboard motor, but upon sudden deceleration, the following wave swamped the boat. His body was never found.
L/Cpl Adam Hugo GWATIRINGA	R44489	C Coy 1RAR	KOAS 5 Apr 1972	Drowned aged 21 on Kariba whilst on border patrol in the Deka area, northern Matabeleland. They had been picked up at the end of a patrol by a small boat with a powerful outboard motor, but upon sudden deceleration, the following wave swamped the boat.
Pte William Jephta MADZIYANYIKA	R44710	C Coy 1RAR	KOAS 5 Apr 1972	Drowned aged 22 on Kariba whilst on border patrol in the Deka area, northern Matabeleland. They had been picked up at the end of a patrol by a small boat with a powerful outboard motor, but upon sudden deceleration, the following wave swamped the boat. His body was never found.

Pte Elton MUSABAYANE	R44831	1RAR	DOAS 27 Apr 1972	Died aged 18 in Bulawayo of septicaemia and multiple lung abscesses. Buried in Bulawayo.
Pte Phinias CHAPANGE	R43804	Regtl Band 1RAR	KOAS 19 May 1972	Drowned aged 32 in the Fuller Forest/Matetsi area. Members of the band were deployed on active service, and as the RL they were travelling in crossed a dam wall the vehicle slipped into the water. The weight of their webbing, and being trapped in the superstructure on the back of the RL, pulled them under. Buried in Gutu.
L/Cpl Silvanos Mashona DUDZIRAYI	R41949	Regtl Band 1RAR	KOAS 19 May 1972	Drowned aged 31 in the Fuller Forest/Matetsi area. Members of the band were deployed on active service, and as the RL they were travelling in crossed a dam wall the vehicle slipped into the water. The weight of their webbing, and being trapped in the superstructure on the back of the RL, pulled them under. Buried in Bikita.
Pte Thomas MANDUNA	R43864	Regtl Band 1RAR	KOAS 19 May 1972	Drowned aged 26 in the Fuller Forest/Matetsi area. Members of the band were deployed on active service, and as the RL they were travelling in crossed a dam wall the vehicle slipped into the water. The weight of their webbing, and being trapped in the superstructure on the back of the RL, pulled them under. Buried in Nuanetsi.
Pte Josephat MANGANDURA	R43761	Regtl Band 1RAR	KOAS 19 May 1972	Drowned aged 29 in the Fuller Forest/Matetsi area. Members of the band were deployed on active service, and as the RL they were travelling in crossed a dam wall the vehicle slipped into the water. The weight of their webbing, and being trapped in the superstructure on the back of the RL, pulled them under. Buried in Gutu.
L/Cpl Kefasi MUCHATO	R42582	Regtl Band 1RAR	KOAS 19 May 1972	Drowned aged 30 in the Fuller Forest/Matetsi area. Members of the band were deployed on active service, and as the RL they were travelling in crossed a dam wall the vehicle slipped into the water. The weight of their webbing, and being trapped in the superstructure on the back of the RL, pulled them under. Buried in Gutu.
Pte Benjamin MURAMBIWA	R43901	Regtl Band 1RAR	KOAS 19 May 1972	Drowned aged 32 in the Fuller Forest/Matetsi area. Members of the band were deployed on active service, and as the RL they were travelling in crossed a dam wall the vehicle slipped into the water. The weight of their webbing, and being trapped in the superstructure on the back of the RL, pulled them under. Buried in Kwe Kwe.

L/Cpl Tshaye **NDAZA**	R53936	Regtl Band 1RAR	KOAS 19 May 1972	Drowned aged 44 in the Fuller Forest/Matetsi area. Members of the band were deployed on active service, and as the RL they were travelling in crossed a dam wall the vehicle slipped into the water. The weight of their webbing, and being trapped in the superstructure on the back of the RL, pulled them under. Buried in Lupane.
Cpl Godfrey **NGORAVANI**	R42764	A Coy 1RAR	KOAS 19 May 1972	Drowned aged 34 in the Fuller Forest/Matetsi area. Cpl Ngorovani had been seconded from A Coy to assist in leading the bandsmen on their deployment. Members of the band were deployed on active service, and as the RL they were travelling in crossed a dam wall the vehicle slipped into the water. The weight of their webbing, and being trapped in the superstructure on the back of the RL, pulled them under. Buried in Gokwe.
Pte Marandu **NYIKADZINO**	R43724	Regtl Band 1RAR	KOAS 19 May 1972	Drowned aged 30 in the Fuller Forest/Matetsi area. Members of the band were deployed on active service, and as the RL they were travelling in crossed a dam wall the vehicle slipped into the water. The weight of their webbing, and being trapped in the superstructure on the back of the RL, pulled them under. Buried in Buhera.
Pte Chirambgwa **RANGANAYI**	R42792	Regtl Band 1RAR	KOAS 19 May 1972	Drowned aged 32 in the Fuller Forest/Matetsi area. Members of the band were deployed on active service, and as the RL they were travelling in crossed a dam wall the vehicle slipped into the water. The weight of their webbing, and being trapped in the superstructure on the back of the RL, pulled them under. Buried in Gutu.
C/Sgt Ernest **TAKAWIRA**	R64741	Regtl Band 1RAR	KOAS 19 May 1972	Drowned aged 38 in the Fuller Forest/Matetsi area. Members of the band were deployed on active service, and as the RL they were travelling in crossed a dam wall the vehicle slipped into the water. The weight of their webbing, and being trapped in the superstructure on the back of the RL, pulled them under. Buried in Gutu.
Pte Maboko **WUNGANAYI**	R43457	Regtl Band 1RAR	KOAS 19 May 1972	Drowned aged 29 in the Fuller Forest/Matetsi area. Members of the band were deployed on active service, and as the RL they were travelling in crossed a dam wall the vehicle slipped into the water. The weight of their webbing, and being trapped in the superstructure on the back of the RL, pulled them under. Buried in Bikita.

Pte Enias NYASALA	R44182	1RAR	DOAS 3 Jul 1972	Died aged 25 of malaria in Bulawayo. Buried in Zvimba.
Pte George MANDIVENGEREYI	R44419	1RAR	KOAS 6 Feb 1973	Killed aged 23 by a gunshot wound, Dande TTL, Sipolilo, Op Hurricane.
Pte George	R44757	1RAR	KOAS 20 Mar 1973	Died of multiple brain lacerations in Sipolilo, Op Hurricane.
Pte Davison HUNYENA	R44904	1RAR	KIA 8 Apr 1973	Died aged 19 from a gunshot wound received in a contact, Mazarabani TTL, Centenary, Op Hurricane.
Pte NHARO	R44846	1RAR	KOAS 9 May 1973	Killed aged 20 by a gunshot wound to the chest, Op Hurricane.
Pte Jere MANASO	R44821	D Coy 1RAR	KIA 24 Jun 1973	Died aged 30 from a gunshot wound received in a contact, Dande TTL, Sipolilo, Op Hurricane.
Cpl Shadreck Misheck CHINYANI	R44156	1RAR	KIA 5 Jul 1973	Died aged 27 from a gunshot wound in a contact in Mozambique. A strap of the radio he was carrying broke while he was crossing a dry river bed. While sorting it out he was shot. Buried in Bulawayo.
Cpl KEMBO	R43731	1RAR	KIA 3 Aug 1973	Died aged 31 from a gunshot wound, Mukumbura, Mount Darwin, Op Hurricane. Buried in Gwanda.
Pte Stephen SEVERINO	R45161	1RAR	KIA 17 Jan 1974	Killed aged 26 in a contact in Centenary, Op Hurricane. Buried in Bulawayo.
Pte Langton	R44535	1RAR	KOAS 3 Mar 1974	Died aged 25 from a cerebral haemorrhage in Mpilo Hospital, Bulawayo. Buried in Kadoma.
L/Cpl John CHOWA	R43210	1RAR	KOAS 21 Mar 1974	Died aged 33 of multiple injuries in Mpilo Hospital, Bulawayo. Buried in Inyanga.
Cpl Henry Rodney ZIRACHA	R43081	1RAR	KOAS 23 Sep 1974	Died aged 36 from severe head injuries sustained in a vehicle accident in Salisbury General Hospital.
Pte John	645313	1RAR	KIA 7 Dec 1974	Killed aged 21 in a contact near Karoi, Op Hurricane. Buried in Bulawayo.
L/Cpl KANGAYI	644157	1RAR	KIA 7 Dec 1974	Killed aged 29 in a contact near Karoi, Op Hurricane. Buried in Bulawayo.
Sgt Manyangire RUNGANO	640353	1RAR	KIA 3 Mar 1975	Died aged 38 in Wankie Hospital from multiple injuries from a landmine explosion.
L/Cpl Poncian MUNEMO	644717	B Coy 1RAR	KIA 2 Apr 1975	Killed aged 22 in a contact in Op Hurricane. 2 Lt Norman Steane, 2 Cdo RLI, was killed in the same contact. L/Cpl Munemo and Pte Zinyemba were part of this very early joint fireforce operation with integrated sticks. All three were killed by a single burst of fire from an RPD. Buried in Hartley.
Pte Saltiel ZINYEMBA	644769	B Coy 1RAR	KIA 2 Apr 1975	Killed aged 21 in a contact in Op Hurricane. 2 Lt Norman Steane, 2 Cdo RLI, was killed in the same contact. L/Cpl Munemo and Pte Zinyemba were part of this very early joint fireforce operation with integrated sticks. All three were killed by a single burst of fire from an RPD. Buried in Gutu.

Pte Celestino BAROPAYI	645270	1RAR	KIA 31 Aug 1975	Killed aged 27 in a contact, Umfurudzi Wildlife Area, Shamva, Op Hurricane.
Cpl Leonard MADZIKA	643553	1RAR	DOAS 8 Sep 1975	Died aged 38 of liver failure at Llewellin Barracks, Bulawayo. Buried in Gutu.
WO2 Sayino Runyowa TSHUMA	640142	1RAR	Murdered 22 Nov 1975	Died aged 37 from gunshot wounds, Mfungo Hills, Nemangwe, Gokwe. He joined 1RAR in 1958, after which his ability and enthusiasm were reflected in his steady promotion through the ranks to his appointment as Platoon Warrant Officer in 1972. From 1973 to 1975 he acted as the Company Sergeant Major of JOC Mtoko. Buried in Gokwe.
Pte Zacharia MUNERI	643811	1RAR	KOAS 13 Dec 1975	Killed aged 33 in a vehicle accident at the Lunga River Bridge on the Essexvale Road. Buried in Zaka.
Pte Amos Sila NCUBE	645250	C Coy 1RAR	KOAS 14 Feb 1976	Killed aged 21 in a vehicle accident on the Umtali-Fort Victoria Road, Bikita, Op Repulse. Buried in Lady Stanley Avenue Cemetery, Bulawayo.
Maj Michael John Forbes AINSLIE	780644	A Coy 1RAR	KIA 27 Mar 1976	Killed aged 28 in a helicopter hit by ground fire whilst commanding a fireforce action, Ngarwe TTL, Mtoko, Op Hurricane. Cremated in Bulawayo.
Pte Masungwa Tobias MVIYO	644546	C Coy 2RAR	KIA 5 May 1976	Killed aged 24 in a contact at Ruda, Honde Valley, Mutasa District, Op Thrasher. As his stick commander stopped to consult his map, the stick came under fire from four enemy positions, and Pte Mviyo was mortally wounded. Buried in Zaka.
Cpl Richard Keni SHAMBANI	644277	1RAR	KIA 6 May 1976	Killed aged 28 in a contact.
Cpl James MAKUWA BCR (Post)	644759	A Coy 1RAR	KIA 9 May 1976	Killed aged 26 in an ambush on his vehicle, when a 60 mm mortar exploded next to him, resulting in massive haemorrhaging, Uzumba, Mrewa, Op Hurricane. His BCR citation states that his success in a fireforce action in April 1976 was attributable to his initiative, personal courage, and leadership qualities. He was due to be promoted to Sgt on 1 Jun 1976.
Pte Dzingarayi MUKONI	646372	1RAR	KIA 13 May 1976	Killed aged 21 in a contact, Mtoko, Op Hurricane.
Pte Michael CHUONDA	644632	1RAR	KOAS 28 May 1976	Killed aged 25 in a vehicle accident on the main Salisbury-Bulawayo road. He was based at the School of Infantry in Gwelo. Buried in Gwelo.
Cpl Alfonse MAKUMBE	645716	1RAR	KOAS 1 Jun 1976	Died aged 19 from head injuries received in a vehicle accident in Gwelo.
Cpl Murira TAVAGURA	644772	C Coy 2RAR	KIA 4 Jun 1976	Died aged 23 in Salisbury Hospital from shrapnel wounds sustained in an ambush at Samutete Store, Op Thrasher
Pte Emmanuel CHAKA	646317	1RAR	KIA 13 Jun 1976	Killed aged 19 in a contact, Op Hurricane.
Pte Charles MAHOGO	646356	2RAR	KOAS 12 Jul 1976	Killed aged 19 by a gunshot wound to the head, Fort Victoria, Op Repulse.

Pte Kumbirayi WUNGANAYI	644817	1RAR	KOAS 26 Sep 1976	Killed aged 24 in Mpilo Hospital, Bulawayo by gunshot wounds to the abdomen, aged 24. Buried in Mazando District.
Pte Julian Chinaka TARUSARIRA	646091	D Coy 2RAR	KOAS 23 Oct 1976	Died in a vehicle accident.
Rct Benjamin CHITIYO	647427	Depot RAR	KOAS 1 Nov 1976	Killed aged 19 by an accidental shooting, Umzingwane area, Op Tangent.
Sgt Constantine Gora MUNANGWA	642671	1RAR	KIA 28 Nov 1976	Killed aged 34 in a contact in Bikita District, Op Repulse. CTs were stopping civilian buses and robbing the occupants. A group of RAR were placed on a 'Q' bus. The 'Q' bus stopped behind another bus that was being robbed. A CT entered the 'Q' bus and was shot. Others outside then raked the 'Q' bus with gunfire. Sgt Munangwa, the commander, was killed, along with L/Cpl Ndaza. Sgt Gora was an outstanding rifle shot. Buried in the Kadoma area.
L/Cpl Tapson Dube NDAZA	644514	1RAR	KIA 28 Nov 1976	Killed aged 27 in a contact in Bikita District, Op Repulse. CTs were stopping civilian buses and robbing the occupants. A group of RAR were placed on a 'Q' bus. The 'Q' bus stopped behind another bus that was being robbed. A CT entered the 'Q' bus and was shot. Others outside then raked the 'Q' bus with gunfire. Sgt Munangwa, the commander, was killed, along with L/Cpl Ndaza. Buried in the Lupane area.
2 Lt Anthony John CARR	V3130	C Coy 2RAR	KIA 17 Dec 1976	Killed aged 25 in a contact, Honde Valley, Op Thrasher. He was a schoolteacher at Vainona High School in Salisbury, and a Hamilton High School old boy.
Pte Dennis (also Kenneth) SIDAMBE	647020	C Coy 2RAR	KIA 17 Dec 1976	Killed aged 16 in a contact, Honde Valley, Op Thrasher. Buried in Bulawayo.
Cpl Peter SHERENI	644678	A Coy 2RAR	KIA 22 Dec 1976	Killed aged 24 in a mortar attack, Matibi TTL, Op Repulse.
Rct Raphael MUCHENJE	647507	Depot RAR	KOAS 25 Dec 1976	Died aged 26 in Binga Hospital from severe injuries he sustained when he fell off a cliff. Recruit Muchenje was part of a deployment from Depot RAR at Balla Balla to the Binga area in response to a CT crossing in the Chete Gorge area. He was deployed by helicopter with three other members to a hilltop radio relay station. He unfortunately went too close to the cliff edge during the night and fell.
Pte Dick TSHABABA	645726	2RAR	KOAS 6 Jan 1977	Killed in a vehicle accident.
Sgt S. Marufu MUCHEMWA	644539	A Coy 2RAR	KOAS 20 Jan 1977	Killed in a vehicle accident en route to Fort Victoria.
Pte Petros SIBANDA	645549	D Coy 1RAR	KOAS 22 Feb 1977	Killed in a shooting accident.

Pte Stanford DUBE	646539	2RAR	KIA 1 Mar 1977	Killed in a contact.
Pte Murove HUMANIKWA	646914	A Coy 1RAR	KOAS 10 Mar 1977	Killed in a vehicle accident.
Lt Gerald William Andrew BELL	V2973	1RAR	KIA 22 Mar 1977	Killed aged 23 in a vehicle ambush in the Zambezi Valley, Op Hurricane. He was returning from a call-up to his job with National Parks when they were ambushed by a group of ZIPRA CTs. A single bullet entered his door-less Land Rover, striking him in the chest. Buried in Masvingo.
Cpl Mashona MASARAKUFA	645522	2RAR	Murdered 24 Mar 1977	Murdered by CTs while on leave.
Cpl Boyina MAGARA	644660	1RAR	KOAS 8 Apr 1977	Killed in a vehicle accident.
Pte Tadios MUCHEKA	645381	2RAR	DOAS 17 Apr 1977	Died of natural causes.
Rct R. MAGOGO		Depot RAR	DOAS 1 May 1977	Died of natural causes.
Pte David TAUYA	644751	2RAR	KOAS 3 May 1977	Killed in a vehicle accident.
Pte Tinarwo MUTEMA	646312	B Coy 2RAR	KOAS 3 May 1977	Killed in a vehicle accident
Cpl Shati JONGWE	643975	1RAR	Murdered 29 May 1977	Murdered by CTs while on leave.
Cpl Mugara Zakaria MHUKA	644517	1RAR	KIA 12 Jun 1977	Killed in a contact.
Pte Stanley NCUBE	647576	1RAR	KIA 12 Jun 1977	Killed in a contact.
Pte Isaac JAKATA	643690	2RAR	KIA 13 Jun 1977	Killed in a contact in the Honde Valley, Op Thrasher.
Pte Michael CHIKOZHO	646432	2RAR	Murdered 24 Jul 1977	Murdered by CTs.
Pte Fibion DZIMBA	646192	2RAR	KOAS 31 Jul 1977	Buried in Balla Balla.
Pte Patrick MANUNURE	646896	2RAR	Murdered 8 Aug 1977	Pte Manunure, together with his older brother from 1RAR, were on R&R when they were taken off their bus and shot by CTs. Their bodies were only found weeks later.
WO2 Tongesayi Callisto MANUNURE	642555	1RAR	Murdered 8 Aug 1977	WO2 Manunure, together with his younger brother from 2RAR, were on R&R when they were taken off their bus and shot by CTs. Their bodies were only found weeks later.
Pte Fanny Kudakwashe RUWANA	644922	1RAR	KIA 8 Aug 1977	Died of wounds received in a contact.
Pte Patrick MLALAZI	648073	Sp Coy 2RAR	KOAS 8 Aug 1977	Killed in a vehicle accident.
Pte Wereki Charles Mafuse KUFAKOWENYU	645951	1RAR	KIA 9 Aug 1977	Killed in an ambush.
Pte Morgan NDHLOVU	647573	B Coy 1RAR	KIA 29 Aug 1977	Killed in a contact near Matetsi in Wankie District Op Tangent. Elements of B Company encountered 20-30 ZIPRA CTs. Pte Ndhlovu was fatally wounded.

Pte Elaja SENGU	648150	2RAR	DOAS 5 Sep 1977	Died of natural causes.
2 Lt Godfrey James Glanville WEBBER	781165	C Coy 1RAR	KIA 7 Sep 1977	Killed in an ambush in the Gwanda area, Op Tangent. 2 Lt Webber and four trackers followed the spoor of CTs for four days after the CTs had abducted a fellow RAR soldier. They entered a village where they were ambushed.
Cpl Jerasi GWAUYA	643839	1RAR	DOAS 26 Sep 1977	Died of natural causes.
Lt Jeremy Lionel FISHER	781005	A Coy 1RAR	KIA 28 Sep 1977	Killed aged 22 in a contact. His patrol had discovered CTs holed up in a cave. After efforts to flush them out had failed, Lt Fisher went in but was shot and killed. He was from Mangula. One of RLI men in the fireforce - L/Cpl Russell Phillips, was awarded the SCR for his action in entering the cave to retrieve Fisher. Phillips refused to wear his SCR ribbon at his investiture and was threatened by his OC with being charged for being incorrectly dressed. Phillips said that he could not wear the ribbon because he believed he did not deserve it as he had failed to save Lt Fisher's life.
L/Cpl Thomas BANGA	646305	2RAR	DOAS 4 Oct 1977	Died of natural causes.
Pte Tarirayi KUREBWA	648005	2RAR	DOAS 14 Oct 1977	Died of natural causes.
Rct L. HLABISO	648526	Depot RAR	KOAS 14 Oct 1977	(Possibly the RAR soldier accidentally shot near Inungu in the Matopos while undergoing integration training with NS soldiers before joining the rebadged RAR independent companies.)
Pte Aaron MUKAPANDA	647516	2RAR	DOAS 5 Nov 1977	Died of natural causes.
L/Cpl Cephas SIBANDA	643896	Att. 2RR	KOAS 6 Nov 1977	
Pte A. MABHENA		2RAR	DOAS 1 Dec 1977	Died of natural causes.
2 Lt Albany Charles BICKLE	V3678	1RAR	KOAS 8 Dec 1977	Killed aged 23 in a vehicle accident on the Bulawayo-Vic Falls road, Op Tangent. Cremated at West Park, Bulawayo.
L/Cpl Toperson MUTARGOZA	646018	A Coy 2RAR	KIA 29 Dec 1977	Killed in an ambush on a stores vehicle and escort TCV by 30 ZANLA in the Mshawasha African Purchase Area just south of Fort Victoria, Op Repulse.
L/Cpl Crispen NGOMANYONI	646067	A Coy 2RAR	KIA 29 Dec 1977	Killed in an ambush on a stores vehicle and escort TCV by 30 ZANLA in the Mshawasha African Purchase Area just south of Fort Victoria, Op Repulse.
Pte Onias ZINYAKATIRI	648169	2RAR	DOAS 15 Jan 1978	Died of natural causes.
Pte Arthur MKANDLA	649421	Att. 8RR	DOAS 6 Feb 1978	Died of natural causes.
Rfn Aleck DE BARRETO	112744	2 (Indep) Coy RAR	DOAS 7 Feb 1978	Died of natural causes

Pte Erisha CHIKEYA	646358	C Coy 1RAR	KIA 19 Feb 1978	Killed in a contact.
Pte Clemence NYENYE	650729	Att. B Coy 1RR	KIA 20 Feb 1978	Killed in a contact.
Pte Isaac DOMBO	651008	Att. 1RR	DOAS 26 Feb 1978	Died of natural causes
Pte Langton MATAMBO	660025	Att. D Coy 1RR	DOAS 1 Mar 1978	Died of natural causes.
Cpl Rashikayi CHIMBIDZUKAYI	643492	C Coy 1RAR	KIA 3 Mar 1978	Killed in a contact.
Cpl Robert Hugh CERFF	106161	3 (Indep) Coy RAR	KIA 18 Mar 1978	Killed in a contact near Nyamaropa, Op Thrasher. Operating from the old Police Camp, a stick of four, a stick of four encountered a very large group of CTs. In the ensuing contact, and in spite of Cpl Cerff's pleas for help over the radio, the stick was overrun and only the MAG gunner, having run out of ammunition, managed to escape, returning to base a couple of days later.
Pte Elson MAKONDE	648811	3 (Indep) Coy RAR	KIA 8 Mar 1978	Killed in a contact near Nyamaropa, Op Thrasher. Operating from the old Police Camp, a stick of four, a stick of four encountered a very large group of CTs. In the ensuing contact, and in spite of Cpl Cerff's pleas for help over the radio, the stick was overrun and only the MAG gunner, having run out of ammunition, managed to escape, returning to base a couple of days later.
Pte Jacob NKOMO	649246	3 (Indep) Coy RAR	KIA 8 Mar 1978	Killed in a contact near Nyamaropa, Op Thrasher. Operating from the old Police Camp, a stick of four, a stick of four encountered a very large group of CTs. In the ensuing contact, and in spite of Cpl Cerff's pleas for help over the radio, the stick was overrun and only the MAG gunner, having run out of ammunition, managed to escape, returning to base a couple of days later.
Pte M. NYANGANI	651152	Att. 6RR	DOAS 22 Mar 1978	Died of natural causes.
Pte Royal MPOFU	647122	C Coy 1RAR	KIA 25 Mar 1978	Killed in a contact.
Pte Cephas MTANDWA	651418	Att. C Coy 9RR	KIA 28 Mar 1978	Killed about 40 minutes flying time south of Shabani and to the west of Buchwa Mine, Op Repulse. Elements of C Coy 9RR on protection duty at a nearby mine were called to assist with a 3 Cdo RLI fireforce action. Contact was made with 8 ZIPRA CTs. 4 were killed and 2 captured. 3 TF members of 9RR were also killed: Cpl Leonidas Andriolakis, Rfn John Rodney Hancock, and Rfn Ugo Boschin. Cpl Andriolakis was posthumously awarded the BCR.
Pte G. CHIRAMBA	650775	Depot RAR	KOAS Apr 1978	

Sgt Owen GUMBO	644835	B Coy 1RAR	KOAS 3 Apr 1978	Died in an accident near Wankie. Sgt Gumbo had been marching all night in the Lupane District, taking his men into a stop position of an HDF. When the operation wound up, they RV'd with the transport. Sgt Gumbo, sitting at the back of the TCV, nodded off and fell out of the back, only to be driven over by the following vehicle. Buried in Lady Stanley Avenue Cemetery, Bulawayo.
Pte Emmanuel MANDEYA	650974	Att. 8RR	KOAS 3 Apr 1978	Pte Mandeya had stepped out during the night to relieve himself without properly notifying the guard and on his return he was mistaken for enemy.
Pte Joseph NTINDINDI	650061	6 (Indep) Coy RAR	KIA 5 Apr 1978	Killed in a contact.
Pte Boniface TUZAYI	648153	2RAR	DOAS 8 Apr 1978	Died of natural causes.
Pte Aleck NKIWANE	651444	Att. A Coy 4RR	KOAS 9 Apr 1978	Died aged 17.
Sgt Kevin Howard BICKNELL	113536	1 (Indep) Coy RAR	KOAS 10 Apr 1978	Killed in a shooting incident at the Essexvale Battle Camp, Op Tangent. Upon returning from R&R, twenty members of 1 (Indep) Coy RAR had drawn rifles and live ammunition. They assembled to strip their weapons for cleaning. Once the group had disassembled their FNs, Private Robert Nyamini Mapfumo suddenly cocked his rifle and opened fire on automatic at his fellow soldiers. As Mapfumo's magazine emptied, and before he could replace it with a fully charged one, Privates Mawonda and Zevezene overpowered and disarmed Mapfumo. Four were killed and four were seriously wounded. In spite of claiming insanity, Mapfumo was found guilty of murder and sentenced to death.
L/Cpl Stephen William RANDALL	114232	1 (Indep) Coy RAR	KOAS 10 Apr 1978	Killed in a shooting incident at the Essexvale Battle Camp, Op Tangent. Upon returning from R&R, twenty members of 1 (Indep) Coy RAR had drawn rifles and live ammunition. They assembled to strip their weapons for cleaning. Once the group had disassembled their FNs, Private Robert Nyamini Mapfumo suddenly cocked his rifle and opened fire on automatic at his fellow soldiers. As Mapfumo's magazine emptied, and before he could replace it with a fully charged one, Privates Mawonda and Zevezene overpowered and disarmed Mapfumo. Four were killed and four were seriously wounded. In spite of claiming insanity, Mapfumo was found guilty of murder and sentenced to death.

Pte Johani **TSHUMA**	649222	1 (Indep) Coy RAR	KOAS 10 Apr 1978	Killed in a shooting incident at the Essexvale Battle Camp, Op Tangent. Upon returning from R&R, twenty members of 1 (Indep) Coy RAR had drawn rifles and live ammunition. They assembled to strip their weapons for cleaning. Once the group had disassembled their FNs, Private Robert Nyamini Mapfumo suddenly cocked his rifle and opened fire on automatic at his fellow soldiers. As Mapfumo's magazine emptied, and before he could replace it with a fully charged one, Privates Mawonda and Zevezene overpowered and disarmed Mapfumo. Four were killed and four were seriously wounded. In spite of claiming insanity, Mapfumo was found guilty of murder and sentenced to death.
L/Cpl Michael Anthony **WALL**	118425	1 (Indep) Coy RAR	KOAS 10 Apr 1978	Killed in a shooting incident at the Essexvale Battle Camp, Op Tangent. Upon returning from R&R, twenty members of 1 (Indep) Coy RAR had drawn rifles and live ammunition. They assembled to strip their weapons for cleaning. Once the group had disassembled their FNs, Private Robert Nyamini Mapfumo suddenly cocked his rifle and opened fire on automatic at his fellow soldiers. As Mapfumo's magazine emptied, and before he could replace it with a fully charged one, Privates Mawonda and Zevezene overpowered and disarmed Mapfumo. Four were killed and four were seriously wounded. In spite of claiming insanity, Mapfumo was found guilty of murder and sentenced to death.
Pte Rabson **RWAWUYA**	649541	Att. 8RR	KIA 10 Apr 1978	Killed in a contact.
L/Cpl Francis **MARHOVA**	645997	A Coy 2RAR	KIA 12 Apr 1978	Died while being casevaced in a helicopter from a contact north of Mrewa, Op Hurricane, having been shot in the head, chest and leg by two ZANLA. He succeeded in killing a CT before he died.
Pte Aleck **MAJONI**	650724	Att. B Coy 4RR	KIA 17 Apr 1978	Killed in a contact.
L/Cpl Jacob **GWAFA**	645297	C Coy 1RAR	KOAS 19 Apr 1978	Drowned. Buried in Lady Stanley Avenue Cemetery, Bulawayo.
Pte Elias **JONGWE**	650514	Att. A Coy 2RR	KOAS 19 Apr 1978	Killed in an accidental contact with another army unit. Pte Calvin Dube was involved in this incident. He lost a leg, and others were severely wounded in the contact.
Pte Nicholas **NAGO**	650665	Att. A Coy 2RR	KOAS 19 Apr 1978	Killed in an accidental contact with another army unit. Pte Calvin Dube was involved in this incident. He lost a leg, and others were severely wounded in the contact.

Pte John ZVUKUVENDA	650610	Att. A Coy 2RR	KOAS 19 Apr 1978	Killed in an accidental contact with another army unit. Pte Calvin Dube was involved in this incident. He lost a leg, and others were severely wounded in the contact.
Pte John TARWIREYI	650873	Att. 4RR	Murdered 20 Apr 1978	Murdered by CTs.
Pte Godfrey CHIBAMBA		Att. B Coy 1RR	KIA 27 Apr 1978	Killed in a contact.
Rfn Godfrey Kenneth HUSSEY	110016	4 (Indep) Coy RAR	KOAS 27 Apr 1978	Killed in a vehicle accident near Milibizi, Op Tangent.
Pte A. MAKUTUKIRA	661425	Depot RAR	DOAS 9 May 1978	Died of natural causes.
Pte Lovemore MAPFUMO	660123	Att. D Coy 9RR	DOAS 10 May 1978	Died of natural causes.
Pte Jenamiso KHUPE	648897	5 (Indep) Coy RAR	KIA 12 May 1978	Killed aged 24 in a contact. Buried in Lady Stanley Avenue Cemetery, Bulawayo.
Pte Phinias M. RUTUNGA	648580	5 (Indep) Coy RAR	DOAS 13 May 1978	Died of natural causes.
Pte Cephas MPOFU	660222	Att. 2RR	KIA 20 May 1978	Killed by a landmine. Buried in the Lady Stanley Avenue Cemetery, Bulawayo.
Cpl Anthony Charles CARROLL	114666	3 (Indep) Coy RAR	KIA 4 Jun 1978	Killed in a vehicle ambush. Cpl Carroll and Sgt Kelly were sitting back to back on a 2.5 when they were hit with an RPG7. Russell Lieberman of SB was also killed.
Sgt Michael David KELLY	81145	3 (Indep) Coy RAR	KIA 4 Jun 1978	Killed in a vehicle ambush. Cpl Carroll and Sgt Kelly were sitting back to back on a 2.5 when they were hit with an RPG7. Russell Lieberman of SB was also killed.
Pte Augustine MAPFUMO	649991	1RAR	Murdered 4 Jun 1978	Murdered by CTs. Buried in the Lady Stanley Avenue Cemetery, Bulawayo.
Pte Robert TICHAZVIGADZIRA	660577	Att. 4RR	KOAS 4 Jun 1978	Killed by friendly fire. A mix-up in navigation resulted in two sticks opening fire on each other. Rfn David de Courpalay was also killed in the same incident.
Pte S. SIBANDA	660531	8RR	KOAS 12 Jun 1978	Killed in an accidental shooting.
Pte Benedict NYONI	649269	Att, C Coy 1RR	KIA 13 Jun 1978	Killed in a contact.
Pte Cossum NDLOVU	651128	Att. D Coy 2RR	KIA 23 Jun 1978	Killed in a contact.
Pte Macdonald PHIRI	660602	Att. 4RR	KIA 26 Jun 1978	Killed in a contact.
Pte Leonard MPOFU	649979	A Coy 2RAR	KIA 27 Jun 1978	Killed by a single round from an SKS rifle in a contact on Devuli Ranch, Op Repulse. Pte D. Njovo, an MAG gunner, was badly wounded, and 2 Lt Bruce Thompson was killed in the same incident.
2 Lt Bruce Malcolm THOMPSON (SCR (Post)	781139	A Coy 2RAR	KIA 27 Jun 1978	Killed in a contact on Devuli Ranch, Op Repulse. His SCR citation states that he was involved in 35 contacts in which 170 CTs were killed. In a contact on 27 June 1978, under heavy fire, he went to the rescue of his wounded machine gunner. He accounted for 2 CTs, but in the follow-up he was fatally shot.

Pte Peter NDLOVU	650639	Att. B Coy 4RR	KIA 12 Jul 1978	Killed in a contact. Buried in Lady Stanley Avenue Cemetery, Bulawayo.
Pte Johanne PHIRI	647601	D Coy 1RAR	KOAS 27 Jul 1978	Killed in a parachute training accident. He failed to jump out of the Dakota door correctly. The parachute static line wrapped around the butt of his MAG, and this caused the static line to break which then failed to deploy the parachute. Pte Phiri's reserve parachute then also failed to deploy properly.
Pte Oliver RANGARIRAYI	650650	Att. A Coy 5RR	KIA 27 Jul 1978	Killed in a contact near Sipolilo, Op Hurricane.
Pte P.C. MUREFU	651488	Att. 5RR	DOAS 28 Jul 1978	Died of natural causes.
Pte Denny MADZIVIRIDZO	661615	2RAR	DOAS 30 Jul 1978	Died of natural causes.
Pte Felix TICHAONA		Att. D Coy 2RR	DOAS 1 Aug 1978	Died of natural causes.
Cpl Isaac NGULUBE	646059	A Coy 2RAR	KIA 5 Aug 1978	Killed in an ambush, Matibi 2 TTL, Op Repulse.
Cpl Victor Carl MEYER	98858	1 (Indep) Coy RAR	KOAS 12 Aug 1978	Drowned in the Zambezi River, Op Tangent. Cpl Meyer's stick was ordered to OP an arms cache on an island downstream from Victoria Falls but, after several days of inactivity his 2 Lt decided they should swim to the island for an inspection. Cpl Meyer made it to the island only to realise his officer was in difficulty and returned to the water to save the officer's life - which he did, but lost his own in the process. His body was never found.
Pte Maxwell MATAVIRE	647515	C Coy 2RAR	KIA 17 Aug 1978	Killed in a contact, Matibi 2 TTL, Op Repulse.
Pte Christopher TAZVIVINGA		Att. D Coy 9RR	DOAS 22 Aug 1978	Died of natural causes.
L/Cpl Peter Hendrick J. FAIRBANKS	110590	5 (Indep) Coy RAR	KIA 2 Sep 1978	Killed in a contact in Chipinga District, Op Thrasher.
Pte Eriazere BHERE	646343	C Coy 2RAR	KIA 8 Sep 1978	Killed in a contact, Sengwe TTL, Op Repulse.
Pte Maphios KWAYARIRA	660408	C Coy 2RAR	KIA 8 Sep 1978	Killed in a contact, Sengwe TTL, Op Repulse.
Pte Clever NYATHI	660254	C Coy 2RAR	KIA 9 Sep 1978	Died aged 20 of wounds received the previous day in a contact in the Sengwe TTL, Op Repulse.
Pte Cladious CHIRAU	660903	A Coy 2RAR	KOAS 10 Sep 1978	Killed in a vehicle accident at Fort Victoria, Op Repulse.
Pte Abednico NGWENYA	648114	Sp Coy 2RAR	KOAS 10 Sep 1978	Believed to have been killed in the same vehicle accident as Pte Chirau at Fort Victoria, Op Repulse.
Pte Frederick NYAMAYABO	646316	Sp Coy 1RAR	KOAS 16 Sep 1978	Killed by a badly aimed frantan canister dropped on the OP of which he was a part.
Cpl Alan John GRANDLUND	118328	2 (Indep) Coy RAR	KOAS 17 Sep 1978	Killed in a vehicle accident. He was the Coy Medic.

Pte Isaac Ronny NEMANWA	646066	Sp Coy 1RAR	KOAS 18 Sep 1978	Died of injuries sustained in the frantan strike which killed Pte Nyamayabo two days previously. WO2 Francis Charamba was awarded an MFC (Ops) for his efforts to try and save Pte Nemanwa.
L/Cpl F. ZIMUNYA	663849	4 (Indep) Coy RAR	DOAS 8 Oct 1978	Died of natural causes.
Pte Christopher NKALA	646995	D Coy 1RAR	KOAS 11 Oct 1978	Died from injuries received in a parachute drop near Shamva, Op Hurricane on 9 Oct 1978. The soldiers were dropped from only 168ft above a rising ground level. This error was caused by the second pilot setting the wrong QFE to the altimeter when flying in for the drop. Operational static line drops were usually from 500ft above ground level. Of the stick of 16, two men both broke legs and one died.
Pte Shandare GANDANGA	648478	D Coy 1RAR	KOAS 12 Oct 1978	Died after falling from a helicopter, Mangwende TTL, Op Hurricane. A rifle magazine slipped from his hand, and as he tried to grab it he lost balance and fell out. Buried in the Lady Stanley Avenue Cemetery, Bulawayo.
Rfn Edward James HARTLEY	124628	6 (Indep) Coy RAR	KIA 12 Oct 1978	Killed in a contact in Op Thrasher.
Sgt Mudzingwa MWENEZIKO	644740	2RAR	KIA 25 Oct 1978	Killed in a contact.
Pte Reason NCUBE	650996	Att, C Coy 4RR	KIA 12 Nov 1978	Killed in a contact.
Pte Rabson TAKARUVINGA	648732	Att. 4RR	KIA 12 Nov 1978	Killed in a contact.
Capt James William HARDY (MFC (Ops))	781083	Sp Coy 1RAR	KIA 14 Nov 1978	Killed in the Mtoko area, Op Hurricane. During a sweep through a dry river bed in search of a group of 40-50 CTs, Capt Hardy was shot in the head and killed. It would have been his last day with the battalion as 2 i/c Sp Coy 1RAR before being posted to Army HQ. He had asked to join Lt Pat Lawless's stick for "one last fling" with Sp Coy. He was an Australian who had served in Vietnam with 1 Royal Australian Regiment. He was awarded the MFC (Ops) three days before he died.
Pte Nabot MAGEDE	661566	Att. 8RR	KIA 18 Nov 1978	Killed in a contact.
Pte Richard EREKANI	660853	2RAR	KOAS 20 Nov 1978	Killed in a shooting accident.
Pte Clever CHINGOZA	651003	Att. 4RR	KOAS 20 Nov 1978	Killed in a vehicle accident.
L/Cpl Timothy Joseph MURDOCK	118553	3 (Indep) Coy RAR	KIA 28 Nov 1978	Killed in an ambush, Inyanga, Op Thrasher. A truck escorting sticks back from Nyamaropa was hit by a landmine, followed by an ambush. L/Cpl Murdock was the MAG gunner. He stood up to clear a jam in the gun and was shot.
Pte Samuel CHILENJE	662021	1 (Indep) Coy RAR	KOAS 29 Nov 1978	Killed aged 17 in a vehicle accident as the Company was going on R&R. Buried in Athlone Cemetery, Bulawayo.

Pte A. **NYONI**	649326	1 (Indep) Coy RAR	KOAS 29 Nov 1978	Killed aged 28 in a vehicle accident as the Company was going on R&R. Buried in Lady Stanley Avenue Cemetery, Bulawayo.
Pte Basilio **TONGAYI**	646355	1RAR	KOAS 2 Dec 1978	Killed in a vehicle accident. Buried in Lady Stanley Avenue Cemetery, Bulawayo.
Pte Levy **MUJERE**	647540	2RAR	KIA 7 Dec 1978	Killed in a contact.
Rfn Johannes Cornelius **VAN HESS**	121553	2 (Indep) Coy RAR	DOAS 7 Dec 1978	
L/Cpl Gwaze **MARUFU**	654735	1RAR	DOAS 27 Dec 1978	
Pte Samuel **KHOLA**	660573	Att. D Coy 4RR	KIA 22 Dec 1978	Killed in a contact.
L/Cpl Clements **MUKARO**	659054	Att. 1RR	KIA 24 Dec 1978	Killed in a contact.
Pte Lovemore **TOTOHWIYO**	660798	2RAR	KOAS 29 Dec 1978	
Pte Baron **GUMBO**	650669	Att. B Coy 4RR	KIA 4 Jan 1979	Killed aged 20 in a contact. Buried in Lady Stanley Avenue Cemetery, Bulawayo.
Pte Jetro **CHIPO**	649229	2 (Indep) Coy RAR	DOAS 12 Jan 1979	
L/Cpl Bethrod **ZHONJA**	647794	Att. 1RR	Murdered 17 Jan 1979	Murdered by CTs while off duty.
Pte Gifyniso Peter **MATHE**	650820	Att. 5RR	KIA 19 Jan 1979	Killed in a contact.
Sgt Thomas **SHERENI**	644939	1RAR	KIA 19 Jan 1979	Killed aged 24 in a contact. Buried in Lady Stanley Avenue Cemetery Bulawayo. From Zaka.
Pte Tamba **CHIVISI**	649194	2 (Indep) Coy RAR	KIA 21 Jan 1979	Killed in a contact near Karoi, Op Hurricane.
Pte Marko **WHAMI**	646099	2RAR	Murdered 21 Jan 1979	Murdered by CTs while off duty.
Pte Mastaff **MUTANGA**	649775	2 (Indep) Coy RAR	KIA 23 Jan 1979	Died of wounds received in a contact near Karoi, Op Hurricane. He was casevaced to Kariba where he subsequently died.
Pte Tobias **KUTINYU**	650629	Att. 4RR	KIA 27 Jan 1979	Killed by a landmine.
Rct Thembikile Bubi **SHABANI**	662465	Depot RAR	KIA 11 Feb 1979	Killed in a contact. It was their last deployment and two weeks before Passing Out Parade. Confronted by a large number of CTs he had to stand up in a maize field and shot 8-10 before he was shot himself. He was MAG gunner in his section.
Pte Obert **MBAMBO**	651250	Att. 4RR	KOAS 16 Feb 1979	Killed aged 24. Buried in the Lady Stanley Cemetery, Bulawayo.
Pte Pondai **CHINDUMA**	649372	3 (Indep) Coy RAR	KIA 19 Feb 1979	Killed in a contact near Avila Mission, in the Ruwangwe area north of Inyanga, Op Thrasher.
Rfn Desmond Kenneth **WASHINGTON**	123353	3 (Indep) Coy RAR	KIA 19 Feb 1979	Killed in a contact near Avila Mission, in the Ruwangwe area north of Inyanga, Op Thrasher.

Sgt George Mathias MLEYA	644704	A Coy 1RAR	KOAS 21 Feb 1979	Killed when he fell from a moving vehicle. Buried in Lady Stanley Avenue Cemetery, Bulawayo.
Pte Matanda NCUBE	660415	Att. B Coy 10RR	KIA 22 Feb 1979	Killed in a contact.
Pte F.A. SARAOGA	660406	Att. B Coy 10RR	KIA 22 Feb 1979	Killed in a contact.
Pte Ruben MUZINGI	647532	2RAR	KIA 27 Feb 1979	Killed in a contact.
Pte Munikwi MUKANDATSAMA	645534	C Coy 2RAR	KIA 28 Feb 1979	Killed in a vehicle ambush between Zaka and Fort Victoria, in Ndanga TTL, Op Repulse. Pte Runodada, killed in the same ambush, was driving the lead vehicle in a three-vehicle ration-run convoy, which came under fire from a group of CTs, later estimated to number about 70.
Pte Chibomba RUNODADA	644239	C Coy 2RAR	KIA 28 Feb 1979	Killed in a vehicle ambush between Zaka and Fort Victoria, in Ndanga TTL, Op Repulse. Pte Runodada was driving the lead vehicle in a three-vehicle ration-run convoy, which came under fire from a group of CTs, later estimated to number about 70. Private Mukandatsama was killed in the same ambush.
Pte Charles SIZIBA	651215	Att. C Coy 4RR	KIA 1 Mar 1979	Killed in a contact.
Cpl Jeche TARUPUWA	649536	Att. 8RR	KIA 5 Mar 1979	Killed in a contact.
Pte Enoch MARAVANYIKA	650969	Att. 4RR	KIA 6 Mar 1979	Killed in a contact.
Pte Kevin MUCHORE	649175	2 (Indep) Coy RAR	KOAS 9 Mar 1979	Pte Muchore had stepped out during the night to relieve himself without properly notifying the guard and on his return he was mistaken for enemy.
Pte Tamusanga Clever MOYO	660414	A Coy 2RAR	KIA 9 Mar 1979	A callsign was attacked in Berejena TTL, Op Repulse with 82mm mortars. Around 20 bombs were fired. Pte Moyo sustained heavy injuries to his head, and died in the helicopter on the way to hospital. Pte Sibanda was killed in the same incident.
Pte Notice Nickson SIBANDA	661746	A Coy 2RAR	KIA 9 Mar 1979	A callsign was attacked in Berejena TTL, Op Repulse with 82mm mortars. Around 20 bombs were fired. Pte Sibanda was killed by a direct hit. Pte Moyo died of wounds from the same incident.
Pte Maxwell E. MUSINDO	648028	B Coy 2RAR	KIA 10 Mar 1979	Died of a fatal gunshot wound to the abdomen during an attack on a CT camp in Maranda TTL, OP Repulse.
L/Cpl Honda Rujada MARWISHA	645734	2RAR	DOAS 16 Mar 1979	
Pte Freddy MARUFU	648036	2RAR	KOAS 19 Mar 1979	Killed in a vehicle accident.
Sgt John Zindoga HAMANDISHE	644775	B Coy 1RAR	KIA 31 Mar 1979	Killed in a contact in Urungwe TTL, near Karoi, Op Hurricane. Sgt Hamandishe was leading a patrol when suddenly he bumped into soldiers wearing army camouflage. In that second or two when he shouted to see if they were "friendlies" he was shot and

				killed. An investigation uncovered that a private shop had sold the CTs the uniforms, purchased on the black market. He was due to start officer training.
Pte Christopher MANYIKA	663508	2RAR	KIA 2 Apr 1979	Killed in a contact.
Pte Zenzo NDLOVU	660078	Att. 8RR	KIA 2 Apr 1979	Killed in a contact.
Pte Obert Tapson	650515	Att. D Coy 10RR	KIA 6 Apr 1979	Killed in a contact.
Pte Emerson HUNGWE	647997	D Coy 2RAR	KIA 8 Apr 1979	Killed by an RPG7 in a vehicle ambush.
Pte Chitanda MATEBWE	645267	C Coy 1RAR	KIA 8 Apr 1979	Killed in a contact.
Pte Patrick NCUBE	661155	C Coy 1RAR	KIA 9 Apr 1979	Killed in a contact.
Cpl Rodwell MOYO	646048	A Coy 2RAR	KIA 10 Apr 1979	Died of wounds sustained while the helicopter he was flying in orbited on a fireforce call-out in Berejena TTL, Op Repulse. Delays at Fort Victoria hospital and the airport meant he couldn't be treated in time to save his life, and he died on the flight to Salisbury.
Pte Hughes NGANDU	660578	Att. 4RR	KIA 14 Apr 1979	Killed in a contact.
Pte Robert SIBANDA	651106	Att. C Coy 10RR	KIA 16 Apr 1979	Killed aged 23 in a contact. Buried in Athlone Cemetery, Bulawayo.
Pte G. WUTETE	662106	Att. 10RR	KIA 16 Apr 1979	Killed in a contact.
Pte Watch DUMAI	647816	1RAR	KIA 21 Apr 1979	Killed in a contact.
Pte Silindile GWENEZI	662754	1RAR	KOAS 14 May 1979	Killed in an accidental shooting.
L/Cpl Gift MUNYORWA	647478	D Coy 2RAR	KIA 17 May 1979	Killed in a contact.
Maj Andre DENNISON MLM, BCR, (MFC (Ops))	781030	A Coy 2RAR	KOAS 3 Jun 1979	Killed by friendly fire. Maj Dennison and others were in the pub of the Zimbabwe Ruins Hotel when it came under CT attack. He reacted with two others from 2RAR and two from the BSAP. One of the policemen heard a noise on front of him and opened fire, hitting Dennison. He was awarded the BCR as a result of his actions in a contact in October 1978. Despite having a shattered femur and bleeding heavily, he refused to be casevaced and continued to direct the fight. His bravery and dedication was far beyond the normal call of duty. His MFC (Ops) was awarded for dragging a wounded soldier, under heavy fire, out of a cave where a CT had established himself.
Rct Raphael S. SIBANDA	662177	Depot RAR	DOAS 8 Jun 1979	Died aged 17. Buried in Lady Stanley Avenue Cemetery, Bulawayo.
L/Cpl Andreas MAMBUNE	655901	1RAR	KOAS 11 Jun 1979	Killed in a vehicle accident.

Pte Fibion SIBANDA	645730	1RAR	KOAS 11 Jun 1979	Killed in a vehicle accident.
Pte Simon CHISORA	661442	1RAR	KIA 12 Jun 1979	Killed in a contact.
L/Cpl Raphael MATHE	645552	1RAR	KOAS 14 Jun 1979	Killed in a vehicle accident in Urungwe TTL, north of Karoi, Op Hurricane.
L/Cpl Samuel MUTENGANI	646163	1RAR	KIA 14 Jun 1979	Died of wounds received in a contact on 12 June. He was casevaced to Mangula, Op Hurricane where he died two days later.
Sgt Pieter Jacobus Stephanus NEL	119582	6 (Indep) Coy RAR	KOAS 16 Jun 1979	Killed aged 21 while trying to disarm an RPG rocket, Inyanga. The rocket was to be kept for a souvenir, but it exploded and killed him instantly.
L/Cpl Richard MAWORERA	645554	B Coy 1RAR	KIA 28 Jun 1979	Killed in a contact in Urungwe TTL, Op Hurricane. L/Cpl Mawowera was in B Coy. He was on patrol when he was shot in the chest during a contact. Unfortunately there were no helicopters in the area to casevac him out and he succumbed to his wound before he could be casevaced by road. The relief vehicles were themselves ambushed as they returned, a soldier being badly wounded in the legs.
Pte Patrick TSIKUYADZI	651360	Att. A Coy 5RR	KIA 30 Jun 1979	Killed in a contact.
WO2 John MATAGA	644475	1RAR	DOAS 6 Jul 1979	Died of natural causes.
Cpl John MARUFU	645300	2RAR	Missing 9 Jul 1979	Pronounced dead in terms of the Missing Persons Act.
Pte Claude Herbert SANDERS	600469	1RAR	DOAS 10 Jul 1979	Died of natural causes.
Pte T. CHAKA		2RAR	DOAS 3 Aug 1979	
Pte Musikwa RUBVA	662147	D Coy 1RAR	KIA 3 Aug 1979	Killed in a landmine explosion
Pte Isaac CHIRWA	660774	D Coy 2RAR	KIA 6 Aug 1979	Killed in a contact in the Rutenga area, Op Repulse. He died instantly when fired on from close range by a hidden CT, who was himself killed shortly afterwards.
Pte Dennis GOVO	665337	Depot RAR	KOAS 7 Sep 1979	Died of gunshot wounds.
Pte Ignatius MAPURANGA (also NCUBE)	650899	Att. 8RR	KIA 9 Sep 1979	Killed in an ambush near St Triashill Mission, Zimbiti TTL, Inyanga District, Op Thrasher.
Pte Freddy MPOFU	660434	Att. B Coy 8RR	KOAS 1 Oct 1979	Killed in a collision with a train. Buried in the Bulawayo Cemetery.
Pte Robert PASINA	649610	1 (Indep) Coy RAR	KIA 3 Oct 1979	Killed in a contact.
L/Cpl Pineal MUTASA	645043	Sp Coy 1RAR	Murdered 15 Oct 1979	Murdered by CTs. L/Cpl Mutasa was in a taxi outside the Zimbabwe Ruins Hotel when a CT fired a rifle grenade into it.
Pte George KHANYE	648867	2 (Indep) Coy RAR	KOAS 22 Oct 1979	Killed in a vehicle accident.
Pte Stone SHADRECK	650333	Att. A Coy 9RR	KOAS 29 Oct 1979	Died from head injuries.

Pte Michael KANJANI	661417	A Coy 2RAR	KIA 12 Nov 1979	Killed in a contact.
L/Cpl Peter MAGONDA	648069	2RAR	KIA 22 Nov 1979	Killed in a contact.
L/Cpl Gideon MUVANGANI	660236	Att. C Coy 2RR	KIA 22 Nov 1979	Killed in a contact.
Pte Simon SITHOLE	649849	Att. 8RR	KIA 22 Nov 1979	Killed in a contact.
Pte L. URAYAYI	660221	Att. 2RR	KIA 23 Nov 1979	Killed in a contact.
L/Cpl Jerifanosi CHAPUTIKA	645914	2RAR	DOAS 26 Nov 1979	
Pte Balenkani CHITSOVI	663508	Att. 8RR	DOAS 27 Nov 1979	
Rfn Grant Stewart MATTHEWS	107475	1 (Indep) Coy RAR	KIA 8 Dec 1979	Killed in a contact at Fort Victoria, Op Repulse.
Pte Phineas MPOFU	649609	1 (Indep) Coy RAR	KIA 8 Dec 1979	Killed in a contact at Fort Victoria, Op Repulse.
Pte Killian MUTAMBURI	661448	Sp Coy 2RAR	KIA 9 Dec 1979	Killed in a contact.
Pte Peter CHIONESO	662343	2RAR	KIA 22 Dec 1979	Killed in a contact.
Pte Felix GOKO	647457	2RAR	KIA 22 Dec 1979	Killed by shrapnel in a contact. L/Cpl Moyo and Pte Goko were both killed when led by their lieutenant whist on spoor. He led his men, despite warnings to the contrary, across a wide area of open ground towards a small, rocky outcrop. The CTs ambushed them when they were exposed.
Pte John KULARA	661820	Att. 4RR	KIA 22 Dec 1979	Killed in a vehicle ambush.
L/Cpl Canaan MOYO	647489	2RAR	KIA 22 Dec 1979	Killed by shrapnel in a contact. L/Cpl Moyo and Pte Goko were both killed when led by their lieutenant whist on spoor. He led his men, despite warnings to the contrary, across a wide area of open ground towards a small, rocky outcrop. The CTs ambushed them when they were exposed.
Pte John Timothy	660470	Att. 1RR	KOAS 22 Dec 1979	Killed in a vehicle accident.
Pte Michael MLALAZI	660368	Att. 1RR	KOAS 23 Dec 1979	Killed in a vehicle accident.
Pte Stephen ZAWAIRA	660202	Att. 9RR	DOAS 24 Dec 1979	Died of cancer.
2 Lt Andrew Jameson DU TOIT	V5047	3 (Indep) Coy RAR	KIA 27 Dec 1979	Killed in a contact in the Inyanga area, Op Thrasher. Various sticks had been deployed in the commercial wattle plantations in the area. 2 Lt du Toit's stick had gone into a plantation workers' compound when they came under mortar and small arms fire from the nearby forest. As 2 Lt du Toit was running across the edge of the forest in a clearing that carried electricity pylons, he was fatally wounded. He died during the helicopter casevac flight to hospital.

Pte Rams MOYO	651183	Att. 10RR	KOAS 8 Jan 1980	Killed aged 31 from a gunshot wound. Buried in Lady Stanley Avenue Cemetery, Bulawayo.
Pte Norbert MUSHONGA	665035	Att. D Coy 2RR	KOAS 15 Jan 1980	Died of injuries received in a vehicle accident.
Pte L. RAMARU	662600	2RAR	DOAS 15 Jan 1980	
Pte Boniface MAKONI	662205	2RAR	DOAS 6 Feb 1980	Died of a subdural haemorrhage.
Pte Martin MTINSI	650615	Att. 2RR	KOAS 7 Feb 1980	Killed by a gunshot wound.
Cpl Morgan MOYO	647319	4 (HU) RAR	KOAS 14 Feb 1980	Killed aged 27 by an accidental explosion whilst on internal ops, Salisbury, Op Salops when an explosive device in their car detonated. The official record shows him as being a member of 4 (HU) RAR when he died, although the Selous Scouts only changed their name to 4 (HU) RAR more than two months later, on 23 Apr 1980.
Lt Edward Ngwarayi PIRINGONDO SCR	781302	4 (HU) RAR	KOAS 14 Feb 1980	Killed aged 27 by an accidental explosion whilst on internal ops, Salisbury, Op Salops when an explosive device in their car detonated. Lt Piringondo received his SCR before being commissioned. His citation states that he displayed initiative and bravery of the highest order. He personally accounted for 14 CT kills and 8 captures, including high ranking commanders. He was also recommended for the highest award, the Grand Cross of Valour. The official record shows him as being a member of 4 (HU) RAR when he died, although the Selous Scouts only changed their name to 4 (HU) RAR more than two months later, on 23 Apr 1980.
Cpl Cletos CHOTO	647410	2RAR	DOAS 25 Feb 1980	Died of asphyxia.
Pte W. NDHLOVU	660314	Att. 5RR	KOAS 6 Mar 1980	Killed in an accidental shooting.
Pte T. SIBANDA	649901	3RAR	DOAS 14 Mar 1980	Killed by a gunshot wound.
Pte Same CHIPONDERA	662673	3RAR	KOAS 19 Mar 1980	Killed in a vehicle accident.
Pte B. DHANO	651450	Att. 8RR	KOAS 5 May 1980	Killed in a vehicle accident.
Pte M. HLIWAYO	663454	Att. 8RR	KOAS 5 May 1980	Killed in a vehicle accident.
L/Cpl MATIGIMA	663489	Att. 8RR	KOAS 16 May 1980	Killed in a vehicle accident.
Pte E. CHAWAPIWA	665300	2RAR	KOAS 21 May 1980	Killed by an accidental grenade explosion.

L/Cpl A. SHONIWA	646070	2RAR	DOAS 15 Jun 1980	
L/Cpl R. CHIDOMBE	646818	2RAR	DOAS 15 Jun 1980	
Pte C. TONGOGARA	648521	2RAR	DOAS 15 Jun 1980	
Pte Thomas MUTEMA	666296	HQ Coy 1RAR	KOAS 6 Jul 1980	Killed by a civilian vehicle.
Pte J. MUDONGO	663375	2RAR	DOAS 5 Sep 1980	
Pte M. MURWISI	661212	2RAR	DOAS 5 Sep 1980	
Pte T. TIGERE	661388	2RAR	DOAS 7 Sep 1980	
WO1 Siwenga Hlabano NKOMO	640569	HQ Coy 1RAR	KOAS 17 Sep 1980	Killed in a vehicle accident.
C/Sgt Edmond CHAWIRA	644172	HQ Coy 1RAR	KOAS 19 Sep 1980	Killed in a vehicle accident. From Charter.
Sgt T.H.C. MURIGO	661498	3RAR	DOAS 8 Oct 1980	
Pte J. PENYEKE	660519	3RAR	DOAS 8 Oct 1980	
L/Cpl Joseph PECHENGA	645310	B Coy 1RAR	DOAS 10 Nov 1980	Died of natural causes. From Nkai.
Pte George CHIWANZA	647946	HQ Coy 1RAR	Murdered 10 Nov 1980	Shot at a ZIPRA motorized infantry column roadblock at Magwegwe Cemetery near Entumbane while off-duty in civilian clothes. The ZIPRA column had moved to Entumbane from Gwaai River Mine in support of their comrades in the Entumbane camps. From Mrewa.
L/Cpl Robson KUJINGA	645503	HQ Coy 1RAR	Murdered 10 Nov 1980	Shot at a ZIPRA motorized infantry column roadblock at Magwegwe Cemetery near Entumbane while off-duty in civilian clothes. The ZIPRA column had moved to Entumbane from Gwaai River Mine in support of their comrades in the Entumbane camps. From Ndanga.
Pte Matthew SIZIBA	647625	HQ Coy 1RAR	Murdered 10 Nov 1980	Shot at a motorized infantry column roadblock at Magwegwe Cemetery near Entumbane while off-duty in civilian clothes. The ZIPRA column had moved to Entumbane from Gwaai River Mine in support of their comrades in the Entumbane camps. From Selukwe.
Pte Chengerayi MATANBUDZIKO	647961	B Coy 1RAR	Murdered 15 Dec 1980	Grenade thrown into his house. From Gokwe.
Pte Japhet MUDARE	663338	C Coy 1RAR	KOAS 30 Mar 1981	From Hartley.
Pte Peter MUDUNGWE	662556	D Coy 1RAR	Murdered 16 Apr 1981	Murdered by his wife. From Selukwe.

INDEX

PHOTO CONTRIBUTORS

Rob Anderson
Roy Amm
Jo Amos
Andrew Barrett
Markham Batstone
Iain Bowen
Ralph Cant
Alan Doyle
Craig Fourie
John Garland
Peter Gill
Bruce Greetham
Adrian Haggett
David Heppenstall
Keith Holshausen

Clive Hooper
John Hopkins
Mike Jones
Andrew Krajewski
Pat Lawless
Brian Lennon-Smith
Alf Logan
Anthony Manning
Mike Matthews
The Peter Morris Collection
Don Price
Mark Sasman
Andy Todd
Sean von Stranz
Ian Wood

Cuttings from the Bulawayo Chronicle, and stills
from video footage, in the RAR archive and other
collections.

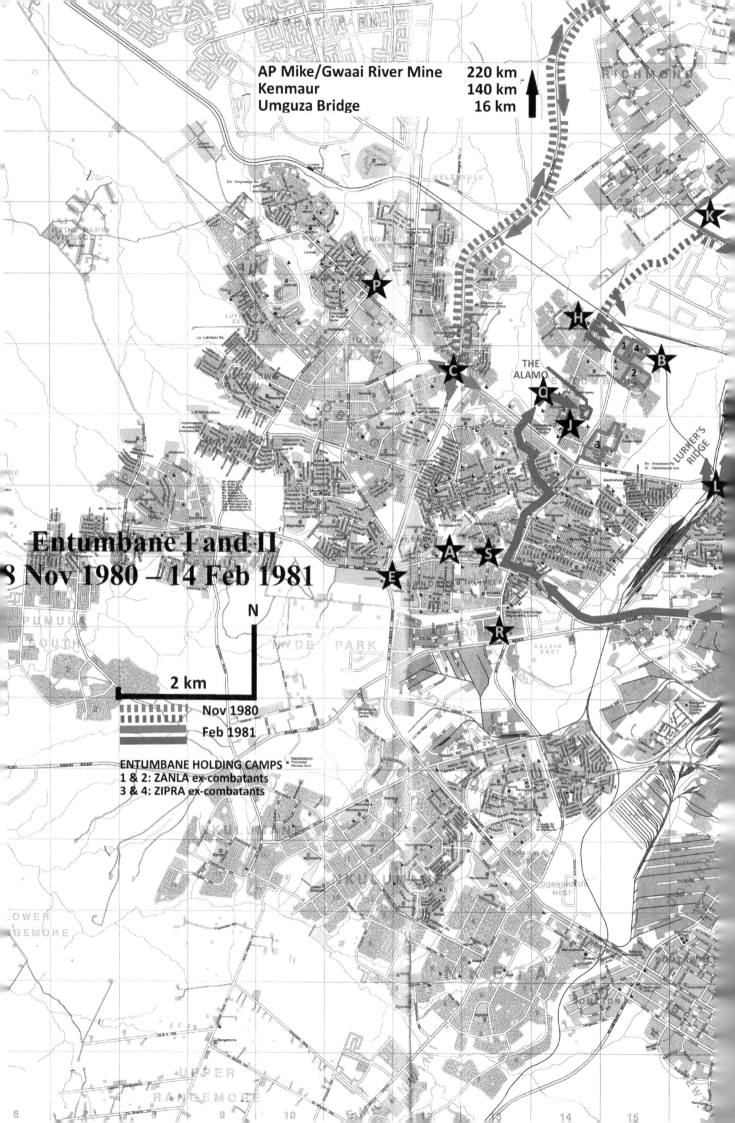

AP Mike/Gwaai River Mine 220 km
Kenmaur 140 km
Umguza Bridge 16 km

Entumbane I and II
8 Nov 1980 – 14 Feb 1981

N

2 km

Nov 1980
Feb 1981

ENTUMBANE HOLDING CAMPS
1 & 2: ZANLA ex-combatants
3 & 4: ZIPRA ex-combatants

THE ALAMO

LURMER'S RIDGE

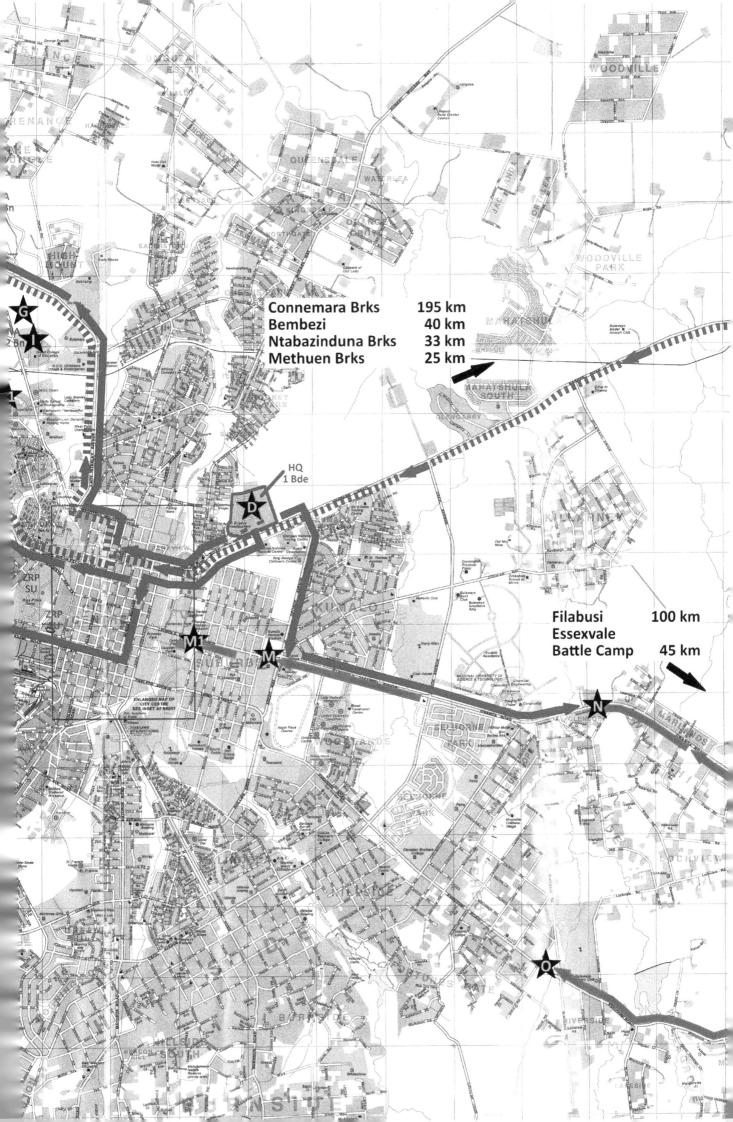

Connemara Brks   195 km
Bembezi   40 km
Ntabazinduna Brks   33 km
Methuen Brks   25 km

HQ
1 Bde

Filabusi   100 km
Essexvale
Battle Camp   45 km

9 781527 286894